By

LOUIS KRONENBERGER

The Republic of Letters 1955
ESSAYS ON VARIOUS WRITERS

The Thread of Laughter 1952
CHAPTERS ON ENGLISH STAGE COMEDY
FROM JONSON TO MAUGHAM

The Pleasure of Their Company 1946
AN ANTHOLOGY
OF URBANE AND SOPHISTICATED WRITINGS
FROM THE CLASSIC TO THE MODERN

Kings and Desperate Men 1942
LIFE IN EIGHTEENTH-CENTURY ENGLAND

THESE ARE *Borzoi Books*
PUBLISHED BY *Alfred A. Knopf* IN NEW YORK

THE REPUBLIC OF LETTERS

Louis Kronenberger

THE
REPUBLIC
OF
LETTERS

Essays on Various Writers

NEW YORK: ALFRED A. KNOPF

1955

THIS IS A BORZOI BOOK,
PUBLISHED BY ALFRED A. KNOPF, INC.

FIRST EDITION

To Newton Arvin

Author's Note

THE ARTICLES brought together here can hardly not betray their rather varied origins. Some were straightforward essays in criticism and appreciation; some first appeared as introductions to books; two or three were originally lectures; two or three others were parts of symposiums or of texts by many hands. Nor was my approach always predominantly literary: in treating of Gibbon, or Boswell, or Pope, I have been far more concerned with the man than the writer.

There was a natural temptation to revise parts, at least, of many of these essays; but except to make the lectures more concise, or to omit from the introductions what was umbilical to the text that followed, I have contented myself with only a few slight changes.

For kindly permitting me to reprint material, I am indebted to *The New Republic*, *The Nation*, the *New York Times Book Review*, *Life*, *The Atlantic Monthly*, and *The Saturday Review;* and to Random House, The World Publishing Company, The Viking Press, Stackpole Sons, The Limited Editions Club, and Alfred A. Knopf, Inc. For a number of editorial suggestions I am greatly indebted to Herbert Weinstock.

CONTENTS

I

II

PART

I

La Rochefoucauld

OF the two dukes who have gained immortality by letters, one depicted the follies and vanities of mankind in almost the lengthiest of human masterpieces, the other in almost the briefest. Each had experience of the great world during a celebrated age, and Saint-Simon in his voluminous memoirs called back to life an endless variety of scenes and characters; but for La Rochefoucauld it was enough to sum up the reactions of a lifetime within the boundaries of epigram. He stripped the stage of scenery, the actors of costume; smoked out the perfume, extinguished the fire, iced the flesh; and to express in full his opinion of the world granted himself no more than the deadly acid of wit.

As a master of serious epigram, of epigram which puts truth before cleverness, he remains unrivaled. So little, at bottom, was he concerned with being merely clever that where he misses fire it is through sententiousness rather than levity. So true is this again that, compact as he is in expression, the brilliance of his maxims lies less in their verbal polish than in their naked meaning. A man more eager for startling effects would have cut his phrases even more sharply, heightened his contrasts even more bitingly, and thrust farther with the rapier simply to exhibit his skill. La Rochefoucauld has indeed the name for dazzling wit, and up to a point deserves it; but he might easily have been far wittier had he been fundamentally less serious.

His passion to express the truth as he saw it with unsparing accuracy distinguishes La Rochefoucauld from all mere phrase-makers, even the brilliant ones like Wilde. Wilde, of course, was essentially a showman, but even had he pursued truth with as much devotion as La Rochefoucauld, he must have tracked it down, by virtue of the medium he chose, less often. For most of Wilde's epigrams, lightly tossed into his plays though they are, are not absolute statements, but statements in a context, statements performing a dramatic function. It may be part of their job to help characterize a cynic, a man about town, a woman of the world; they may be flashy because the person who utters them himself is flashy, or shocking because the person has an inclination to shock. In just such a manner, at any rate, some of our wittiest analysts of human conduct have had other aims in mind while spinning out epigrams; but La Rochefoucauld the straightforward moralist never adorned his morals—he set down his discoveries without dramatizing or even collating them, and though all of them are dominated by one note, each must be examined and judged by itself.

That La Rochefoucauld was one of the most thoughtful and indefatigable moralists who ever lived is in no wise contradicted by the immoral and disillusioning spectacle he never relented from uncovering. To begin with, he was the creature of an age far more alive to "honor" than to highmindedness, and he spent his life among privileged and emulous people. They had been born to sufficient position always to thirst after more: more wealth, more power, more pleasure, more prestige. Naturally rivals, inevitably they became intriguers; in such an era and atmosphere, compliments were conjoined to rapiers, and men bowed with a civility that took nobody in and could scarcely have tried to. La Rochefoucauld shared in this dishonest spectacle—for a time as a rather formidable participant; for a longer time, and at length for all time, as its hawklike observer. He saw it for exactly what it was worth and exposed it exactly as he saw it; but this was no easy thing to do and had to be done, not simply by a master of surfaces, but by someone who could peer beneath them into a realm of tangled and unsightly motives, into hearts concealed from their owners and minds concealed from the world.

What he saw there, and what became the burden of these maxims, is of course the love of self which dominates, consciously or unconsciously, naïvely or craftily, all we think and do; and which, though it operates with great force upon others, operates with even greater force upon ourselves. The reason why so much of La Rochefoucauld shocks us is not that we have failed to examine other people's motives but that we have shrunk from examining our own. For La Rochefoucauld, unlike the great philosophers, does not widen our horizons with truths we have been unable to perceive; he merely illuminates them, with truths we have been unwilling to admit. And as he does, all the cant and pretense and false virtue by which we contrive to hold our heads up in the world are brutally and lastingly put on display. Afterward we may once again go on pretending (La Rochefoucauld would be the first to insist that we do), but we cannot help knowing that someone has detected our motives.

The verdict of these maxims is almost sinister. All in all, this is the most pulverizing cynicism that literature can offer, and it grinds even a little finer because it is spoken with such glacial impersonality, with such sweeping lack of apology. Could we only suspect its author of bearing life a grudge, of scheming toward an end, of seeking to justify his conduct, of attempting to show off his wit, even of laughing at those in the wrong—as Voltaire was laughing in *Candide*—we might see some hope of refuting him; did he even so much as paint himself somewhere into the picture, we might see some chance of retouching it. But these are the most disembodied of sentiments; they exist alone; and where they are incorrect, they are incorrect without reference to personal desires, like errors of Nature. The author has totally—or almost totally—effaced himself. The one thing about him that betrays his presence is his pride of self-effacement.

It is because these sayings have a perfect disinterestedness that, whatever we may presently think of La Rochefoucauld's philosophy, we need never disinfect it of suspicious origins. If a knowledge of human failings evolved it, no personal prejudices muddied its flow; and between the scientific cynicism of La Rochefoucauld, which inspected vanity in a test-tube, and the self-interested cynicism of a Chesterfield, there is a tremendous difference. Chesterfield was a cynic partly out of temperament no doubt, but consciously because it paid the best dividends, and the counsel he bestowed upon his son was profoundly mischievous. From his contemplation of the world's low altitudes La Rochefoucauld at least had learned not to stoop; furthermore, he was too proud.

Again, whatever we may presently think of his philosophy, his little book is one of the very few which really leave us different from what they found us. Though we fancy ourselves much influenced by the books we read, almost none of them impress us even enough to recur again to mind, whereas La Rochefoucauld, with his stealthy smile and riveting eye, can dog our steps for weeks. For, because he gives our self-esteem a blow from which it never quite recovers, the impact of his knowledge rather increases than abates. He has pitilessly ferreted out many of our truest feelings in such matters as envy, jealousy, coquetry, friendship, love, gratitude, ambition; and whoever attempts to deny the veracity of those feelings offers La Rochefoucauld an even better proof of his wisdom than his own wise remarks.

He leaves us with a miserably low opinion of ourselves and the world, with a sense that there is little real kindness or integrity possible in life, with the crushing thought that we are not even so well disposed as our sternest detractors would find us. He leaves us almost without hope for ourselves or faith in our fellow men; with nothing more than the cold comfort that, selfish and designing as we are, no one else is much better. But he leaves us, at any rate, with the discoveries of a great explorer; at whatever cost, we have learned some part of the real, the immitigable, truth. There are many bitterer and more terrible books in our libraries than La Rochefoucauld's, picturing life as even more vicious and degraded; but we can usually brush them aside as the morbid and unbalanced conceptions of people so unlike us as to have no bearing on our lives. The *Maxims*, conversely, are one book from which no man can feel quite exempt and they therefore constitute one of the most disillusioning of human documents.

Only it so happens that, for all the truth they contain, it is not the whole truth, and after a first reading has flayed us into too helpless submission we shall find a second reading partly recuperative. For, correct as he was in many essentials, La Rochefoucauld simplified too much; and if pure unselfishness is the rarest thing in the world, pure selfishness is the next rarest. We think first of ourselves, we want the good we do publicized and the bad concealed, we repeat our mistakes, we encourage our follies, we are cocky and vainglorious, malicious and mean; we are pre-eminently the victims of vanity. With all these stated or implied contentions of La Rochefoucauld I do not quarrel—in the face of his evidence I could not if I would; but at the very outset he overlooked one powerful engine of our behavior—conscience and sense of duty. That proves we are good enough, at least, to realize that we are inherently bad. That works its will upon us sufficiently to make us turn the other cheek, humble our pride, denounce our vanity, dilute our malice, strengthen our resolves; it leads us at times to fight for lost causes or causes not quickly won, and to see ourselves as though we were the judges of our conduct and not the instigators. (All this La Rochefoucauld would doubtless still proclaim to be either vanity or pride or fear; but there the way plainly narrows, there our knowledge of ethics gets enmeshed in our ignorance of psychology, virtues and vices become indistinguishable, only our Unconscious knows the exact truth—and whatever La Rochefoucauld might proclaim, we can only insist that at such times we try our best to behave well.)

And if La Rochefoucauld's conclusions are too one-sided, it is partly because his field of operations was too narrow. After all, he formed his judgments from observing a corrupt and pleasure-loving leisure class, encouraged by its own code of honor to be selfish, tempted by having no bread to earn into every skirmish of ambition and subterfuge of amour. Only people with much time on their hands can make an art of insincerity; only people who need never think of self-preservation can think perpetually of self-indulgence. For that reason La Rochefoucauld was brought face to face, day after day, with selfishness, vanity, treachery, shallowness in their most naked forms; he knew much less about people who have modest ambitions because they have modest hopes, to whom sacrifice is no test of virtue and disappointment no cause for vengeance. As a result, the better part of his indictment is more applicable to the well-placed than to humanity in general— though humanity in general is not to be acquitted.

A full diet of La Rochefoucauld would therefore be very misleading. We must not rank him, even as a psychologist, too high. Once he came to the well-formed conclusion that self-love is the mainspring of our conduct, he rode it as a hobby; perhaps it is not unfair to say that he never afterward could look with the same sharpness, the same curiosity, on the human scene. But if his philosophy must in the end be guarded against, it remains a magnificent antidote to all the fuzzy idealism, all the disingenuous play-acting, all the noble verbiage and sanctimonious sitting in judgment that tend to color our thoughts and speech and action. It remains, besides, a magnificent flagellant for the good of our natures, for if there is any chance of our becoming better than we are, it is through perceiving that we are worse than we think. The grandiose mottoes on the wall are more likely than not to increase our cynicism, but the cynicism of La Rochefoucauld, if we have any of the moral earnestness which produced it, must sting us with a certain shame and make *us* less cynical.

(1936)

CHAPTER II

The Eighteenth-Century Ideal

RICH young William Beckford put down the Deist tome he had been reading and scribbled gaily in the margin: "Hurrah! no Hell." To him (and he typified the more fortunate eighteenth-century Englishman) the news removed the one dark cloud, the one discordant element, from his universe. Everything else—everything in this world—was very pretty and very much of a piece, very solid and harmonious and handsome. Nor is it difficult for us to see what he meant; for though Beckford's England has been dead for over a century, it stares out at us a dozen times a day—in the architecture of houses, the furniture of rooms, the prints on people's walls, the plates on their dinner tables. It is the chief glory of many museums, the first prize at many fancy-dress balls; while a single grandee of the period, Lord Chesterfield, has conferred his name on a style of sofa, a type of overcoat, and a brand of cigarettes.

Eighteenth-century England is still scattered all about us because, to an extent unequaled by any other era, it signifies a *way* of life. Even before we think of it as the century when England became Great Britain, or when Great Britain lost the Thirteen Colonies, or launched the Industrial Revolution, or fully achieved parliamentary government—even before eighteenth-century England suggests any of these momentous facts, it evokes a scene, it suggests an age when men were reasonable, and life was leisurely, and things had elegance. It was the last stop before the modern world was reached; the last time that a hundred years did not alter a picture almost beyond recognition. Eighteenth-century England has about it an ordered sense of movement, something between a march and a minuet; it has equally about it an atmosphere of light— the reign of superstition was ending, and that of smoke had not yet begun.

It was less an era of growth than of superb consolidation. The previous era had seethed with violence; the coming one would boil with activity. England, between-times, grew rich as she grew restrained, and embossed common sense with style. The seventeenth century had been sanguinary and bigoted and intense; it was unruly enough to precipitate rebellions and revolutions, Gunpowder Plots and Bloody Assizes. For asserting the divine right of kings, Charles I went magnificently to the block; while to be rid of divine right England had to submit to dictatorship. Presently—after a dozen years of the Cromwells—the Stuarts were on the throne again; but James II not only believed in divine right, he paid allegiance to Rome; and at length he too had to go. At his going, something like the seventeenth century went also; for spiritually eighteenth-century England begins with 1688, as it concludes with 1789. The Revolution Settlement firmly established the Established Church, forever denied the divine right of kings. But 1688 did more than bring James's Protestant son-in-law and daughter, William and Mary, over from Holland. Thanks in great part to its principal interpreter, John Locke, it meant individual liberty and religious tolerance, and it produced a spirit of militant common sense.

It would be hard to say whether this new spirit chiefly set up fences or pulled them down. For if it put an end to abuses that had hemmed man in, it suddenly set limits to his vision of the world. But the fences that came down were of much the greater significance, because they had actually been like walls. The Englishman, during the eighteenth century, was to become a great deal more the slave of convention, but a great deal less the victim of authority. He was to be free, at any rate, to enslave himself: where, throughout history, he had always been harangued about his duties, Locke now would remind him of his rights. Hand in hand with the Age of Reason go the Rights of Man; goes the great watchword of the century—liberty; freedom; "not to be subject to the inconstant, uncertain, unknown, Arbitrary Will of another Man." The Rights of Man, to be sure, are in great part property rights; it is not an age when the poor will be offered much chance or much charity.

But while the walls of arbitrary authority were coming down, and those of religious intolerance were being breached, neat hedges and palings were everywhere going up. For a century England's desires had been either sadly starved or violently gorged. Under the Puritans—who "hated bear-baiting, not because it gave pain to the bear, but because it gave pleasure to the spectators"—enjoyment had been driven underground. But life, having been all morality under Cromwell, understandably became all license under Charles II. For hundreds of years, moreover, life in England and Europe had been splendidly but dangerously dramatic; there had been no end of violence, of exaltation, of conspiracy, of bloodshed. Now men were sick of drama, and they rebounded to the idea of life as civilized comedy; so it was already being regarded in France, and France was but another name for Fashion. But civilized comedy cannot be played without rules; without, in fact, quite strict ones. So, at this particular turn of time, the policy arose not of driving the Devil out but of fencing him in; not of thirsting after omniscience but of resting happy in reason; and of shrugging the shoulder in preference to unsheathing the sword. The eighteenth-century gentleman thus set up, in the common interest, a great many thou-shalt-nots. Thus it was commanded: *Thou shalt not talk about thyself lest thou bore thy neighbor;* or it was enjoined: *Thou shalt not become overzealous lest thou disturb the peace:* no word was a greater slur in Augustan England than the word "enthusiasm." All this tended to make social life unusually harmonious; the possible drawback was that it raised etiquette a good deal higher than ethics.

Certainly in its search for harmony eighteenth-century England constantly resorted to compromise; but no one can begin to understand the period until he understands that compromise was a quality it *admired.* In its experience, two men with strongly opposed ideas of the truth would certainly shout, and might very well shoot, at each other; whereas two men trying to find a common area of agreement seldom raised their voices and usually achieved their ends. The Age of Reason was willing to give up some of the grandeur in life to get rid of most of the muddle; eighteenth-century people saw no more point to squandering energy than to squandering money.

Their guide, their god, was common sense; which, when joined to natural British pluck, they felt would solve any difficulty—even Robinson Crusoe's on an island. They were not wrong; the combination gave England tremendous security and power. No doubt it cost something; it led to a certain stifling of the imagination, a certain withering of the emotions, a certain contraction of the soul. What saved the age from aridness and unbearable philistinism was the quality that gives it a retrospective glamour, a lingering bouquet—its enormous sense of style.

For, though common sense was its god, it worshipped it with elaborate ceremony. It cared terribly—in a moral view, it cared far too much—about appearances; velvet gloves concealed not only mailed fists but itching palms. Yet much else, beyond prudence and hypocrisy, contrived to give the life of eighteenth-century England an air. It was, for one thing, very much the age of the aristocrat; it was, for another, *not* the age of the machine. The aristocrat brought distinguished manners into everyday life; you might see in a hundred drawing-rooms what in a slapdash age is only to be seen on the stage. An aristocrat spent all his leisure hours acquiring style, and *ton;* and his leisure hours, to steal a phrase of Heine's, generally amounted to twenty-four a day. His education was in many respects a disgrace; he might quite possibly attend Oxford or Cambridge for years without setting foot in a lecture room or even meeting his tutor. But he did learn there how to cut a figure in the world; no one could saunter more charmingly, or philander with more grace.

But at its best the sense of style went well beyond this; went far, indeed, toward fulfilling a high aristocratic ideal. Probably the aristocratic ideal came closest to being personally achieved in Lord Chesterfield, who is most famous for his letters to his son, but whose greatest feat, as Charles Whibley said, was to "create himself." For what Chesterfield did went a good deal beyond Nature, and a little outside it; such was the noble Earl's view of distinction that he forbade many harmless amusements; a gentleman, for example, must on no account ever laugh out loud. The possible objection to all this is that it is so harmonious it has rather ceased to be human, and the Earl himself, in the end, is less a man than a work of art. But his life does genuinely have all the form and polish of a work of art, just as the life of his far greater contemporary, Gibbon, has all the movement of a minuet.

And style in eighteenth-century England was not just a matter of stance and stride, of paying a compliment or wearing a coat. It was something men commanded in the stress of business, in the teeth of adversity. They snubbed with style: "The honorable gentleman," retorted one M.P. upon another, "would seem to be indebted to his memory for his jests, and to his imagination for his facts." They plundered with style: Clive, confronted with the proofs of his huge Indian haul, confessed himself "amazed" at his own moderation. They died, nay, went to the scaffold, with style: the Jacobite Lord Balmerino "lay down; but being told he was on the wrong side, vaulted round, and immediately gave the signal by tossing up his arm, as if he were giving the signal for battle."

As it was perhaps the most lustrous period of the aristocrat, in a sense it was the last. The eighteenth-century aristocrat owned everything, it might be said, except the future. For quite as much as he set the fashion and the pace, he made the laws and held the offices and scooped up the money and owned the land. (For being of middle-class origin, even so great a statesman as Burke was never permitted high political office.) Because the patrician had outstanding style, it is easy to forget that he often had uncommon ability. Chesterfield was indeed a great gentleman; but he was also an admirable governor-general. Charles Fox was clearly the most dashing of good fellows; but he was also the deadliest of parliamentary debaters. During the eighteenth century the aristocratic ideal was a vivid conception, but the Whig oligarchy was an overwhelming *fact*. For almost fifty years, from the day Anne quitted the throne to the day George III ascended it, the great Whig lords, immense owners of land and undeviating supporters of trade, ran England. They were so powerful they really constituted government and opposition both; indeed, had they not quarreled among themselves, even George III could probably not have ousted them. And while the great Whigs administered, their kinsmen and disciples and dependents legislated; for in class terms the House of Commons was no offset to the House of Lords; it was a sort of gentleman's club, its seats mostly in the gift, its sitters mostly at the service, of the great aristocrats. It was an age of pocket boroughs and rotten boroughs, and of very *un*representative government. John Wilkes once tried to show how, in a country of some 7,000,000 people, the votes of 5,723 could yield a majority in the Commons.

The great eighteenth-century aristocrats had their very serious faults, but it would not be easy to find a comparable body of men with more varied talents. The best of them were really spectacular performers, endowed with a fantastic energy that they monstrously abused: they were like sets of human fireworks, crackling and glittering and illuminating the heavens, and suddenly blazing forth again after they were supposed extinct. It was not so much that they went round the clock without even pausing for sleep, but rather how much and how many kinds of things they could pack into twenty-four hours. On no condition would they, to begin with, forgo their normal pleasures, their dalliance and their drinking and their gambling; but, having emptied a sensational number of bottles, they were quite likely to issue forth and electrify the House; also, in the same day, help design a grotto, compose an epigram, translate an ode, amuse a great lady, assist an author, exercise a horse, perpetrate a hoax, administer a province, and read for an hour in Mr. Pope.

Considering what these men did, there were startlingly many of them; but in actual numbers there were relatively few. The aristocratic ideal was far more a dream than it was ever a reality, just as the Age of Reason far better expresses the desire to be rational than the ability. This is not to minimize either thing. The very dream and the very desire are in themselves large achievements in the history of civilization; nor, taking the long view, did eighteenth-century England dream or desire in vain. Eighteenth-century England, today, is a byword for aristocratic art, a synonym for rationalist thought. But it must also be confessed that the age which made a god of decorum all too frequently made a beast of itself; and that the century which stood dedicated to reason produced some of the most unbalanced of all human beings.

The age teems with references to *aurea mediocritas* and *ne quid nimis*, the golden mean and "Enough is as good as feast." All the same, any chronicle of England during those years is almost equally a chronicle of excesses, a chronicle of extremes. The rich were very rich: "A man," conceded one of their tribe, "can jog along on forty thousand pounds a year"—at a time when an income of forty thousand pounds was like a million dollars today. The poor were very poor: an industrious laborer earned nine shillings—what today would be ten dollars—a week. The grand were very grand: the "Proud Duke" of Somerset had the roads cleared of bystanders when he traveled; and, his second wife happening one day to tap him playfully with her fan, "Madam," said the Duke sternly, "my first wife was a *Percy*, and she never dared take such liberties." And the disciplined, it is only fair to add, were very disciplined. The youthful romance that his father opposed, Gibbon reduced to a frigid antithesis: "I sighed as a lover, I obeyed as a son."

Nor was there ever such immoderacy. Scholars fought duels over a Greek accent; a great-uncle of Lord Byron's killed a man over how many manor houses one of their neighbors owned. Everywhere men drank prodigiously: so far from remarkable was it to toss off three bottles of wine at a sitting, it was hardly respectable not to. The brave fellows tossed off six. The Methuen Treaty of 1703, which spelled the domination of Portugal by England, spelled equally the domination of England by port. "Claret," pontificated Dr. Johnson, "is for boys." And while the comfortable classes got gouty from port, the poor went to pieces from gin. During the first half of the century, gin-drinking reached ghastly proportions; inside 15 years the consumption of spirits doubled, and the author of *Tom Jones* wrote that a hundred thousand Londoners lived on gin alone. In vain did parsons denounce "Gin, Cursed Fiend with Fury frought" in favor of "Beer, happy Produce of our isle." While their wives and children starved, a multitude of wretches grew vicious, turned criminal, went mad.

It was, indeed, a brutal and audacious age of crime, with pickpockets in every crowd and highwaymen along every road; a stealthy and menacing age, a bloody and murdering one. Even so, the punishments were incredibly harsh, and grew harsher as the century went on. There came to be 160 offenses punishable by death—among them, chopping down a tree in a garden or being seen for a month with gypsies. Since the mildest of misdemeanors meant the gallows, the eighteenth-century wrongdoer felt he had nothing to lose through the blackest of crimes, and (like as not) burned the house he ransacked or killed the man he robbed. Juries, to be sure, were often too appalled by the punishments to invoke them. But convictions, for all that, were plentiful enough: many condemned men had to be transported because on "hanging days" at Tyburn there just wasn't time or room to hang them all.

Low and high life alike were exceedingly profligate, in particular early in the century when there was hardly a public figure not stained with scandal. When the glittering Viscount Bolingbroke became Secretary of State, the madam of a bawdy house crowed: "Five thousand a year, my girls—and all for us!" Great ladies often had little better reputation than their lords; the paternity of men like Horace Walpole is to this day a subject of doubt. "Nobody's son," sniffed Chesterfield of a certain marriage, "has married Everybody's daughter."

But the worst excess of all in eighteenth-century England was the gambling; never have men played for higher stakes or stranger ones. The great clubs—whether Whig or Tory, Brooks's or White's—were essentially gambling-houses where time and again an ancestral estate hung on a throw of the dice. From Brooks's a member retired in disgust because he had won only twelve thousand pounds in two months. The gambling debts of the celebrated Duchess of Devonshire approximated twenty million dollars in today's money. Nor was it only money people gambled with. One man gambled away, with her consent, his wife; another gambled his child; still another, his freedom; while two others gambled their lives—the winner to string up the loser.

Nor has reason a notably better record than decorum. Emotion, to be sure, was very often repressed; but that just meant that, denied a natural outlet, it periodically exploded. The Age of Reason might almost as accurately be termed the Age of Riots—riots, moreover, of every kind: riots over popery, riots over gin, riots over wages, riots over Wilkes. For all its high manners, it was hardly less an age of quarrels. There was even a kind of chain-squabbling in vogue: Steele quarreled with Addison, Addison with Pope, Pope with Lady Mary Montagu, Lady Mary with half her friends. Again, the Age of Reason seemed very often like an Age of Madness. Bedlam was so much one of the sights of London that tea was served there—while the rage to visit it might be thought a touch eccentric in itself. Beginning with Dean Swift, a whole procession of the century's poets—Smart, Collins, Cowper, Blake—went mad; perhaps to go mad was the only polite thing to do, since His Majesty George III often went very mad indeed.

Again, as the century wore on, England's era of enlightenment craved the creepy spells of the Dark Ages; built "Gothic" piles and abbeys; wrote Gothic romances where, in a world of vaults and midnight, everything clanked and shrieked and groaned. But even more than it wanted to shudder, a too-long-repressed England wanted to weep. And weep it did—and in time, all Europe after it—when a milksop printer of genius, Samuel Richardson, wrote *Pamela* and *Clarissa*. As *Clarissa* came out in installments and Clarissa's virtue became ever more gravely endangered, all England pleaded that the poor girl should not be ravished; but Richardson was relentless, and presently all England wept buckets of tears.

Assaulted by feeling, reason was next to be shaken by faith. The deism of Locke and Bolingbroke, and later the outright skepticism of Gibbon and Hume, prevailed, in high society and the intellectual world, right through the century. But midway through it the rest of England, which a lazy Church had rendered apathetic, began to hearken to the blazing call of John Wesley and George Whitefield, who, denied a pulpit, preached in the open fields and converted thousands and then tens of thousands to Methodism.

What perhaps it all came down to was that, like the British monarch, reason and decorum reigned but did not govern. They, like kingship, represented something tremendously important; but they could no more withstand the pressures of emotion than the throne could override the voice of the people. The impeccable Lord Chesterfield was all very well; but even had they the desire, few men had the ability to convert themselves into works of art. No one was ever turned out so flawlessly as Beau Brummell; but then it took Brummell, with the aid of a valet, four hours to get dressed, and he got dressed three times a day. As for reason, the age made a truly magnificent effort to be rational; if the age yet fell short, the moral appears to be that man cannot live by head alone. His body, for one thing, is always intruding; his heart, for another, is always objecting.

All this eighteenth-century background is of a piece with the "plot." In political and economic terms, eighteenth-century England is much less a high and violent drama than a now and then agitated success story. Without spilling a drop of blood, the Revolution of 1688 had completely determined the political structure of the country. Not everything, to be sure, was instantly settled by the Revolution Settlement; there was to ensue an era of conspiracy and unrest. The Tories had agreed to the Settlement because they would not tolerate James II as a Catholic; but they had never for a moment objected to him as a king. To them, quite as much as to him, divine right seemed the very essence of royalty—and the Stuart name seemed more essential still. As long as a Stuart—James's daughter Mary or his daughter Anne—occupied the throne, the Tories might endure the thought that not God but Parliament had put her there. But when all Anne's children predeceased her and Parliament chose the obscure House of Hanover as her successor, many Tories began glancing "over the water" toward James's exiled son; they preferred a Catholic Stuart to a Protestant nonentity. Besides, the Whigs were in the saddle now, waging a costly war in Flanders to keep a French prince off the Spanish throne; war that bled the land-poor Tory squires white from taxes; war that, thanks to Marlborough's genius, was already won, only the Whig profiteers insisted on prolonging it; war abroad that intensified party war at home. The party war itself was inescapable. For the Tories did not merely stand for divine right or the Established Church or the old landed interests, and the Whigs for parliamentary government or religious toleration or commercial enterprise; quite plainly, the Tories symbolized the past and the Whigs the future. That, among other things, is why a constitutional-minded House of Hanover came to stay; and why feudal-minded Jacobite uprisings came to nothing.

Queen Anne's reign, however fractious, was also resplendent; by dint of arms Marlborough raised England, after a century of subservience and struggle, to the most commanding position in Europe. But internally things were still far from sound. France had been brought to her knees by Marlborough, but it remained for Robert Walpole to put England on her feet. This burly Norfolk squire who invented the long parliamentary week-end so that he could indulge his love of fox-hunting; this cynical manipulator who always talked smut at his dinner table because he insisted it was the one form of conversation that everybody could enjoy; this supremely efficient Whig statesman who managed to hold the reins of power for over twenty ticklish years, is anything but eighteenth-century England's best-known figure; but he is conceivably her cardinal one. Even the Great Commoner, Pitt, means rather less; for though Pitt means Empire, Walpole means England.

For Walpole did two tremendously vital things for England: he set it on its feet, and then set those feet squarely along the path of the future. He first of all put the Hanoverians firmly on the throne—firmly, so that the nation was spared serious upheaval; and yet as figureheads, so that George I and George II stayed put without ever acting up. As a result, the form of government Walpole evolved became the government of Britain for good and all—strictly parliamentary government functioning through the party system, with the administration made up of ministers of the same political stripe.

But Walpole chiefly put England on her feet by giving her—actually, by compelling upon her—a long interval of peace. Many and great were the temptations to dabble in the dynastic ructions and political ups and downs of the Continent, but Walpole sternly resisted them. Time and again he had the country, and even his own Cabinet, against him; and in the end public pressure forced him into war with Spain. But by then his aim was accomplished; a whole generation of peace had reaped for England a rich harvest of plenty. Trade had grown, commerce had multiplied, the middle class had gained steadily in wealth, self-confidence, and power. Under Walpole, England kept shop with wonderful success; and so became, for good and all, a nation of shopkeepers.

Walpole has not come down the years enhaloed, for his methods have sadly tarnished his achievements. In politics he put a welcome end to the treacherous cabals and revenges of Stuart times; in politics he is bluff, hearty, modern. But if he put an end to conspiracy, he gave an enormous boost to corruption. Utter realist and complete cynic, he accepted the maxim that one must govern by either corruption or force, and unblinkingly chose corruption. He never made the one remark he is universally famous for—that "every man has his price"—but he would scarcely have jibed at it, he who said he had to bribe members of Parliament "not to vote against, but *for* their conscience." Walpole, moreover, left England not only more corrupt than he found it, but crasser and more philistine. But he gave it a modern impulse, he gave it sinew and direction, and while he cooled, he also fortified its blood; as somebody said, the best tribute to his administration was the ten bungling years that came after it. Only hams and supers filled the stage until Pitt's majestic entrance.

Walpole was not merely the antithesis of Pitt; he was also the very necessary antecedent. He had to make England prosper through peace before Pitt could make her powerful through war. The two men—so alike in their masterfulness, so utterly different in their methods, the one all rudder, the other all sail—offer in the eighteenth-century that mixture of the hardheaded and the heroic which has been, in almost every century, the key to England's success. But where Walpole worked grubbily behind the scenes, Pitt performed with the utmost éclat on a brilliantly lighted stage. Joining Frederick the Great against half of Europe in the Seven Years War, Pitt devised a global strategy to match England's vast ambitions, and made the year 1759—the year of Quebec, and Madras, and Minden, and Guadeloupe, and Quiberon Bay—England's most triumphant since the Middle Ages. The whole thing crowned an era.

It also ended one. For in 1760 a new king, George III, came to the throne with a most decided conviction that it *was* a throne. The handsome young man did not need to believe in the divine right of kings; sufficient, to his mind, was their purely human opportunities. He did not need to challenge the belief that Parliament ruled the country; he, in his turn, would simply rule Parliament—by bullying it where he could, by bribing it where he must. So, with a craft that equaled his purposefulness, George set about regaining the lost glories of the Crown. After much dabbling in ministers, George found the mouthpiece he wanted in Lord North, a decenter man and more competent minister than most Americans are given to believe at school, but one who could never get George's permission to resign and could never muster the courage to resign without it.

Always asserting to the utmost what power he technically possessed, forever using money, sinecures, pensions, promotions, promises, threats to buy up votes, George was at length in a fair way to achieve his ambition of running the country. It really took the American Revolution to foil him. The real cause of the Revolution was economic and stemmed out of Britain's mercantilist policy, out of a nation of shopkeepers condemning her colonies to be a "nation of customers." We could buy only from—or by way of—Britain, while Britain did not have to buy from us and no other country was permitted to. Hence we were more and more becoming a nation of smugglers; and now that England owned Canada and there was no longer any danger of a French invasion, our strongest tie with the mother country fell away. George III or no George III, the colonies would sooner or later have had to be given considerably more rope; but had George and his ministers not bullied and bungled, had there been no Stamp Act or uproars over Taxation without Representation, the colonies might have been appeased with something like dominion status. As it was, the drain on their purses stung them less than the slaps at their pride.

George's pigheaded methods made all Britain's enlight-

ened statesmen regard the rebels less as enemies than al-
lies; to a Chatham or a Burke, the Americans were defend-
ing the British Constitution against itself, while Charles
James Fox could characterize a British victory as "the *bad
news* from Long Island." Lord North's attempt (1778) to
offer us a kind of dominion status came too late; by then
we were committed to independence, and by then, with
France, Holland, and Spain all at war with her, England
was clearly doomed to "the most damaging and humiliat-
ing defeat" in her history. But the loss of the colonies possibly saved England from something worse; for had George
won the war, he would have become so highhanded that
the English might have had to rebel against him themselves. It was a great try, this last grab of a British monarch
for extensive power; but it was a decisive one, for as a result no subsequent British monarch was to have any power
at all. When the younger Pitt finally drew the royal claws,
monarchy in England became little more than a synonym
for pageantry.

Indeed, the danger for the aristocratic ruling class was
all in the other direction. On the heels of the American
Revolution came two far more momentous ones—the
French Revolution, which was the agitated dawn of
democracy; the Industrial Revolution, which meant the
transfer of power to the middle class. The whole tune, and
still more the whole orchestration, of life was to be immensely altered.

(1948)

CHAPTER III

Pope

EVEN today, even after two hundred years, Pope's name continues to be ringed with controversy, as Chatterton's with pathos or Byron's with scandal. Moreover, the world goes on loudly and heatedly disputing not only how good Pope was as a poet, but how bad he was as a man. It goes on playing the detective at least as zestfully as it plays the critic; and whatever conclusions it arrives at, it goes on being fascinated. Great poet or very special poet or no poet at all, Pope—it will nowhere, I think, be denied—charged his couplets with intense and insistent life; aggressor or victim, demi-devil or child of pain, Pope everywhere still makes his presence passionately felt.

Like Chatterton, like Byron, Pope boasts a "story" as well as an achievement: indeed, his character was so devious and his career so dazzling that they have often shifted the limelight from the poetry to the poet, and made the "little monster" who hobnobbed with dukes rather more of a figure than the author of *The Dunciad* and the *Epilogue to the Satires*. Furthermore, the "story" and the achievement have forcibly affected each other. Thus some of the Victorians, quite sure that very little about Pope was creditable, went on to wonder how much of him could be great; and today there are those who act as if whitewashing his character were a *sine qua non* to appreciating his art.

Today, at any rate, Pope's goodness is far more in question than his greatness: his greatness, I think it might even be ventured, is no longer in question at all. Classicism has only needed a friendly hearing for so famous a classicist to be once more acclaimed. Abuse has only needed to be considered as "poetic" as, say, eulogy, for the most telling of our satirists to exert on the twentieth century some of the force he exerted on the eighteenth. It is even possible that Pope may become too fashionable for a time, though not that he will ever become widely popular. (For some reason, a Pope or a Dryden is usually recommended to the public as a "change" from Keats or Shelley: but the great mass of readers don't want a change from Keats and Shelley.) Meanwhile the man—and no one can care much about the poet without coming to be interested in the man—continues to be wrangled over, and I suspect that any jury chosen to pass judgment on him would wind up failing to agree. *Were* his provocations greater than his revenges? Do his handicaps on the whole excuse his faults? Was he more sinned against than sinning—and quite as much the victim of his age as of his ailments? Or was he most of all the victim of a succeeding age—of Victorian smugness and self-righteousness and of that Victorianism which, resenting its repressions, so frequently managed to be cruel while it pretended to be moral?

Alexander Pope was born in London on the 21st of May, 1688. Both his parents were then past forty and both (his father by conversion) Roman Catholics. Both were also of what we should now describe as middle-class origin; for Pope's claims that on his father's side he descended down

some circular staircase from an earl were long ago disposed
of. Pope's father had prospered as a linen-draper and was
able, soon after the poet's birth—it was also (a matter of
some importance to papists) soon after the Revolution—to
retire from business and quietly remove to the country.
The boy received a very jumbled and discontinuous school-
ing, hardly so much at school as among priests and tutors,
and in later life could claim with some accuracy to be
largely self-taught. He made a good-looking child who at
ten had a "plump, pretty face" and a "fresh complexion";
but soon after—and as the tale runs through "perpetual application"—Pope began to suffer from ill-health and in particular from a tuberculous infection that in time caused
him to be deformed. Condemned to be a hunchback not
five feet tall, tormented with headaches and other recurring ailments, the youth was early set apart from most of
his kind as much by his disabilities as by his genius; and
was also to bear the burden of his religion at a time when
it could be particularly heavy.

Shut off by his faith from many callings, and by his
health from many others, and by his appearance moreover
from some of the primary gratifications of life, the young
Pope was yet not altogether unfortunate. He could be what
alone he seems ever to have wanted to be; he could be a
poet. As yet, as we all remember—

> As yet a child, nor yet a fool to fame,
> I lisp'd in numbers, for the numbers came.

Fortunately, too, his parents raised no objections—indeed,
his father so far encouraged him as to be critical of his
"rhimes"; and there was the family purse to give substance
to the family blessing.

Thus Pope was started on a grown-up career at an age
when even most serious boys are satisfied with collecting

coins. It is possible that, as he in later life maintained, Pope saw Dryden kinging it at Will's Coffee House: Pope was just twelve when Dryden died. It is certain that by his middle teens—there were "intellectual" and influential country neighbors to introduce him about—he had begun to know a number of established writers. Before he was seventeen, Pope was exchanging letters with the aging Wycherley; and it was about then that he received from the poet Walsh a piece of very famous advice. "He . . . used to tell me, that there was one way left of excelling: for though we had several great poets, we never had any one great poet that was correct, and he desired me to make that my study and aim." Both Walsh and Congreve, moreover, sufficiently admired Pope's youthful *Pastorals* to bring them to the attention of the well-known bookseller—we should say publisher—Jacob Tonson; and in 1708, when Pope was twenty, Tonson published them in one of his Miscellanies. Now Pope was really launched; another five years and, having published both the *Essay on Criticism* and *The Rape of the Lock*, he would be really famous.

Yet another five years, which brings us to Pope at thirty, and he had not only become the most celebrated poet of his age, he had also revolutionized the poet's place in the world. He was something much rarer, for a poet, than illustrious; he was independent. He had made, or would very soon have made, well over five thousand pounds from his translation of the *Iliad*—which is much like making over a hundred thousand dollars in America today. This was the pivotal, the decisive, thing in Pope's life. It saved him from ever having to be a hack. It enabled him to regard the lords he moved among as friends rather than patrons. It made it possible for him to settle down for the rest of his life at Twickenham, where he might busy himself with his garden and his grotto, care for his mother, receive his guests, polish his verse, touch up his letters, nurse his feuds, and amplify his fame.

It can only be because Pope is so extremely notorious for his enmities that he is not remarkably famous for his friendships. Few men, certainly, have had more glittering connections—and these include connections with writers. The greatest writer of the age, Dean Swift, was very nearly Pope's greatest friend. Gay, Congreve, Prior, Thomson, Steele—were all men with whom Pope moved on easy or affectionate terms. One sentence from a letter of Pope's written when he was twenty-nine, and rather near the foot than at the apex of his glory, will aptly enough convey how well he did in the great world: "After some attendance on my Lord Burlington, I have been at the Duke of Shrewsbury's, Duke of Argyle's, Lady Rochester's, Lord Percival's, Mr. Stonor's, Lord Winchelsea's, Sir Godfrey Kneller, who has made me a fine present of a picture, and Duchess Hamilton's." To each of these moreover he had gone, not as one might reasonably imagine, for dinner, but for a visit of "some days."

Pope followed his translation of the *Iliad* with his edition of Shakespeare and his translation of the *Odyssey*. These three undertakings—and while they were performing, he did only very minor work besides—bring us to 1726 and to Pope at thirty-eight. It is to be noted that though for a number of years he had been easily the first poet of the age, of the poetry for which we really value him today he had written nothing but *The Rape of the Lock* and some scattered verses. It is to be noted further that though Pope, long before 1726, had become the center of numerous feuds, he had almost never retorted upon his enemies in print. Barring some early pieces, there was only—and at its first appearance it fell upon barren ground—the "Atticus" portrait of Addison. Indeed, Pope's career as a satirist, which is in the vital sense his career as a poet, was only now to begin. From the first version of *The Dunciad* in 1729 to the final version of *The Dunciad* in 1743, Pope produced a body of work, a succession of masterpieces, which do something to justify the existence of malice in this world, and which include, so far as that goes, not simply the vitriol Pope threw so unerringly in the faces of his personal enemies, but a massive onslaught against mediocrity, incompetence, and dullness. In the design and much of the detail of *The Dunciad;* in the Moral Essays; and most of all in the Satires and Epistles, Pope brought his genius to its fullest flower.

Life, all in all, had perhaps not grown sunnier as it grew more distinguished. The Prince of Wales might come to visit Pope at Twickenham and the Queen of England hint that she would like to come; and every year Pope might make the circuit of patrician country houses, as too he might enjoy the devotion of his friends and that final homage, the quaking terror of his enemies. Still, there was a good deal amiss. Though the hump might grow no bigger on Pope's back, it loomed larger and larger in Pope's mind. From the outset of his career he had never been allowed to forget his appearance; he had had to endure such taunts in print as Dennis's about "a young, squab, short Gentleman . . . the very bow of the God of Love." Even more painfully, he had had to endure the common fate of the misshapen, becoming in the eyes of the other sex an object of pity when he was not an outright object of scorn. The story goes—and the hardness of the age, not to speak of the hardness of the lady, tends to support it—that upon Pope's declaring his feelings for Lady Mary Montagu, she was seized with laughter. The story of his love for Martha Blount has doubtless been much embroidered, lacking solid facts to build on; but very possibly Pope did love her, and if so, loved in vain.

All this, as time went on, could have made Pope no happier: nor must we forget that he was chronically ill as well as deformed, and that there is no great exaggeration in his celebrated reference to "that long disease, my life." The little fellow who used to pad out his rickety legs with three pairs of stockings, used too to need a servant within call, for whom he might have to ring a dozen times a night. From boyhood the headaches had been agonies, and as life wore on there were more serious ailments as well. Then, too, one after another of his closest friends began dropping away: Gay died, and Arbuthnot; Atterbury was sentenced to exile, and Swift, after a time, sentenced himself. Doubtless the enmities remained more fixed. There had always been dunces to flay, and Dennises to be flayed by. There was to the very end—Pope died of a dropsy when he was fifty-six—the need and the ability to have the last word.

The need to have the last word is a common enough and never very engaging trait; and though the source of it is occasionally pride, it is infinitely oftener vanity. Pope was one of the vainest and hence one of the touchiest men who ever lived. Edith Sitwell, the most ardent champion of Pope to have yet appeared, says that vanity was "the one grave fault in his character." This in a sense is quite true, but hardly redeems Pope so much as Miss Sitwell fancies. After all, vanity is the one grave fault in most people's characters; being, surely, the *fons et origo* of almost everything unpleasant or evil in their actions. Nevertheless, even though Miss Sitwell shuts her eyes to the enormity of Pope's misbehavior, it is good to find her understanding the nature of it. It keeps Pope altogether human; it quite disproves him a monster. And it explains, without necessarily justifying, much that Pope's own age found inexplicable and the Victorian age found shocking.

All the same, we need not pretend that the world of his time was the prettier for having Pope in it. His talent for getting in the last word must have made him loom a perpetual menace; just about what a vastly malicious columnist of brilliant gifts and immense reputation—who had little to fear from the laws of libel—would be today. For it was very evident that because of Pope anybody might wake up of a morning to find himself infamous. Pope, moreover—it is one of the most extraordinary things about him as an artist, but most damning as a man—seldom lashed out in the heat of anger; he knew how to bide his time, how to age his resentments. One thing was certain: whoever stepped on his toes could not sidestep his anger. As I am perhaps too fond of saying, it was Pope's instinct to take offense, and he made it his trade.

But Pope was not just vindictive. His vanity demanded that he preen as well as protect himself; that he lose no chance of seeming generous or kindhearted or wise or rakish or precocious [1] or indifferent to fame. He went to great lengths that people (and posterity) should think so, and to even greater lengths lest they think otherwise. His desire to seem nobler than he was; [2] his indulgence in what Dr. Johnson, and not Dr. Johnson alone, would have termed cant; his carefully limelighted admiration for the

---

[1] He pretended, for example, to have written a great many poems earlier than he actually wrote them, "so that he might be admired as a prodigy."

[2] Which rubs us the wrong way in even the most polished of his moralizings; for example:

When Truth or Virtue an affront endures,
The affront is mine, my Friend, and should be yours . . .
Mine, as a Friend to every worthy mind,
And mine as Man, who feels for all Mankind.

good life, are much harder to bear than his malice. Vanity, moreover, made Pope fantastically devious, involving him in almost as much conspiracy as cant. As Lady Bolingbroke once remarked, the little man couldn't have resisted playing the politician with cabbages and turnips. The key to much of Pope's life is the character of many of Pope's letters. He not only wrote a vast number, full of fancy sentiments, in a ceremonious style; he not only used the same ones more than once: but later in life he tried wherever possible to get his letters back, that he might ink out what was injurious and touch up what was not. And all this was merely preliminary to Pope's real object: getting his letters published. But, it being impossible for Pope to do this in a forthright manner—or even, as someone has said, for him to be normally arch and pretend that he was giving in to the urgings of "friends"—Pope cooked up the most elaborate of plots. I have not the space, and am by no means certain that I have the skill, to set forth the famous "P.T." saga in all its detail. Very briefly, however, Pope—to quote Macaulay—"robbed himself of his own letters, and then raised the hue and cry after them." Pope, in other words, invented a person named P.T. who, through a flesh-and-blood intermediary of Pope's hiring, secretly supplied a piratical publisher, Edmund Curll, with a good many Pope letters. These being in due course published, Pope now stepped forth to denounce the correspondence as unauthorized and inaccurate; and soon after brought out, in "self-defense," the authorized version that had been his object from the first. Using much the same tactics, he pursued much the same stratagems with some of his best friends, notably Swift.

It need not surprise us that a man who from vanity could trick his closest friends should from pique, or genuine pain, contrive harsh revenges against his enemies. Once, for example, Pope pretended to seal a reconcilation with Curll by "civilly" drinking sack with him: shortly afterward the bookseller was griped by the emetic Pope had dropped into his wine. Usually, however, Pope chose to pay off old scores with from a couplet's worth to a column's worth of verse. Sometimes, as with Hervey or Lady Mary, the repayment went on, in this poem and that, for years; sometimes, as with Theobald—or Cibber, who displaced him—the victim of Pope's displeasure became the very hero of his poem. Sometimes, as with many of the dunces, the victims had sinned not so much against Pope as against poetry, and the thwacking was administered in the name of Art. But whatever the provocation, and whether mere concentrated venom or sheer malicious magic—

> *Pox'd by her love, or libelled by her hate*

or

> *Silence, ye wolves! while Ralph to Cynthia howls*
> *And makes night hideous—Answer him, ye owls!*

or

> *Beauty that shocks you, Parts that none will trust,*
> *Wit that can creep, and Pride that licks the dust*

—the punishment always more than fits the crime.

Diligent in implying the best about himself, Pope shrank—more than a satirist strictly needs to do—from owning up to his more questionable impulses. Having anonymously published something licentious or sharp-toothed, Pope did not merely deny having written it when asked; with a pious look he would deny having written it unasked, and would sometimes go so far as to abuse the poem or "identify" the anonymous author.

Such duplicity, though there may have been an element of self-protection in it, was chiefly grounded in a nature that had to throw dust in people's eyes, had to mislead, had to lie. The letters are filled with pointless lying, often in the form of needlessly fervent or solemn assertions; the life is a tissue of ambiguities and falsifications. Having lied like many another man about his ancestry, Pope proceeded to lie, like very few others, about almost everything else. Professor Sherburn, the foremost living authority on Pope, is indignant that Leslie Stephen should have characterized Pope as "the most untruthful man of his age." It is indeed a whopping indictment, for the age of Pope, furious with faction and intrigue, was outrageously untruthful, outstandingly treacherous. All the same, if Pope was not "the most untruthful man of his age," I do not know who could have been except the man Pope saluted (in the phrase he coined for the occasion) as his "guide, philosopher and friend"—Lord Bolingbroke.

There were other very disagreeable and unworthy qualities—petty plagiarisms, rather shabby dealings with collaborators, a snide withholding of full credit from people who helped Pope as a matter of business or of friendship, a tendency toward smirking and even nasty-mindedness. Yet even to ask the question today, *Was Pope a bad man?* is obviously to beg it. Doubly to beg it: for on the one side there juts up all that tends to redeem Alexander Pope, and on the other, all that helps to explain him. We must seek as much of a medical as of a moral judgment for a man who nearly all his life had a sick crooked body and hence a sick crooked mind. Nor need we be sanctimonious about a man who, endowed with an incomparable talent for vituperation, was prodded time and again into making use of it. We must see Pope, furthermore, in relation to his age: he was enormously sensitive, and the age was coarse; incredibly vain, and the age was cruel. But all the same we must deplore a general lack of forbearance and an almost utter lack of charity in Pope, who, be it noted, put into polished form virtually every cliché of morality except *Love thine enemies,* and who considered the ability "to forgive" as not human but "divine."

The Victorians—most notably the Rev. Whitwell Elwin, who grew so abusive he had to be disbarred from completing what is still the standard edition of Pope's works— went at Pope all wrong. Men so very respectable, and so very repressed, got an almost pathological enjoyment out of being scandalized; and in Pope's endless mendacities, in his overflowing malice, in his habitual and sometimes smirking indecencies, there was much to scandalize them. Moreover, the Victorians railed against Pope as a man during an era when it was safest to depreciate him as an artist. And railed with little restraint: the Rev. Whitwell Elwin displays almost all of Pope's venom without any of his wit. Today the pendulum has rather swung to the other extreme. Since Elwin, who attempted to crucify him, Pope's most biased biographer is Miss Sitwell, who did all she could to make him out a martyr.

But he was even less a martyr than he was a fiend. His hateful qualities are very glaring indeed: there is simply no means of arguing them away, and not much reason to suppose that had other people been habitually sympathetic, Pope would have been habitually kind. His provocations were sometimes great, but in the perspective of a lifetime his revenges seem highly disproportionate. Yet, and not at all from any desire to soften an indictment or throw a sop, it must be made very clear that, beyond a gay and witty side, Pope had a charming side, a kindly side, even a truly loyal and generous side. It was once the custom, after painting Pope at full length as a monster, to concede that he had been good to his family. We can do better than that. The extremely affectionate and devoted son was also, toward a surprising number of people, an

extremely affectionate and devoted friend. He was deeply
and generously attached to Martha Blount. His flattery (as
manifested in his letters) can be degrading, but Pope had
a good deal of social grace, and as a talker and host must
have had a good deal of personal charm. No doubt, like all
the other writers of his age, and most writers in every age,
Pope was a climber and a snob; yet from a very early period of his career he was certainly as much sought after as
seeking; nor would great lords have annually solicited the
honor of housing a difficult semi-invalid had it not been a
pleasure as well.

The man knew how to please almost as artfully as he
knew how to wound. The best of his compliments are very
different from his habitual flatteries—in fact, they do not
rank too far below the best of his barbs. And if Pope loved
a lord, it was not without gallantry: for his loyalties were,
on the whole, much less toward lords in power than toward
lords in opposition, or in retirement, or even in disgrace.
Pope was not at all put off by unpopular causes—you may
say, but I think in this case injudiciously, that a satirist
cannot afford to be—and he was not upset by a worse than
unpopular, by a downright unsafe, religion. More than one
friend bade Pope mend his faith lest it might mar his fortune; but first and last, and as the real victim of some of
its slighter and the potential victim of some of its severer
disabilities, Pope remained an avowed Roman Catholic.
He remained one, moreover, despite being by temperament pretty much a skeptic and by conviction pretty
much a deist. It holds true, I think, that for all that was
sick in Pope, and deceitful, and done for effect, and almost
fiendishly rancorous, he had a quite impressive amount of
character. "That long disease, my life" was spent, not in a
bed, but on a battlefield.

. . .

The Pope we have so far discussed as though he were a rather fascinating character in a novel happened to be a great poet. He happened to be the greatest master of rhymed vituperation in the history of letters; so that even to prick him with a pin was a sure if not very enviable way of achieving immortality. He was also the greatest master of the heroic couplet in the English language; and he was, finally, a great master of words, in sound and in sense, in combination and in opposition: indeed, so much and so mainly an artist that, though spectacularly unlike them in his vision of the world, Pope is commonly grouped with such other pre-eminent artists as Spenser, Milton, Keats, and Tennyson.

How then, we may ask, can there have raged so long and shrill and *à outrance* a conflict over whether this thrice-great poet was a poet at all? How came he, for something like a century, to be so often disparaged or damned with faint praise: was this most conspiratorial of writers himself the victim of a long-drawn-out conspiracy?

I am beginning to give the air of a mystery melodrama to what, after all, is one of the most celebrated reversals of judgment and reflections on shifting taste in literary annals; but there is even now something dramatic, as well as ironical and instructive, about Pope's being toppled from the heights where he reigned so long. Yet, up to a point, what happened to Pope was bound to happen. "Every hero," Emerson remarked, "at last becomes a bore"; and if heroes, how much more readily heroic couplets. People got fed up with heroic couplets, particularly when written by other hands than Pope's; people got fed up with "correctness," particularly when not reinforced by skill; people got fed up with the eighteenth century, particularly if they happened to be living in the nineteenth. It was time an old age was out: poetry, like music, was now to have a darker, dreamier, lusher, and in many ways grander orchestration.

In the new age, unfortunately, Pope was not merely condescended to for writing unfashionable poetry; he was all but ostracized for not writing poetry at all. For he made no appeal to the feelings, or to the senses, or to the soul. One could read him for hours without breathing a larger air, or issuing upon a more glowing landscape; all too often Pope's adjectives were opprobrious, and his figures of speech sheer objects of revulsion. To a century hardly less exalted by Arnold's doubts than by Wordsworth's affirmations, a century equally entranced by the visions of Coleridge and the music of Swinburne, Pope seemed frivolous, mundane, besmirched—and as far removed from poetry as Scott seemed adjacent to it.

All this is so very old a story that it doubtless seems an outmoded one as well. But it is really not: the business of abusing Pope may have stopped, but the business of appreciating him has scarcely been resumed. His poetry remains a stumbling-block; which is to say that while it is safe to call Pope great—in fact very unsafe to call him anything less—the usual yardsticks will never confirm his greatness; nor will a sincere lover of poetry necessarily be a lover of Pope. If he quite reasonably seeks in Pope something that appeals to the feelings or the senses or the soul, he will seldom find it. It is important to state, and even to stress, what Pope was not; and it could possibly be maintained that, in a very restricted and Romantic view, he was not a poet. But there is no view by which it could possibly be maintained that he was not a great genius; and on those grounds Matthew Arnold's dictum that Pope is not a classic of our poetry but a classic of our prose will not hold up. For Arnold clearly meant to demote him to a lower level, and the most that anyone may permissibly do is to exclude him at a corresponding one. At the very least, he is a classic—and a great classic—of our literature.

In the wake of Arnold's calling Pope a classic of our prose, his admirers have been at some pains to exhibit him as—*by Arnold's standards*—a classic of our poetry. They have quoted, over and over, such lines as

> *Die of a rose in aromatic pain*

or

> *Lo! where Maeotis sleeps, and hardly flows*
> *The freezing Tanais thro' a waste of snows.*

And no doubt, had he cared to, Pope might have written, quite consummately, more of Arnold's—or the average poetry-lover's—kind of poetry. But what he happened to write on "poetical" subjects was most of it conventional and even counterfeit, and we are much better off to face the fact. His real glory lies in a different sphere.

That sphere is not, again, the part of Pope that comes readiest to men's lips or bulks largest in Bartlett. Literally anybody who can quote anything can quote (or misquote) Pope:

> *A little learning is a dangerous thing;*

> *To err is human; to forgive divine;*

> *For fools rush in where angels fear to tread.*

It was in giving so sharp a turn to the better-explored truths of life that the twenty-three-year-old Pope achieved his first important success, the *Essay on Criticism;* and of this side of him there is little to add to his own nine-word précis of the subject:

> *What oft was thought, but ne'er so well expressed.*

He reclothed clichés of thought so vividly that they long ago became clichés of language; he became as great an

aphorist and expounder of worldly wisdom as any Poor
Richard in prose. At its own level all this is remarkable;
but all this plainly never made Pope great, or a poet.

What made him both, of course, was his satire—a body
of work in which he mingles autobiography and abuse, is
equally master of the scalpel and the poisoned dart, and
proves himself the most brilliant student of manners of
the age, and the most artful scandalmonger. His is not the
noblest tradition of satire; chastising evildoers interested
him far more than reforming them. He is often very malicious and sometimes very unjust; but he can be as lynx-
eyed as any Saint-Simon, as worldly as La Rochefoucauld,
as witty as Voltaire, as conscientious an artist as Flaubert
and (in his own field)as consummate a one as Virgil.

The artist, indeed, is the important thing about the satirist. Though Pope's stock-in-trade was the famous figures
of his day, as a social historian he can seldom be trusted:
he has La Rochefoucauld's worldliness without his disinterestedness, Saint-Simon's sharp eyesight without his
honesty. And though he may very often happen to be
speaking the truth, once we cease to count on his doing so,
we can approach his satires, and come to value them, as
works of art.[3] The grudges that start off in Pope as goads
wind up as catalysts, converting flawed eighteenth-century

---

[3] The point of many of Pope's jibes is now quite lost, and the point
of many others depends on a detailed knowledge of Pope's era. A full
appreciation of Pope's work is possible only to someone up to his neck
in the social and political, the literary and artistic, history and gossip of
seventeenth- and eighteenth-century England and Europe, with a further
very ripe background of antiquity; and—since Pope "imitated" on an
immense scale—with a solid knowledge of four or five literatures to boot.
The perfectly equipped reader of the Satires or *The Dunciad*, effortlessly catching the point of each reference as he reads along, is indeed
to be envied; but the non-scholar cannot achieve the same experience by
boning up, by constantly grappling with footnotes. It is better, on the
whole, to miss many of Pope's allusions than, by fussing over them, to
miss any of Pope's art.

figures into flawless characters of fiction. Pope's Sporus is no more Lord Hervey than Dickens's Harold Skimpole is Leigh Hunt: Sporus is a good deal more wicked and immeasurably more wonderful. Yet it is not quite true that Pope always had to invent or exaggerate or unscrupulously "arrange" his portraits in order to triumph: the resemblance between Atticus and Addison, for example, is uncomfortably close.

Moreover, though Pope took revenge in print—and superb revenge—upon his enemies, it was his essential self as much as particular circumstances that made a great satirist of him; which is to say that it came quite as naturally to him to be abusive as to feel abused. Consider his portrait of Narcissa:

> *Narcissa's nature, tolerably mild,*
> *To make a wash, would hardly stew a child;*
> *Has even been proved to grant a lover's prayer,*
> *And paid a tradesman once to make him stare;*
> *Gave alms at Easter, in a Christian trim,*
> *And made a widow happy, for a whim.*

"Narcissa" may be a sobriquet for somebody Pope disliked; but we feel here a malice—if malice it be—that has been so completely aërated into sheer wit, we feel here so much greater an impulse to create a portrait than to destroy a person, that no animus seems involved.

Pope furthermore proves himself quite as brilliant a satiric artist when pure worldling as when pure wasp: it is the hundreds upon hundreds of lines in the style and at the level of

> *A saint in crape is twice a saint in lawn*

or

> *Proud to catch cold at a Venetian door*

that are most representative of Pope's skill and most indica-
tive of his temperament. He had a "sophisticated" knowledge of the world that contained much truth, even if too
much cynicism: indeed, so easily wounded by particular
men that he could never be very wise about them, Pope
was wisest about mankind in the mass.

Mankind for Pope—the mankind, at any rate, that Pope
has any first-hand understanding of—is chiefly the society
world, whose follies feel the cold hard glare of his wit:

> *Pleasure the sex, as children Birds, pursue,*
> *Still out of reach, yet never out of view . . .*
> *At last, to follies Youth could scarce defend,*
> *It grows their Age's prudence to pretend . . .*
> *As Hags hold Sabbaths, less for joy than spite,*
> *So these their merry, miserable Night;*
> *Still round and round the Ghosts of Beauty glide,*
> *And haunt the places where their Honour died.*
> *See how the World its Veterans rewards!*
> *A Youth of Frolics, an old Age of Cards;*
> *Fair to no purpose, artful to no end,*
> *Young without Lovers, old without a Friend;*
> *A Fop their Passion, but their Prize a Sot;*
> *Alive, ridiculous, and dead, forgot!*

Now and then, as in his great parody that comes so close
to being great poetry, Pope—and not just because Pope's
Homer is reverberating in our ear—manages to transform
the tarnished social spectacle into a kind of fairyland of
regret, to give things a true moral coloration, to bring them
to a delicate emotional pitch:

> *Oh; if to dance all night, and dress all day*
> *Charm'd the small-pox, or chas'd old-age away;*
> *Who would not scorn what housewife's cares produce,*

Or who would learn one earthly thing of use?
To patch, nay ogle, might become a saint,
Nor could it sure be such a sin to paint.
But since, alas! frail beauty must decay,
Curl'd or uncurl'd, since locks will turn to grey;
Since painted, or not painted, all shall fade,
And she who scorns a man, must die a maid;
What then remains, but well our pow'r to use,
And keep good-humor still whate'er we lose?
And trust me, dear! good-humour can prevail,
When airs, and flights, and screams, and scolding fail.

Here we have a sensibility apprehended through the gauze of worldly wit that is one of the finest things about Pope.

And let us note in passing another fine thing about him. That Pope's war against the dunces was fundamentally a Holy War in the service of art is so beyond serious dispute as to have become a critical commonplace; but I think it is very far from well known generally. Unfortunately, the "little monster" squirting his poison at his Grub-Street ill-wishers has quite effaced the fiery poet brandishing his sword in a great cause. Yet Pope's sniping at his very large circle of enemies, and even his deplorable sneering at those "sons of a day," the starveling hacks, is incidental to his grand mock-epic design of attacking dullness and incapacity. Pope's record in the matter of appraising his contemporaries would do credit to the most disinterested and distinguished of professional critics: whom Pope abandoned, few subsequent critics have defended; and whom Pope praised—though here the record is far less remarkable—usually deserved to be praised. He was "moral" about writers, *qua* writers, because he was passionate about literature.

As a moralist about life, Pope seems to me to have infinitely less importance. Until quite recently, in fact, it would scarcely have occurred to me to discuss the point. But it was no doubt inevitable that one kind of excess about Pope should be followed by another; that he should come to be acclaimed, as he had formerly been assailed, on quite the wrong grounds; and that, while we were most of us absolving Pope of a number of his sins and labeling the rest of them sickness, some few should actually find him a moral poet in as grave and positive a sense as Dr. Johnson is. For a particularly earnest example of this sort, turn to *The Moral Poetry of Pope,* by Geoffrey Tillotson. Professor Tillotson labors to show, not only that Pope's was a "sound morality," but that when he moralized in couplets he produced genuine poetry. Now Pope, like other mixed and malignant beings, possessed intense moral sensibility and saw all that was beautiful in virtue; he was quite as "moral" as the next man who aims high but only fitfully practices what he preaches. And no doubt what Pope preached was sound enough: but sound preaching is a very different matter from sound poetry. Out-and-out didactic verse has poetic impact, as a rule, only to the extent that it has personal impact, whether of vision or of style. Pope, borrowing and embroidering the standard texts—Pope, producing "what oft was thought but ne'er so well expressed"—quite fails to write good poetry, though he frequently writes good epigrams. Even Dr. Johnson's second-best manner, even

> *Still raise for good the supplicating voice,*
> *But leave to Heaven the measure and the choice*

has an accent that Pope quite lacks. It required, not a moral philosopher, but a great poet like Homer to raise Pope to a "poetically" serious level (and even there, Pope is neat where Homer is spacious):

> *But since, alas! ignoble age must come,*
> *Disease, and death's inexorable doom,*
> *The life which others pay, let us bestow,*
> *And give to fame what we to Nature owe.*

The poet usually slumbers in Pope when he is formulating moral laws, and only comes broad awake when he can single out who broke them; when he can tag Addison as

> *Willing to wound, and yet afraid to strike*

or dub Bacon

> *The wisest, brightest, meanest of mankind.*

Professor Tillotson's praise of Pope as a moral poet seems to me the kind of thing from which Pope—and particularly now, when he is being restored to much of his former glory—must be saved. Exactly as Matthew Arnold insisted that it is not in his moral effusions but in the roaring bestiality of *The Jolly Beggars* that Burns achieves superb poetry, so we may insist that Pope being moral usually writes smooth couplets, but Pope being malicious usually writes glorious verse. It is much to be hoped that Pope will not come back in style as a sort of tarnished saint, or an Interesting Mind. Ours is an age with, critically, a greater capacity to analyze than to appreciate. It is an age very good at reducing a work of art to its social and political, or its religious and psychological elements; an age very apt at telling us what a given work of art signifies, or symbolizes, or suggests; or whence it derives or toward what it is moving. It is just not a very splendid age for telling us what a work of art *is;* what it, so to speak, tastes like. And with Pope, even though he palpably derives from dozens of earlier poets and tremendously influenced dozens of later ones, the only very important thing is the poetry itself. Compared with what there is to appreciate in him, there is

little to analyze. Technically, yes: Pope's metrics will repay endless study; but his "meaning" demands almost
none. Goethe said of Byron: "Whenever he thinks, he is a
child"; and it might be as fairly said of Pope: "Whenever
he thinks, he is a plagiarist." His works are a sort of anthology of other men's thoughts and beliefs and moral sentiments; only the language is Pope's, only the language
really mattered to him, and only the language, for the most
part, need matter for us. On the other hand, and it involves nothing contradictory, Pope is enormously cerebral
as an *artist*.

In almost every way, in fact, he is one of the most
astounding technicians, one of the most astounding artists,
in the whole history of verse. (It is to be hoped that our
many distinguished critic-poets—one or two of whom, like
Mr. Auden, have already written well but too briefly of
Pope—will turn their attention to him.) He scarcely needed
to think, or to appeal very strongly to the feelings or the
senses or the soul, in order to be great; and whoever
doubts that a supreme gift for verse and vituperation adds
up to greatness, had better steer clear of him. Deliberately
I have left to the very end mention of certain qualities of
Pope which one would sometimes gather are beneath notice in literature, but which I am bound to think are above
praise—his great energy, gaiety, verve. They are the qualities that keep Pope—and most literature—fresh; that make
Pope—and much literature—fun.

(1948)

CHAPTER IV

Robinson Crusoe

AMONG the world's great writers, scarcely any has cared so much about expediency, has been so philistine and calculating in his methods, as Daniel Defoe; and yet none, in a sense, has calculated so badly. For though his works of fiction run to sixteen solid volumes, to the world at large he is simply and solely the author of *Robinson Crusoe*. The rays of that blinding sun have quite extinguished even such brilliant stars as *Moll Flanders* and *Roxana* and *A Journal of the Plague Year*. But that is hardly the worst of it. To the world at large, *Robinson Crusoe*, however celebrated, is not a book for men but a book for boys; lore, not literature. It is something that everybody has read, though perhaps not everybody can remember reading it; it is, or was until recently, as much a part of boyhood as the slingshot and the circus. But it can hardly be said to rank with the indispensable, or with even the most popular, novels for grown-ups. The reason why—or, better yet, the instinct why, is easy to grasp. If one is not a sentimentalist, one may well wonder whether even the very greatest of boys' books will constitute an exhilarating experience for men. And if one is a sentimentalist, one may wonder whether anything one loved so much in childhood should be touched, tampered with, re-examined—how can it help letting one down?

Well, one can only speak for oneself; but when some years ago I went back to *Robinson Crusoe*, I was enthralled. I'm sure it helped that I went back rather expecting to be disappointed, as it may hinder if, after reading this essay, you pick up the book expecting to be instantly dazzled. But I doubt whether it helped, and I doubt whether it can hinder, much. I can understand (though not easily) anyone quitting the story before Crusoe gets shipwrecked on the island, or again after Crusoe sails away from it. And I can understand (quite easily) anyone who should impatiently toss aside the succeeding volume of Crusoe's adventures—because I have twice done that myself. But in *Robinson Crusoe* itself, so long as Robinson is held fast on the island, so long must the reader be too. For just that long he is in the presence of a masterpiece, and of what might almost be declared a miracle: for a situation that has, in itself, an intense and universal lure is somehow handled exactly as it should be. The only thing that for me has the same kind of magnetism as the island section of *Robinson Crusoe* is the piloting chapters of *Life on the Mississippi*. In both we are offered what might be called a discourse on method; and in the plain utilitarian details of both there is something immensely romantic, something that fires our youth, and then long after rekindles it.

For however grim and disconsolate the situation of a man all alone on an island, who ever saw Crusoe there in any such light? So far from making his hero tragic, Defoe makes us—or at least the eternal boy in us—not pity but envy him. Crusoe is not only monarch of all he surveys; but by virtue of his experiences and his predicament he acquires for us something like the rank of a mighty hunter or a great explorer. What were in truth quite back-breaking obstacles are time and again made to seem like glorious opportunities; he is no realist who pursues *Crusoe* as realism. This is no poor devil who while under sentence, as it were, of solitary confinement must also forage for food and beware of cannibals. This, rather, is a man with a whole island for a toy, who may build him as many residences and pleasuredoms as he fancies, and trek lordlike through his own forests and sail along his coasts and herd his goats and harvest his crops and ransack the ship for plunder. There is something of the morning of the world about it all; yet together with the unspotted opportunities of the first man, Crusoe has all the ingrained skill and knowledge of many generations of Britons. Hence, single-handed, he converts a rough-hewn Eden into a rough-hewn England. From one point of view, it is odd that we should find all this romantic; for Crusoe's stubborn resistance to the call of the wild is so outside Nature that it could only be believed of something so equally outside Nature as the trueborn Englishman. We can be very glad of this, however. For it would need a rather diseased taste to enjoy watching Robinson sink to the level of the brute and perhaps below it; whereas there is a healthy and creative satisfaction in watching him turn his island into a tidy Little England.

Which brings us to something stranger still—the fact that Crusoe's story is so intensely interesting only because Crusoe himself is so incredibly dull. But then, to do what he did, he had to be what he was; to make a second England, he had to believe fanatically in the first; not to go mad at the end, he had to be a trifle mad from the outset; in the midst of abounding self-pity he had to be sustained by consuming self-interest; even God had to be a sort of

Magnate with whom, in effect, a lesser businessman could bargain. Of all the great heroes of fiction, Crusoe is surely the one who would have bored us the most in the flesh. With me, indeed, it is a nice point whether I should prefer to be shipwrecked, as he was, alone; or with him alone for company. He has no humor, no charm, no sensibility, no reach of mind, no grace of perception. Dickens truly remarked that *Crusoe* is the one great novel that never calls forth either laughter or tears. Robinson is smug, he is crass, he is—like Defoe himself—hypocritical in grain. But if he contains almost everything that is arid and coarse in the British character, he exemplifies, as well, everything that is admirable. He is plucky, sturdy, self-reliant, practical, imperturbable—the very essence of that race which thinks it unmanly to grumble and ungentlemanly to gloat.

Others have noted how cleverly Defoe allowed Crusoe just enough in the way of equipment and fodder and tools for him at the outset to stay alive, and in the course of time to be made comfortable. And to a nicety too, I would add, Defoe has contrived when total solitude shall cease. For at length the point is reached where Robinson has achieved as much in the way of civilization as he finds possible, or we find fun; it is the point where, in a commoner run of novel, the hero after long and arduous struggle has made his pile and is ready for a mate. Defoe cannot in the circumstances offer Crusoe a mate; and he need not—a companion, for the reader at any rate, does quite as well. So lo! there appears in the sand that single footprint which is still, after two centuries, more dramatic and thrilling than all the fingerprints in the very best whodunits; and presently there appears on the scene that savage who is still, after two centuries, the most famous of all servants. Once he has Friday to educate, Crusoe can embark on his great secondary English role; having contrived all by himself a Little England, he turns Friday all by himself into a Little India. After that and a round of skirmishing with cannibals, it is permitted to sail for home.

After that, there are further adventures, of course—as there had been a whole slew of them before the ship-wreck. But the picaresque parts of the book, though lively, are no part of the miracle; the miracle belongs to the island, where neither Crusoe nor Defoe can go astray, nor Robinson be ever anywhere but at home. And this is of enormous help to a teller of stories who is absolutely incapable of constructing a genuine plot. Defoe can invent endlessly, but hardly integrate at all; one thing does not come out of another, it merely comes after it. The artistic shortcomings, the essential discontinuity of such a method are obvious; and it can be truthfully maintained that Defoe's genius most expands where his geography least does—in the island parts of *Crusoe* and in the *Plague Year*. For these two works have something of the concentration of interest, the intensive force that distinguish the novel from the tale, and the work of art from the mere irruption of talent. On the other hand, by the singularity of their subject-matter, they have had not the slightest influence on the serious novel itself; whereas *Moll Flanders* and *Roxana* have probably had a good deal.

No doubt there is much to say of the exotic fascination of *Robinson Crusoe;* of the oppressive sense of danger and appalling sense of solitude; of the flora and fauna, the parrots and cats. But this side of the story counted much more for me in boyhood than it does now. What lures me on is much less the creepiness of the island noises at midnight than tomorrow's straightforward effort to build a fence or bake a pot; the given A and B, how to contrive C; the given A, B, and C, how to bring off D—straight on to ampersand. This marvelous resourcefulness on Crusoe's part, this determination to wrest comfort out of chaos, this transforming a wilderness into a one-man state, in which he is both architect and builder, husbandman and housewife, management and labor, commoner and king, awakens in us a very delighted response. But of course *Crusoe* does have much also in the way of thrills and suspense—consider the blood-curdling encounter with the wolves; and it is the greatest of all boys' books because it is about equally compounded of derring-do and "Do and Dare," the adventure yarn and the Alger story. Accordingly, this dullard whom one would in real life run screaming from has caught and forever held the imagination of mankind.

(1949)

CHAPTER V

Lady Mary Wortley Montagu

THE LIFE and Letters of Lady Mary Wortley Montagu must be accounted two very dissimilar things. In the flesh, Lady Mary had her numerous and quite serious drawbacks: her progress through the world was neither sweet-tempered, nor tranquil, nor at all *comme il faut*. In her letters, on the other hand, she possessed almost every qualification for making people wish to know her. To begin with, she had contrived to belong to England's finest age of letter-writing and hence to partake of all its predominant merits—a prose that combined elegance with ease; a courtesy that, if superficial, endowed the surface with a brilliant gloss; a worldliness that relished gossip, appreciated comedy, sniffed at highfalutin avowals, and moralized brightly in epigrams In addition, Lady Mary shared in that leisure which made it possible for privileged people to write their friends letters at considerable length with considerable regularity. But as a letter-writer Lady Mary not only enjoyed all the best gifts of the eighteenth-century patrician; she had special and picturesque virtues of her own. There was her highly charged, instantly perceptible personality, which in her correspondence she kept on leash. There was her wit, by no means first-rate, but frequent and enlivening; there was her born talent for words. Finally, she knew everyone and went everywhere. A superb letter-writer like Byron, she was also like Byron a genuine cosmopolite. For almost fifty years, from the time she set out, an ambassador's wife, to cross Europe in her coach, till, looking more like a witch than a woman, she crept home to die, Lady Mary moved from one European spa and private villa and provincial court to another, an unwearied traveler, an indefatigable correspondent.

Almost from her cradle Lady Mary had had opportunities to see the world and savor its worldliness. By her own confession, the happiest day of her life came when she was not yet eight—when, on a whim, her father proposed her as a toast at the celebrated Kit-Kat Club and, to prove she was pretty enough to deserve that honor, had her fetched to the clubrooms. There, passed from lap to lap of the most eminent personages in England, "she was received with acclamations, her claim unanimously allowed, her health drunk by everyone present, and her name engraved, in due form, upon a drinking glass." The incident sheds, too, a certain light upon her father. Plainly, to belong to the Kit-Kat, he was very much of a Whig and at least something of a wit; also a capricious and indulgent man with more paternal vanity than love; and, as one possibly might guess, a widower. Her father, Evelyn Pierrepont, who later became Duke of Kingston, did not indeed much concern himself with Lady Mary's childhood. Her education was put into the hands of a governess, though its success was due largely to herself—it was through her own efforts, for example, that she learned Latin; while for warmth and affection there was happily her maternal grandmother, the Countess of Denbigh. Her literary ties of blood almost outstrip her social ones: as the daughter of a Fielding, she was the great novelist's cousin; as the granddaughter of an Evelyn, she was the great diarist's. And already in girlhood she read many ponderous classics and—from our point of view—even more ponderous trash.

It was indeed owing to her criticisms of a new play, when at fourteen she first met her future husband, that she immediately riveted his interest. This incident, too, sheds a certain light. Edward Wortley Montagu was just the sort of man to be brought round to what might pass, on his part, for love through what might pass, on Lady Mary's, for learning. He confessed he could not have been more thunderstruck had he heard a waxwork speak.

Of their romance, their elopement, their many years of married life together, their many years of married life apart, very much comes out in Lady Mary's letters, though some things have never been explained. At the outset, in any case, Mr. Wortley [1]—a stuffy fellow in our view, but a handsome one in Lady Mary's—plainly captivated the young girl. "A slow man with a taste for quick companions," he for the most part made love to Lady Mary by forcing Lady Mary to make love to him. But the courtship, whether or not truly ardent, was in all respects sufficiently arduous. The cautious, priggish Wortley—who carried everything, even romance, to the fourth decimal place—refused to settle money on an unknown heir who might turn out to be an idiot; wherefore Lady Mary's

---

[1] His family name was Montagu; but his father assumed his mother's name of Wortley on marrying her. The name was later made into Wortley Montagu.

father refused to sanction the match. Having disqualified himself with her father, the thoroughgoing Wortley next subjected Lady Mary to stout trials of character and stern tests of devotion, all of which roused her to high-mettled but not very resolute chidings and farewells; and after the lovers had exchanged any number of letters in which love assumed all kinds of prosaic and querulous shapes, they finally (just as Lady Mary's father had brought forth a suitor of his own) eloped.

During the first weeks after the elopement, the bride was kept not too acquiescently in the country while her husband transacted business and politics in town; but soon after, marriage opened the door for her on an active social life in London and Twickenham. Wortley was already the friend of Addison and Steele, and Lady Mary presently became the friend of Pope. As a devout Whig, Mr. Wortley benefited from the Whig triumph at the accession of George I, and was soon after made ambassador to Constantinople. He did not shine as an ambassador—he apparently did not shine at anything but the hoarding of money—and, after no great while, was recalled to England. But the ambassadorship had started Lady Mary on her travels, and occasioned indeed her longest journey and most famous sojourn. Nothing is better known about her than that in Turkey she penetrated the harem, or that on her return to England she introduced the Turkish custom of inoculation against smallpox. This latter act, which caused furious opposition in Britain until it was shown to work, was Lady Mary's one indisputable service to humanity.

The Wortleys returned to London in 1718, when Lady Mary was not quite thirty; and for twenty years thereafter she was part of the life of the Court and the town, pursuing her highhanded, steadily quarrelsome, increas-

ingly eccentric way. Much the most chronicled event of
those years is her quarrel with Pope. The exact cause of
the quarrel has never been determined: perhaps, as Ma-
lone and others would have it, Lady Mary borrowed some
sheets of Pope's mother and sent them back unwashed;
perhaps, as is rather more commonly held, Lady Mary
burst out laughing when Pope made love to her. Probably
there *was* no single cause, only a final collision: as Bagehot
has suggested, it was inevitable for two people who quarreled with everybody else to quarrel with each other. The
quarrel survives, in any case, as one of the most rancorous
in history, with Lady Mary (in the guise of "Sappho")
hounded down the centuries by the greatest of all masters
of personal attack. On the other hand, Lady Mary got on
swimmingly during her London days with the one other
person equal to Pope and her in quarrelsomeness, and no
less equal in renown—the Duchess of Marlborough.

Just what Lady Mary's relations with her husband had
come to be is less certain—whether the two had gradually
drifted apart, or whether something specific now abruptly
divided them. Their separating has long been a matter for
speculation, with the strongest hints of scandal.[2] Perhaps
tongues were wagging over Lady Mary's having love affairs, and Mr. Wortley would have no more of it; perhaps
she only wished to have her love affairs where tongue-
wagging would not signify. At any rate, in 1739 when she
was just past fifty, she set forth for the Continent, and
only returned at seventy-two, soon after her husband's
death and not long before her own. Though she and
Wortley wrote to each other for many years, and Wortley

---

[2] Professor Robert Halsband, an authority on Lady Mary whose
forthcoming *Life* promises to become the standard one, has uncovered
proofs of Lady Mary's passionate involvement with an Italian, which explains the break with Wortley and their joint desire for her to remove to
the Continent.

preserved and made a précis of every letter he received from her, they never met again.

Nothing of great moment happened to Lady Mary during her twenty-odd years abroad. The varieties of scenery, the changes of air, the now elegant now impromptu diversions of an English lady of fashion turned bohemian and eccentric; turned conceivably sluttish and slatternly beyond all doubt; and at last turned ill-favored and elderly —all this is the stuff of her most brightly colored letters. And there might be a greater temptation to philosophize about it all, did not Lady Mary philosophize so stridently herself. In any case, it is these wayside habitations, these halts in a procession to nowhere, that strike us as possibly Lady Mary's most characteristic homes. If she lacks the tragic dignity of the exile, she possesses the rather splendid isolation of the nonconformist. Of such a person, always spiritually in motion, it is hard to say whether each new movement constitutes exploration or flight. Such a person is never, at any rate, commonplace; and Lady Mary must in her own day have been one of those characters who, if struck by the arrows of scandal, are yet a little protected by the armor of legend. When she finally dragged herself back to London to die, she was not so much sought out as a once-celebrated grande dame as stared at as a kind of distinguished freak.

Her connections with Constantinople and Pope aside, Lady Mary's career has scarcely a footnote's worth of historical value. Her fame stems altogether from literature, by virtue of the letters she wrote, the history she *recorded*. And indeed the most noticeable value she has now, the greatest use to which with the passing of time she has come to be put, is that of social historian. One cannot read much about eighteenth-century life—or write, really, anything at all—without meeting or drawing upon her. She had large social opportunities which she fully seized upon, and others that she might be said (for she did not lack aggressiveness) to have created. She had sharp eyesight, keen hearing, a malicious tongue, and not too squeamish a nature or lurid an imagination—so that she is almost always diverting and surprisingly often reliable. Neither in amplitude nor range, to be sure—nor yet in centrality—is she the equal of Horace Walpole. But she did not eye posterity with the same ambition as Walpole; she did not try to *chronicle* an age. She eyed posterity fixedly enough, however: speaking of Mme de Sévigné's letters, "Very pretty they are," she remarked, "but I assert without the least vanity, that mine will be full as entertaining forty years hence." Yet it is important to note that it was precisely with another great lady that she compared herself; with a letter-writer whose touch is quite personal, whose province quite feminine. In just such directions lay her real strength. Lady Mary's Turkish letters, self-conscious to begin with and extremely self-conscious as finally revised, still have much interest and value of a sort; but set beside Lady Mary at her best, the letters become stiff and over-literary and have all the drawbacks of set pieces. Like most good memorialists of an age, Lady Mary is as notable for what she *didn't* know would some day seem striking as for what she did. In the main, however, she knew quite enough—she knew, which is indeed almost everything, the difference between the lively and the dull. And because she was writing from abroad, she had reason to set down contrasts between life in England and on the Continent, a practice that furnishes contrasts today between life in her century and in ours. The letters are full of such particulars as that in Constantinople a lady's position derives from her lover's rank rather than her husband's, or that "it is indecent for a widow ever to wear green or rose color." Again, with Lady Mary living at such a distance from London, her daughter had the obligation to pass along current gossip and society chatter; and much of this gossip Lady Mary annotates or retorts upon, tossing in here an anecdote and there a generality. As social historian she is, indeed, among that small company who, ranking as "primary sources" of information, are also primary sources of enjoyment.

For my own part, however, the portraiture of these letters counts for less than the portrait-painter: what is most valuable in the end is not Lady Mary's record of the world about her, but what she reveals and conceals, fancies and fails to notice about herself. She writes with a good deal of care, partly out of politeness to her correspondent, partly out of deference to an audience unborn; but frequently, too, she writes in haste, in irritation, in anger, in no mood to soften her language or polish her style, but simply to be vocal about what interests or discommodes her, to find an outlet for her energy, or (one would guess) an escape from boredom. She was much alone, and even she might well sometimes be lonely: clearly one motive she had in writing letters was to receive them. And of course writing letters was of immense service to her: it was not only her greatest talent, it was equally her safest form of contact. She and Mr. Wortley could contrive no satisfactory relationship in flesh and blood, but they did handsomely, for twenty years, with pen and ink. At home, Lady Mary had got on rather badly with her daughter: from abroad she got on very well. It was indeed to everybody's advantage—the family's and the future's—that she chose to put the best of herself in writing: it enabled her contemporaries to steer clear of her faults; it allows us, even today, to rejoice in her virtues. Writing, as she so often did, to close connections, she could comment without restraint, disparage and dissent at will;

and we are drawn very close to a woman who, while always herself, was still a true part of her age. These letters are as valid autobiography as they are social chronicles or records of travel.

Very graphic autobiography, in fact. To begin with, Lady Mary draws so good a self-portrait as to enforce the impression that we could not have helped disliking her. A little ironically, we would in part have disliked Lady Mary for qualities that almost do her credit: a refusal to be sentimental; a tendency to be blunt; a kind of willingness to pay the price of her prejudices and inclinations. She was, even for her own day, a hard woman, with the insensibilities of the privileged, the callousness of the cynical, the weak affections of the selfish. Though one has a most decided feeling that her whole life breathes an intense frustration—that she aspired to eminence, and to trifling gave up what was meant for career—she nevertheless, so far as she knew how, brusquely commandeered what she wanted. She was a true aristocrat in the old Renaissance sense, when privilege signified, above everything else, participation, and disdained the kind of exclusiveness that cuts one off from half the enjoyments of life. In Lady Mary, the careless bohemian, we can still sniff the feudal appetites of the barbarian. She is an aristocrat in the exact sense that her contemporary Horace Walpole was not one; and to begin with, of course, Walpole was not one even by blood. Walpole, with his squeamishness, his fussiness, his need of a life all hedges and palings, all conventions and gambits, is overbred—a predestined dilettante. His whole *human* make-up is conditioned by vanity and fear—a fear of emotion, of exposure, of ridicule, of bad taste: he darts and improvises and experiments, to be sure, but inside a cosmos with the dimensions of a bird cage, and with all the fluttering movements of a bird. This is to define, not to condemn, a man who certainly had genius— and by stating what he was, to insist on what the normal patrician was not. Lady Mary shows absolutely nothing of Walpole's uneasiness, but has rather an unshatterable aplomb. Her very coarseness suggests the true aristocrat, whose stigmata is co-ordination rather than sensibility; manner rather than mannerliness; the ability to dominate a situation rather than endow it with grace. Lady Mary had a good deal of personal self-esteem, but also a good deal of pure class assurance. She was very often impelled to be courteous, and even here and there to be kind; but she was far oftener merely unfeeling or arrogant. Doubtless she was extremely ill-served by some of her closest relationships: her father set her a wretched example of self-indulgence; her husband put her to the utmost extremes of forbearance; her son was an utter and by no means engaging scamp. To what extent all this affected her character is hard to determine; what is quite clear is that it never weakened her spirit. She disregarded her father, she shook herself free of her husband, she turned her back on her son. She had not the slightest ability to be tragic, but at least she made no fraudulent efforts to seem so.

If she had the hardness of the age, she had also the clear-sightedness and good sense; and the three qualities together made her a thoroughgoing worldling. Lady Oxford would seem to be the only woman she ever counted on, or cared about, as a friend; and as she looked upon friendship, so she looked upon love. In her letters to her daughter she manages to be a good, indeed a sagacious, mother; but we can't help feeling that hers were very temperate maternal emotions, and that if she was resolved not to burden Lady Bute with filial responsibilities, she was equally resolved that Lady Bute should confer no anxieties upon her. "You are no more obliged to me," she writes, "for bringing you into the world, than I am to you for coming into it, and I never made use of that common-place (and like most common-place, false) argument, as exacting any return of affection." This makes excellent sense, but hardly argues deep feeling. In her relations with her son, of course, Lady Mary shows an utter lack of sentimentalism that has a good deal of character, but also a touch of monstrousness, about it. Having taken young Wortley's measure, she coldly condemned him, accepting her own share of the punishment: "I look upon it as on the loss of a limb, which ceases to give solicitude by being irretrievable." Toward people in general, toward life in the mass, she shows a corresponding clear-sightedness: "As the world is, and will be, 'tis a sort of duty to be rich."—"The world never believes it possible for people to act out of the common track; and whoever is not employed by the public, may talk what they please of having refused or slighted great offers; but they are always looked upon, either as neglected, or discontented."—"It is the common doctrine of (what are called) good books, to inspire a contempt of beauty, richness, greatness, &c. which has done as much mischief . . . as an over eager desire of them."

Out of a lifetime's experience she could fish back, for counseling courtiers, to a Turkish maxim: "Caress the favorites, avoid the unfortunate, and trust nobody." Yet, though doubtless cynical in grain, she was perhaps not altogether resigned to the coldhearted way of the world: her quarreling, her wandering, her moralizing all hint at an unfulfilled vision of life as it might be lived. There may have been no real aspiration, only personal ambitiousness; there may have been no better reason for her quarrels than a determination to have her own way: yet to have been so signally disappointed in one's father, and then in one's husband, and then in one's son, is to some degree to have been disappointed in life itself—and to have chosen insensibility as a way to escape unhappiness. With insensibility, at any rate, she went well armed; and she was certainly no more blessed with illusions than she was burdened. To *prefer* the Continent, where life was more sinuous, decadent, personally isolated, sexually free; where, as a foreigner, one was in continuous danger of being bilked, blackmailed, lied to, looked askance at, spied upon; where what devotion existed sprang from ancient local attachments, where what religion was practiced was alien to one's own—to do this, one must have indeed determined the exact price of things and decided to pay it; to have ceased to care, no doubt, but if so to have in some sense ceased to complain.

And though, despite all her philosophizing, Lady Mary was not altogether philosophical about life, she does seem—more fully and competently than most—to have been self-sufficient. She valued her own opinions, she trusted her own reactions, she enjoyed her own society, more than she did other people's; and she had, after all, those two traits that no one feigns and that people who are unsure of themselves particularly fear—she was closefisted and she was physically dirty. Her behavior in money matters was a real bond with her husband, who lived one of the stingiest and died one of the wealthiest commoners in England. Her slatternliness is, of course, proverbial: it is what lends most credence to the story of the unwashed sheets. It is clinched by her confession, at the age of sixty-eight, that she had not looked in a mirror for eleven years; and it is immortalized by her remarking, to someone who told her at the opera that her hands were dirty: "You should see my feet." [3] If there is any very good argument for acquitting her, at least in after years, of loose living, it is her appearance and personal habits. Who, after all, would have become the lover of a woman so repulsive—since she was so penny-pinching into the bargain?

The whole spectacle—social, moral, physical—of her later life is a tarnished and even messy one: yet this too has some sort of odd basis in good sense, as though in parting with her illusions about life, she was damned if thenceforth she would suffer its inconveniences. Whatever she did (she doubtless told herself), she was bound to be gossiped about; whatever her motives, they were likely to be thought bad; so that as time went on she showed less and less concern for the proprieties and tossed her reputation to the winds of chance. Already as a girl she had written: "I believe more follies are committed out of complaisance to the world, than in following our own inclinations—Nature is seldom wrong, custom always. . . . I am amazed to see . . . that people of good sense in other things can make their happiness consist in the opinions of others, and sacrifice everything in the desire of appearing in fashion." She became in some respects almost ostentatiously unconventional. She traded elegance for eccentricity, telling herself perhaps that, though life had to be a burden, living need not be. All the same—as a great many of her letters are the first to show—it was propriety she dispensed with, not good breeding. She preserved her sense of form; she maintained, however erratically, her place in the scheme of things. She was never déclassée; she was always, even if simultaneously a freak, a great lady. And though at its worst her mode of life must have been positively be-

---

[3] It was an age when, on the Continent that Lady Mary inhabited, a young girl showed special favor to a young man by allowing him to pluck the vermin out of her hair.

draggled, her actual life, regarded as an adventure in living, had style. What remained to the very end, so to speak, was bone structure.

Her writing displays it also—has also that sense of a person molded but never submerged by a period. Sometimes, of course, as in her letters to Lady Pomfret, Lady Mary is so glibly ceremonious that she just adds an insincerity of her own to the insipidities of the age. Sometimes, again, she strains to be sprightly and the note is all too forced. Yet there is always something terse, telling, racy in her letters; a sudden thrust; a startling phrase; a passage that delights for its grace; or that evokes, in what it describes or through how it describes it, a vanished age.

Such things—the eloquent detail, the airy unscaffolded use of language—are the signs of the born letter-writer; and it is the abundance of them that makes the eighteenth-century letter-writer supreme. Certain people's letters are, of course, valuable and even fascinating for what they contain, but the value and fascination are in the end documentary. Other people's letters—Pope's most relevantly here—are studied compositions, literary exercises, frauds. Somewhere between the two, and in the occasional touch rather than the whole texture, is the slightly "literary" example of the good letter. Amid so much that is personal, trivial, volatile, there needs to be a pinch of that more profoundly personal quality, style. The whole thing, in other words, must be ever so delicately starched. Lady Mary has just the right pinch of this: she is neither too formal nor too feminine, she clearly likes words, but just as clearly does not live for them. She lacks the sovereign virtures of her era—Walpole's artistry, Chesterfield's urbanity, Gray's beauty of tone; but she equally lacks the defects of these virtues—Walpole's self-consciousness, Chesterfield's punctilio, Gray's thinness of content. Though she almost

never achieves the heights, she keeps to perhaps the pleasantest level of all her century's letter-writers: she summons up her century, but without suppressing herself. She
is thus wonderfully readable. Her letters constitute, in
fact, the only book that Dr. Johnson read through, in later
life, purely for pleasure.

And I suspect that Dr. Johnson read her through not
from concern for her character nor admiration for her
prose: his chief reason, our chief reason, her chief merit
being, in the final analysis, that she is excellent company.
No doubt this is a composite merit, deriving from her
skill as a social chronicler, her vivaciousness as a writer,
her revelations as a human being; yet it is more than precisely the sum of these things, there is yet something else
involved. Swift, in his *Journal to Stella,* is an immensely
valuable social historian, an almost too fascinating autobiographer, a master of colloquial prose; yet, for me at
least, he is *not* excellent company; the *Journal* is always a
little flat and often a little dull. Mrs. Carlyle is perhaps the
most similar instance of "excellent company"; the supreme
instance I would think to be Byron. To be excellent company, a letter-writer ought to be engaging regardless of
subject-matter. He ought, again, not to interest us at too
intense or important a level, as, say, Keats often does; or
to be concerned, save in quick swoops and sudden intima-
tions, with the profundities of life or morals or art. He
might better, too, be good companion than true friend;
with no deep ties, with only kindred taste, between us. All
these terms Lady Mary meets very well; and she is more
truly companionable to boot because she is not a "writer,"
not a wit, not a public figure. We certainly do not despise
her opinions, but we haven't the slightest impulse to defer
to them. One enjoyment in reading her, in fact, is that she
is so obviously to be read for enjoyment—she commands

no personal homage, she suggests no cultural duty; she is not a Significant Figure. But though not significant, she is much better than chatty: she never just buzzes or bumbles, or runs on about trifles, or indulges in nonsense. Like the furniture and architecture of her time, she is solid without being massive. She is also ubiquitous without being much limelighted. Rather than writer, wit, or public figure, she was the companion of all three; she had the entree to the worlds of birth and brains alike, she was never on the fringes, she was always (though she doubtless pushed a little) near the center; and when she withdrew in the flesh, she had high-placed intelligencers to keep her informed. As a result, she still after two hundred years constitutes what might be called perfect light reading for superior minds. She is—well, Lady Mary, a name that evokes something too personal to be mere literature. And, incidentally, there is no one else in English history whose courtesy title constitutes so complete an identification. "Lady Jane" will not safely do for Lady Jane Grey, nor Lord John for Lord John Russell, nor even Lord Randolph, quite, for Lord Randolph Churchill—and if it does, it is because the name Randolph is so uncommon.

Considering how marginally Lady Mary is regarded as a writer, there is, I think, some honor in how continuously she goes on being read; and there is also a certain tribute in how continuously she goes on being discovered. With quite cultivated people who have no great interest in the eighteenth century she is likely to be, for years and years, no more than a name; then, whether through urging or accident, they pick up her letters and become almost noisily charmed. People of many kinds, moreover; for Lady Mary's is not the esoteric appeal of Beckford or Aubrey. Her worst fault is that she is not very likable; yet this is not the drawback it can be with others—with, for example, Henry

Adams. For our deep dislike of Henry Adams as a human being—which penalizes him as a letter-writer—is not the mere result of finding him a querulous snob; it stems much more from his being endowed with such delicate insights and moral sensibilities as a Lady Mary could not boast of; from his being aware, as Lady Mary was not, that there were other choices, even other mandates. Thus Lady Mary sees the futility of war, yet simultaneously thinks it axiomatic that wars must be waged. She thinks with her era, which means that she really doesn't think at all. Henry Adams occupies himself for years with the great ethical problems, then in a moment of disgruntled cynicism merely shrugs his shoulders. Adams had the hardness of those whose pity, in the end, is all for themselves; for Lady Mary, pity—as we conceive it—scarcely exists.

If she is clearly dislikable, she has just as clearly been over-maligned by Walpole and by Pope. As is always pointed out, Walpole had a motive in Lady Mary's—not to speak of Mr. Wortley's—hostility to Walpole's father. "Any foe of Sir Robert's," said Walpole in effect, "is a foe of mine." But though Walpole's treatment of her is spiteful, it is scarcely unfair: he repeated stories that were plainly going the rounds, he pictured her as no worse than she sometimes looked, he ascribed traits to her that she certainly possessed. His portrayal is at worst a legitimate caricature; Pope's, on the other hand, is an unprincipled libel. Pope's treatment stems from two almost contradictory impulses. He had real reason to hate Lady Mary: perhaps she spurned his advances, she probably passed comments at his expense, she definitely joined up with Lord Hervey to outwit him—and for the moment *did* outwit him. But Pope's revenges are more a matter, in the end, of his abilities than his resentments; a line like

Pox'd by her love or libelled by her hate

though inspired by anger was at length achieved through art; the original feeling was simply the impetus.

In any case, the truth about Lady Mary is not to be found in Pope. The truth, so far as I can judge, is that she was as distinctly hard, high-handed, and self-indulging as she was not outrageous, implacable, or blind to common decencies. *Outré* as her life in many ways was, it retained a large measure of health and normality: it was disheveled but not debauched, malicious but not malign. What Lady Mary most lacked was what she most needed—simple, charitable human feeling. It was what the age most lacked, but where the age at its best offered grace and charm in its stead, Lady Mary went on being her somewhat rasping self. Yet that was not, in the end, so bad a thing to be. Doubtless the list of her unattractive qualities runs perilously long. But throughout a century boasting a most lustrous gallery of women—Swift's Stella, Marlborough's duchess and Gay's, Congreve's duchess and Gainsborough's, Dr. Johnson's Mrs. Thrale, Mrs. Crewe, Mrs. Siddons, Fanny Burney, Mary Lepel—it is Lady Mary who bequeaths to *us* the most in the way of enjoyment. She had very few friends, but time was one of them.

(1950)

CHAPTER VI

Fielding: Tom Jones

Tom Jones belongs with those beneficent great novels that can be enjoyed quite as much as they are esteemed. The book is, indeed, so masculine, so solid, so engaging that, delighted as one is to talk it over with a friend, one shies off a little from assessing it as a critic. In a certain sense, one would as soon "assess" a good dinner. There are no dark things to be cleared up in *Tom Jones,* and no deep things to fathom; Fielding's masterpiece must be accounted among the great *simple* novels. One never stops reading the story to reflect on what it means; one never has half the impulse to look back that one has to move forward. For in the very best sense *Tom Jones* is an entertainment; it entertains you with all England at a lusty moment in her history.

Few English novels possess more range and variety; for, compared to Fielding, few English novelists have seen more at first hand, have had a wider arc of experience. Fielding knew the great world by virtue of his birth, and the rest of the world by virtue of his character and his calling. He had been squire and rake, but also debtor and drudge, and as a practicing magistrate had heard the stories of sots and ne'er-do-wells, of pickpockets and highway-men and whores. As a great humorist, moreover, he had as sharp a sense of what was picturesque and odd as of what was virtuous and ignoble. But Fielding was not only tre-mendously observant, with tremendous opportunities to observe; he had what Bagehot said Macaulay lacked, an *experiencing* nature. It is easy to understand that such a man should have packed his book not simply with all the detail of life, but with all the zest and ferment of living. The hum and stir of the world, scarcely muffled after two hundred years, pervade *Tom Jones;* its inns have warmth and its inn doors let in cold; its soldiers march and its coaches lumber.

Happily, beyond painting a great picture, Fielding knew how to tell an uncommonly good story. In the end it is the picture that we value more, not least because it is always a moving picture, because this England of Garrick and Hogarth, of George II and the Young Pretender, is caught vividly on the run, our eye taking in the eloquent detail while our pulse quickens for the next turn of the plot. The plot of *Tom Jones* is very neat and beckoning; Coleridge, indeed, was rash enough to call it one of the three greatest plots in literature. Yet it is not a concern for how Blifil will be unmasked, or Sophia won, or Tom's mysterious birth explained, that counts most with a ma-ture reader. It is as a story in the old picaresque sense, of one highly colored or comic or dramatic episode following another, that *Tom Jones* is most pungent and alive. Yet the book is also picaresque in a certain timeless sense; for, like a hundred recent novels, it is the story of a young man. The story of any warm-blooded young man almost has to be picaresque, for such a hero will not stay put: he must peer and poke and learn what lies on the other side of the hill, consort with high and low, and ferret out the truth—

or some fraction of the truth—about himself. In *Tom Jones* the plot, as it were, creates the story: for in suffering disgrace and being sent from home, Tom is thrown upon the world, is catapulted among soldiers and pettifoggers, gypsies and hermits, innkeepers and cheats and every class of woman; and brought at last to London and Lady Bellaston. And the story in turn creates the picture, for as we follow Jones we ride about England.

The picture is as spacious in extent as it is graphic in effect: for Fielding's special achievement in *Tom Jones* was to transform the picaresque into the panoramic. The book is much the best fictional introduction we have to the diverse manners of its age, to the life of the well-to-do country gentleman with his retainers and sycophants; to the life of the road, where all classes met and mingled; to the life of London, where different classes rarely met and mingled more rarely still. *Tom Jones* is a very "worldly" book, full of conniving servants and bilking innkeepers and selfish gentry and haughty great folk; it combs an age that was scheming, self-seeking, and monumentally hypocritical; yet an age that, compared with ours, seems magnificently healthy.

Fielding, moreover, both inhaled and exhaled its vital spirit. With his resilient temperament and balanced mind, he offers us a great normal view of the world, in which nothing seems expurgated and nothing overemphasized, and of which the final impression is that life is worth living and has many trials but no real terrors. It is an optimistic without being a *Candide*-like view, for it stems out of experience and a humorist's tolerant sense of life. On the other hand, no writer has ever been more aware of the besetting vices of his age, or at greater pains to expose them. His Thwackums and Squares, his Blifils and Lady Bellastons are polished off forever. His onslaught against hypoc-

risy was particularly unremitting. For Fielding, though
not a sanctimonious or copybook moralist, was a genuine
moralist for all that. The moral contrast in *Tom Jones* is
less between conventional virtue and vice than between
forgivable and unforgivable transgressions, between the
animal excesses of a generous nature and the artful malice
of predatory minds. It was men's motives rather than
men's behavior that Fielding cared about—it was decency
he honored, not decorum. His essentially sound values are
one of the things that still draw us to him.

Those sound values—as our approval of them attests—
are modern values: never so much as in the twentieth century has *Tom Jones* been read so little against the bias of
prevailing "morality." All through the nineteenth century
Tom's sexual irregularities, particularly his liaison with
Lady Bellaston, shocked and offended not merely the mass
of readers, but even liberal and discerning critics; and in
the eighteenth century Fielding himself felt obligated to
reform his hero—not that, having sown his wild oats and
won Sophia, Tom mightn't have been distinctly in the
mood to settle down. Indeed, one sometimes wonders
whether Tom would not have settled down too much,
whether he would not have grown at last a little paunchy
and dull. Much, of course, that went into Tom's experience
came out of his creator's; but if the young Jones is the
young Fielding, he is the young Fielding without a whit of
his awareness, let alone his genius. Tom makes a winning
hero, but I have never understood how he could be hailed
as a "whole man." He is hardly, for all his admirable man-
liness, a man at all. It is true that he is loaded down with
experiences; but of a man we ask—in serious fiction—that
there be a reaction to experiences, and the trouble with
Tom is that, in any adult sense, he fails to react. He is lusty,
candid, and chivalrous; but, far from seeming grown-up,

he never even seems to be growing up. Doubtless his child-like values are a retort upon the worldliness of the people around him; nor do they ever keep him from being real. But they do keep him, in some final sense, from being interesting.

The truth is that in contrasting Tom and Blifil, Fielding evolved a contrast that has since degenerated into one of the unhappiest clichés of English fiction. Every schoolboy has read dozens of yarns in which the hero is Tom and the villain Blifil, under another name. Easy is the descent in fiction from Tom Jones to Tom Rover. Yet *Tom Jones* is conventionalized less, perhaps, by its contrast than by its conclusion. Judging it as a story, we should be exceedingly sorry to see it wound up in any other fashion than it is. But of *Tom Jones* as an interpretation of life, we may wonder whether so shipshape an ending is altogether convincing. We may even wonder why Fielding, who had made so many of Tom's mistakes and had to pay for them, should have consented in Tom's case to override his own experience. The comic plan and healthy tone of the book no doubt license its happy ending; yet, even so, that is one of the things that make *Tom Jones* seem primarily a very great entertainment. Another limiting thing is that, though *Tom Jones* has all the multiplicity of life, it quite lacks the mystery. It lacks the accent of those writers who have, not just a knowledge of the world, but a kind of vision of the world.

The reason for this is not what it might seem to be—namely, that Fielding was a comic writer. It is rather that he wasn't *more* of a comic writer, that he was also an earnest human being. The earnestness does honor to the man, but it does damage to the novelist. For it remains creatively unabsorbed: it comes off a little preachy. It is the "serious" side of Fielding that is the weak side, the comic side that is truly expressive. This (suggests the comic side), this is the nature of man—that he sets forth to hunt for his daughter and ends up hunting the fox. Here, and often elsewhere, we get something that seems to make life vibrate. But at other times Fielding failed to produce such vibrations.

All we are saying, in a sense, is that Fielding did not happen to be Tolstoy. Their worlds have a comparable mass, breadth, vigor, populousness. But Tolstoy, beyond brilliantly depicting manners, beyond creating a multitude of scenes and characters, infused into his fiction a far more secret knowledge of the heart, a brooding and dusky sense of life as ultimately a mystery, as ultimately a dream. We feel we know everything there is to know of Fielding's characters; of Tolstoy's, we feel that Tolstoy did not know everything himself. In a certain sense Natasha is as far removed from Sophia as André is from Tom. Yet it is not pointless to bring the lesser novelist into the presence of the greater, for both present life on an epic scale, with a classic wholeness.

And Fielding, on his own ground, could be very great. We may complain of an Allworthy or a Blifil, but about a Partridge or a Squire Western there can be no reservations: the first is a true, the second a triumphant creation. I am not sure that, in his own mind, Fielding ever decided in what vein—humorous or caustic—to treat the Squire: there was much to hate in Western, and much that Fielding hated. But the passion to rush in and create quite swamped any impulse to stand apart and criticize; and Fielding created with magnificent boldness and relish. The sheer vitality of Squire Western makes something unforgettable of all that is robust in him, and again of all that is wrong. His boorishness, his narrowness, his selfishness impale a type without for a moment impairing a person; even in his own hard-drinking, hard-riding, gross, and tyrannic age, we could never have mistaken Western for anyone else.

One further character in *Tom Jones* ought to be remarked upon before I conclude—I mean, of course, Fielding himself, who acts throughout as a kind of Master of the Ceremonies. Many readers find Fielding's little essays even more delightful than the story they interrupt, and no one can fail to find them exceedingly agreeable. Judged on the highest level, Fielding perhaps lacked the delicate artistry that can perfectly merge self with story; or it may just be that his particular method seems a little old-fashioned today. But it certainly fell in very well with the sort of epic narrative that Fielding, in his own day, proposed to write. *Tom Jones* ranks, indeed, with the very finest of prose epics. After it—or, rather, contemporary with it, in Richardson—there began to emerge something else: what we might call the modern novel.

(1949)

CHAPTER VII

Fielding: Jonathan Wild

ALTHOUGH Fielding maintains his place as one of the most popular of English novelists, it cannot be said that *Jonathan Wild* is, or ever was, one of the most popular of English novels. Yet its weak hold on the public reflects much less on its merits than on its method. Sustained irony has no great following anywhere, and among the English-speaking nations its following is very modest indeed. Yet what it lacks in size it often makes up for in fervor; and though you will find that most people have never read *Jonathan Wild* at all, you will find among those who have, many who have read it three or four times. There are a number of authors whose masterpieces everybody reads, but some lesser one of whose books is prized, by the few, almost more highly than the masterpieces. The many esteem Samuel Butler for *The Way of All Flesh*, but the few have an intenser fondness for *Erewhon*. The many love Jane Austen for *Pride and Prejudice,* and Charlotte Brontë for *Jane Eyre,* but there are those, and they are people of marked discrimination, who put a higher value on *Persuasion* or *Villette*. So with Fielding; so with *Tom Jones* and *Jonathan Wild*.

There are good grounds for being more partial to *Jonathan Wild*, even though pure merit is certainly not one of them. *Tom Jones*, we must allow, is decidedly the greater book: yet it is so much in the main tradition of English fiction that it scarcely provides anything unique or irreplaceable in the way of story or hero or background; whereas there is no other book quite like *Jonathan Wild* in the language. Fielding himself had to have a second go at it, had to pick it up again years after he had laid it down, and enlarge and embellish it, before it was transformed from journalism into literature. It bears little relation to his other novels, though it is clearly born of the same mind and imagination; but it bears as much relation as it conceivably could, seeing that its aim was so special and that in one sense it can hardly be considered a novel at all.

In general, we think of Fielding as both the sanest and lustiest of English novelists, someone who, from being well born and ill circumstanced, companion of the great and small, the good and bad alike, saw almost everything there was to see in the world, and made novels of what he had seen. *Tom Jones*, indeed, is a vast, much-changing, many-sided picture of mid-eighteenth-century England. It leaves nothing out: it is so tonic precisely because it is so unexpurgated. Conscious of Fielding's lustiness, of Fielding's sanity, we remember too that he wrote his first novel, the lively *Joseph Andrews*, as a way of retorting the prudential, genteel, mushy *Pamela* of Samuel Richardson. Richardson's heroine was too calculating to get into trouble; Fielding's heroes—Parson Adams and Tom Jones—were too honest not to.

What we perhaps forget, however, in our enjoyment of *Joseph Andrews* and *Tom Jones,* is that Fielding was not less a moralist for being a man of the world. All his books, in a certain sense, are didactic: indeed, the next most palpable thing after their energy is their earnestness. But Fielding does not grow moral in the same way or about the same things that Richardson does. Richardson is concerned that his heroines should be chaste—not least because chastity pays; that his heroes should set good examples and live lives of elegant refinement: one feels that what bothers him most is their behavior. But Fielding is only interested, as a moralist, in their motives. He can forgive all those transgressions that spring from impulse, intemperateness, animality; what he finds unforgivable are meanness and calculation, what he loathes are hypocrisy and pretense. He loves innate goodness, and loves it the more, perhaps, because he finds it so rarely.

This attitude, which is no less moral for its impatience with conventional morality, runs through everything of Fielding's, and is what pre-eminently links *Jonathan Wild* to his other books. For *Jonathan Wild* is concerned with showing that greatness and goodness have nothing to do with each other—which may be a platitude, but is not so platitudinous that people always perceive the distinction. Fielding, moreover, avoided triteness by turning the moral inside out. He decided to show that *true* greatness is hampered by virtue and shuns it as a fault; and as an example of an unapproachably great man he chose the most notorious criminal, the most ruthless and rapacious underworld figure of his time.

Jonathan Wild was, of course, a real person, a man who became the head of a great gang of London thugs and thieves, highwaymen and pickpockets; who appropriated most of their booty without running any of their risks; who squealed on them whenever he felt that they were about to squeal on *him;* who also informed against such criminals as refused to join his gang; and who, in that way, must have got almost as many guilty people hanged as he got innocent people murdered. Utterly fearless, completely coldhearted, he carried out his operations, during many years, on a gigantic scale; being finally hanged himself, however, in 1725.

Eighteen years later, when Fielding published his first and inferior version of this story, Wild had become something of a legend, but his spectacular career of crime suggested in many ways Sir Robert Walpole's corrupt career of statesmanship. As Walpole's political enemy, Fielding was unprepared to give the fallen prime minister the credit that in certain respects he deserved; but there were glaring and egregious faults enough in Walpole to make a comparison with Wild seem apt, and to enable the discerning to transfer to the politician much that Fielding ascribed to the thief. Walpole's career no longer occupies men's minds; but in the "greatness" of Wild we still may see—we can hardly *not* see—the self-interest, treachery, and ruthlessness that adhere to many a later Walpole, to statesmen and bigwigs in every age; we can hardly deny that the story has a permanent application.

To deify Wild's baseness; to treat every flicker of humanity in him as a weakness or a fault; to despise and disparage the good and kindly people whom Wild met and fell upon and fleeced—this was the road of irony down which Fielding proposed to travel. The hangman's victim was indeed to be built up into the most dazzling of heroes. Yet we misread the story if we merely see in it a crude reversal of values, a trick of calling all black things white and white things black. There would soon be no fun left in such a performance, and there would certainly be no point.

Fielding was not concerned with writing mere clever non-sense; he rather meant to show that what seemed like non-sense had in it a disconcerting amount of sober truth. For in the very act of reversing all our copybook maxims, he yet managed to come tolerably near our actual worldly standards of appraisal; he reminded us that many men whom we *do* call great have a good deal in common with Wild, and are only unlike him in achieving through lawful means what he achieved through criminal ones. And Fielding's irony cuts two ways even when he exalts Wild still higher *because* he was a criminal—for a criminal, from facing graver dangers, has need of greater courage. Indeed, the more violent Wild's methods, the more there is to be said for them:

> *Is it not more generous, nay, more good-natured, to send a man to his rest than, after having plundered him all he hath, or from malice or malevolence deprived him of his character, to punish him with a languishing death, or, what is worse, a languishing life?*

This we might almost take literally; for there is something more admirable about crime that swaggers than about crime that skulks, there is more to be said for a blow to the heart than for a stab in the back:

> *Do you imagine [says Jonathan] that guns, and pistols, and swords, and knives are the only instruments of death? Look into the world and see the numbers whom broken fortunes and broken hearts bring untimely to the grave.*

All these things, however, are mere refinements. The story never loses sight of its main theme, which is the contrast between greatness and goodness. The story everywhere excoriates all greatness that is not good—which is most of the greatness that ever has been in the world. Fielding, one imagines, would have agreed with those words that Lord Acton wrote long afterward: "Power corrupts and absolute power corrupts absolutely. . . . All great men are bad men." He meanwhile, as an offset to his hero, created the kindhearted, honest, trusting Heartfree, whom he pretended to abuse. *Jonathan Wild* has horrified a good many people who took it too literally—including Sir Walter Scott; but it is hard to conceive of a more truly moral story, right down to the end.

Fielding's ironic conception was all very well; but it had to be carried off, page after page, chapter after chapter, to almost the length of a full-fledged novel; and that was not so easy. The thing was forever in danger of blowing itself sky-high: it could strike the same note too often and monotonously, or go too slow, or too fast, or too far. A tale must not be less a tale—must not be less interesting, less coherent, less plausible—because it implies the opposite of what it says: irony is not worth having if irony is all we are to have. Happily Fielding contrived to make his story interesting in itself, to vary the feats that made Wild ever more splendid, to shuffle the qualities that made him ever more glorious; he contrived to show us Wild the friend, and Wild the lover, and Wild the husband, as well as Wild the boss and Wild the businessman. Frequently, too, Fielding's irony winds like a serpent through a particular sentence:

> . . . *and when he had stripped him of everything he had, never desired to do him any further mischief; for he carried good-nature to that wonderful and uncommon height that he never did a single injury to man or woman by which he himself did not expect to reap some advantage.*

The irony does not desert Fielding even at the very end, for the gibbeting of Wild is transformed into his apotheosis:

> *Thus fell Jonathan Wild the* GREAT, *by a death as glorious as his life had been, and which was so truly agreeable to it that the latter must have been deplorably maimed and imperfect without the former; a death which hath been alone wanting to complete the characters of several ancient and modern heroes, whose histories would then have been read with much greater pleasure by the wisest in all ages.*

Austin Dobson called *Jonathan Wild* "a model of sustained and sleepless irony," while "a matchless piece of sustained irony" is the recent verdict of Wilbur Cross. It is easier to agree with the second of these judgments than with the first, for "matchless" the book very likely is, there being nothing, at any rate, of equal length to match it; but a "model," I would venture to say, it is not. Considering his difficulties, Fielding did uncommonly well; but he sometimes faltered, and could clearly have done better. For one thing, he reminds us too often and too emphatically that he is being ironic. His methods are sometimes crude and often repetitious; as an ironist no more than as anything else could Fielding achieve a final delicacy. For another thing, there is too much disquisition, too much personal comment in *Jonathan Wild* as, for my taste— though others will disagree—there is in Fielding everywhere. For a third thing, his method breaks down just where it ought most to hold up: too many of the episodes involving the Heartfrees are handled with undisguised and open sympathy, where—in keeping with Fielding's premise—they should always profess contempt. Here Fielding, by violating the tone of his tale, does it great damage.

For the ironic approach could only accentuate the pathos of the Heartfrees' situation, whereas Fielding's humane lapses tend to make it unguardedly sentimental. And certainly, as others before me have noted, there is something a little overblown about Mrs. Heartfree's escaping ravishment five times in twenty-odd pages.

No doubt such flaws and crudities are unavoidable in a work of this nature spun out to this length; and they perhaps exist to remind us that the ironic method can achieve perfection only in a much briefer compass and concerning a much more specific theme—as in the *Modest Proposal* of Swift, or the *Shortest Way with the Dissenters* of Defoe. I suspect that a tale the length of *Jonathan Wild* needs to have its irony streaked with satire and even splashed with burlesque. But there is one further merit, besides its irony and its narrative, that helps keep *Jonathan Wild* alive: I mean its background. A world of thieves and bawds, of sharpers and tricksters and bogus counts, however little we should care for it in the flesh, must always hold and interest us on the printed page.

(1942)

CHAPTER VIII

Johnson & Boswell

UNWEARIED and inseparable, Johnson and Boswell move from one generation to another—the greatest social talker whose talk has been recorded, and the greatest biographer the world has ever known. Each, in the final sense, owes his celebrity to the other. But for Johnson, Boswell would surely be forgotten. But for Boswell, Johnson would simply be a man of letters important to other men of letters and not at all a figure of universal fame. As it is, perhaps no other personality has vaulted farther out of literature into life: hundreds of Johnson's remarks have passed into common cultivated speech; his eccentricities are better known than other great men's solidest achievements; his portrait is one of the very few that everybody can recognize; and he has lent his name to both a discredited style of writing and an immensely distinguished age. Boswell, with greater genius, has had far less luck. Too many people still regard him as a kind of inspired idiot, someone who had an unrivaled opportunity to hear Dr. Johnson talk, and wrote down all he said. Nothing could explain his achievement worse. Even as concerns hearing Dr. Johnson talk, Boswell had fewer opportunities than most of Johnson's other intimate friends; as for merely writing down what his hero said, rather with the most staggering skill he wrote it up.

Yet, though the story will not down that Boswell the biographer was only accidentally great, the greatness of his biography no more requires demonstration than it provokes dispute; while it is Dr. Johnson himself who, outside his disciple's pages, must plead for a hearing. The popular conception of Johnson is of someone as dull in his writing as he was lively in his talk. For he wrote, tradition has it, in stupefying polysyllables on crushingly tiresome themes: his only novel has no plot, and his only play no drama; his journalistic essays suggest the pulpit far more than the press; and his criticism is loaded down with such dicta as that *Lycidas* is "disgusting" and that *Lear* is the better for a happy ending. Thus condemned as arid or unreadable, Johnson goes on—save by scholars and literary men—being virtually unread. And in all this he is to some degree quite fairly condemned. There *are* too many polysyllables, there *is* too much preaching; Johnson's novel is a fraud if read for its story, and his play a burden, however it be read; while some of his critical remarks are as misguided as they are well known. Only it so happens that his often ponderous style can also be extraordinarily powerful; that while Johnson, in *Rasselas*, shows no merit as a story-teller, he shows considerable as a moral philosopher; that the faults which submerge *The Rambler* hardly exist in the best of the *Lives of the Poets;* and that, in spite of many wrongheaded criticisms, he is very nearly a great critic. We shall always go first to Johnson the talker and Johnson the man; but afterward we may find a different sort of pleasure in Johnson the biographer and Johnson the critic and Johnson the poet.

. . .

The greatness of Boswell's *Life of Johnson* rests on a number of things—one of them, very obviously, the wonderful potentialities of its subject. Johnson had, in a surpassing degree, qualities that awaken universal interest. He had massive force, all the bursting vigor of a man seldom given to fear or to forbearance, a man who was in many ways a hero, yet in certain ways a bully. He had enormous color: with his queer habits and grotesque appearance, his odd mannerisms and peculiar superstitions, he was in fact a monumental "character." He had tremendous wit: his comments are among the most striking, and his repartees among the most pulverizing on record. To listen to him must have been—for it still is—a really notable experience; more than any other Englishman, it has been said, he raised "a life of talk to the level of a life of action." Moreover, there was something so unchartable and eruptive about Johnson as to lend to his drawing-room appearances an atmosphere of continuous drama.

To chronicle the life of such a man is clearly to start off with immense advantages. But it does not begin to explain Boswell's achievement, for other men chronicled that life without ever approaching that achievement. Nor does the fact that Boswell slaved away far harder at the job explain it much better. Boswell, to be sure, went to the great trouble of getting down much more about Johnson, and getting it down much more accurately, than anybody else. But all experience favors the judgment that stenography is rather the enemy than the ally of skill; that without selection and arrangement and shading and stress there can be no true effect of art; and few would deny that Boswell's *Life* provides a very powerful effect of art. The more familiar with it one becomes, the surer one feels (even without the evidence of the Notebooks) that it has been creatively worked up; and that even where Boswell may have been no more than faithful in what he recorded, he had earlier been discriminating in what he recalled. Sainte-Beuve said of Mme Récamier that she "remembered with taste"; it might be said of Boswell that he remembered with wit. If nothing about Johnson seemed too trivial to him, some things may, for all that, have seemed too dull; and such things he expunged, not deliberately from his "minutes," but by instinct from his mind. Besides, Boswell's reports of Johnson's conversations are seldom purely stenographic reports; they are for the most part commotion recollected in tranquillity; they have been reconstructed, with the aid of notes, from memory, and are in the final sense the product of Boswell's artistic "ear," of his unerring sense of what constituted the Johnsonian statement and the Johnsonian style.

Thus, in what appears as the most slavish element in the writing of the *Life*—the word-for-word setting down of Johnson's talk—industry was abetted by ingeniousness; and from that known fact we may proceed to facts less knowable in contending that Boswell was far more an artist than an ape. An ape might have caught Johnson's single statements, but only a man of great capacities could have written up, as Boswell wrote them, many-voiced and rounded scenes. Here, in the pauses, the changes of pace, the build of the argument and the sting of the rejoinders, there exists an expert dramatic sense for controlling dialogue. In the most famous of the scenes—Johnson's interview with George III, his first encounter with Wilkes, his meeting with his old schoolfellow Mr. Edwards—Boswell is very great, but we may also concede that the circumstances are very showy: it is rather where the situation is less certainly dramatic that Boswell reveals his true mettle. And of course he reveals it in yet another way on those numerous occasions when he acts as Dr. Johnson's straight man, holding the match to set off the fireworks (and often getting badly burned).

Yet, without industry, without even the worst kind of drudgery, Boswell could never have brought off such a *Life;* for second only to his efforts to get down what he heard were his efforts to get down what he did not hear; his running "half over London . . . to fix a date correctly"; his shaking every tree of knowledge for its possible fruit; his badgering one man for a letter of Johnson's and another man for an anecdote; his sitting up till all hours to rifle his memory and recast his jottings: it was only such assiduity that made possible such a *Life* as Boswell's, composed on such as Boswell's methods.

Though Boswell himself may have idealized Johnson, Boswell's *Life* set out to portray him exactly as he was—to paint in every wart, and every hair on every wart, which at once indicates how realistic the portrait was to be, how intimate, and how detailed. To Boswell himself, Johnson seemed so transcendently great that his foibles and failings could do nothing worse than make him human; but to us, the miracle of Boswell's exact and unsparing portrayal is that Johnson did not issue forth a monster. It is often forgotten, and often perhaps not known, how revolutionary a biographer Boswell was: never before had any biography treated its subject at such close range, in so strong a light, so largely in his own words, so strikingly on his own terms. Despite Boswell's frequent irruptions into eulogy—which oftener than not defeat their purpose by their fatuousness—Johnson must ultimately fend for himself, for he is never accorded either the dignity or the glamour of distance. "I will not," Boswell asserted, "make my tiger a cat to please anybody." In the matter of brushwork, no biographer has ever come close to Boswell, though most subsequent biographers have been in some degree Boswellian. The pudgy Scot is one of the very few men in literature who have managed both to formulate a method and to carry it through to perfection; he is one of even fewer men who, though monstrous egoists, have remained consistently objective artists.

For all its greatness, Boswell's *Life* provides an incomplete and perhaps too simple view of Johnson—other contemporaries saw him in a measurably different light, and later biographers in much clearer perspective. Boswell's *Life* is also, in a sense, too static; and as I venture to think, too long. Boswell did remember some things that are dull, and did (for all his wariness) include some things that interested himself much more than other people, or his own age much more than ours. We could do, I think, without a single one of the lawsuits on which Boswell sought Johnson's advice; with much less about religion, with fewer eulogies, without certain of Johnson's letters and some of other people's.

At any age one can be caught up in Boswell and appreciate the great virtues of his portrait of Johnson; but I suspect that one must be a good way past youth to appreciate the great virtues of Johnson himself. That he was a magnificent talker one knows from the outset; but it needs a certain hard-won knowledge of the world to realize that he was also a magnificent man. For the man represents, on one side, almost everything an enlightened and forward-looking citizen of today must deprecate or condemn. He was not simply a staunch, he was a prejudiced and even to a degree a benighted, Tory. He believed in inequality and championed subordination; Whigs—and all the more as they corresponded to something approaching modern liberals—he detested and denounced; unlike almost every other great Englishman of his day, unlike even such feudal-minded Tories as Boswell, he opposed the claims of Wilkes in the Middlesex elections and the grievances of the American colonists; he supported rank, and showed every formal deference to a lord. Moreover, he was very nearly as great a bigot in religion as he was a Tory in politics—so much an adherent of the Established Church that in Scotland he refused to go of a Sunday to the kirk. And to make matters more difficult, there is not just the rigidity of his beliefs but the violence with which he espoused them. Which calls up that last infirmity of a noble mind—Johnson's often indefensible social behavior. He could be both the worst of boors and the worst of bullies. "Those," said Wraxall, "whom Johnson could not . . . vanquish . . . by his intellect, he silenced by his rudeness." He very often "talked for victory," and then might say anything that came into his head, and less say than shout it. He could get violently angry; he could be shamefully unjust; he could become outrageously insulting; and between being testy and taurine, he could disrupt—it is strange that he did not sometimes empty—a drawing-room. And when he left the drawing-room for the dinner table, he might easily double the offense, for then one might be as disgusted watching him bolt his food as one was appalled hearing him whiplash his neighbors.

Yet if Dr. Johnson was all these things, he was immeasurably more than the sum of them. He had, I think, a larger nature, a truer benignity, a profounder humaneness than any other English writer of his age. Even his faults live understandably inside the framework of his mind, or can be ascribed in part to the infirmities of his body. Johnson's religious bigotry, for example, was actuated not by passionate belief, but by a strong tendency toward disbelief. He, like Swift, had to be a rigid churchman because he was not naturally a religious one; each had a skeptical mind, and sensed that if he ever conceded anything, he might wind up conceding all. Johnson happened also to be weighed down by his moral sense; he was painfully aware of how far he fell short of perfect virtue, and dreaded the thought that at the Judgment Day he might be held to have fallen too far short. Relative goodness offered no consolation: "The better a man is, the more afraid he is of death, having a clearer view of infinite purity." God, for Johnson, was someone not to love but to fear; no man ever got less comfort from his faith, or more perturbation. In the famous colloquy with Dr. Adams there was no talking for effect: Johnson meant literally what he said, "I am afraid," he remarked, "I may be one of those who shall be damned." "What do you mean," inquired Adams, "by being damned?" "Sent to Hell, Sir," Johnson thundered back, "and punished everlastingly." Johnson's morbid horror of death was certainly as much founded on the idea of damnation as on the idea of dissolution. His sort of believer could hardly help being his sort of bigot.

Johnson, again, was a Tory on principles that may be rejected, but need not be misunderstood. To begin with, one can fairly point out that there was almost no self-interest in his Toryism. Rather was it rooted in that perfectly empirical view of life which concludes that all men are created *un*equal—not in worldly position alone, but in physique, in personality, in moral stamina, in intellectual capacity. Johnson saw life so; he also saw life much too pessimistically to have any faith in progress; and so saw nothing iniquitous in making the structure of society loosely conform to a "law" of nature. And in Johnson's view, the more arbitrarily it conformed to it, the less cause there was for individual resentment. If it is by pure accident that a man is born a lord, then the man who is not born one is far less stigmatized than if he had had the chance to become one and failed. Johnson really believed that accepting one's place in society—at least as a convention—tended in the long run to make the individual happier. He saw in "the perpetual struggle for precedence" all the seeds of human dissatisfaction and rancor; while the new democratic conception of equality he thought mere cant. Everybody, he declared, talked of leveling *up*, but nobody of leveling down; and when, to test Mrs. Macaulay's equalitarian professions, he bade her invite her footman sit down and dine with them, he was smugly pleased to note how irritated she became. Moreover, it was one of Johnson's contentions that the ordinary man cares little about political equality; what he wants is personal liberty, the right to live his day-by-day life as he pleases. So far as he went, Johnson was probably right; only it seems never to have occurred to him that the two things might be crucially interdependent; his political obtuseness quite canceled out his psychological insight. The dangers of despotism Johnson airily disposed of by declaring that whenever a ruler becomes too despotic, the people will rise up and cut off his head.

He was, I am afraid—even for his own age—an archconservative. But despite the foolish pamphlets he wrote and the ingenious nonsense he talked (a good deal of it largely for effect), his practices often contraverted his principles, and his ethics were vastly superior to his politics. He could defy a lord as well as defer to one, and denounce injustice even more strenuously than he supported privilege. He would certainly have agreed with that monstrously undemocratic but not irresponsible belief of Burke's, that "though nothing should be done by the people, everything should be done for them." He himself did for them everything he could; whatever must be charged against Johnson's ability to think, very little can be levied against his capacity to feel. For the poor and disinherited and oppressed he had more than profound compassion; he had real understanding. He had lived very much in the world, he had been poor and miserable himself; and in respect of poverty, the pompous moralist was never imposed upon, was always roused to anger, by the glib moralizing of others:

> "Sir [*run the famous words*], *all the arguments which are brought to represent poverty as no evil show it to be evidently a great evil. You never find people laboring to convince you that you may live very happily upon a plentiful fortune.*"

Indeed, the plight of the poor only made him impatient with the dislocations of the well-off:

> "*The sight of people who want food and raiment is so common in great cities, that a surly fellow like me has no compassion to spare for wounds given only to vanity and softness.*"

And Johnson did much more than abhor such outrages as the slave trade or imprisonment for debt; he did much more than relieve such patent distresses as homelessness and hunger. He loathed every pseudo-pious and sanctimonious move to curtail or condemn the pleasures of the poor. He knew to what crumbs of enjoyment the poor were reduced; he knew *why* they got unruly, he knew why they got drunk. He cast no stones, first or last, at them: instead he spoke up for the few "sweeteners of their existence," he consorted with the "Laurindas" and Bet Flints, and took streetwalkers under his own roof to be nursed back to health, and when he came upon better days, spent on himself a mere fraction of his income. We all remember how he filled his house with dependents, but we may have forgotten the sort of atmosphere they created: "Williams hates everybody. Levet hates Desmoulines, and does not love Williams. Desmoulines hates them both. Poll loves none of them." Yet the surly fellow bore patiently with them all.

Johnson, moreover, rather did good by stealth than ever seek to paint himself as better than he was. He detested what seemed to him false or fulsome sentiment. "When a butcher," he remarked, "tells you that his heart bleeds for his country, he has in fact no uneasy feeling." Time and again he insisted that other people's troubles never really disturb our own enjoyments; that one never slept the worse, or ate the less, for this friend's sufferings or that friend's loss. It was in matters of this sort that he rang all the changes on "Clear your mind of cant"; in condemning fictitious virtue, Johnson even contrived a kind of fictitious cynicism. In the matter of "cant," Johnson himself may have indulged in a measure of cant-in-reverse; the word, at any rate, acquired a pretty loose meaning in Johnson's mouth, and was made to embrace some things that simply aroused his impatience. Such a famous statement as "No man but a blockhead ever wrote except for money" is not to be taken quite literally. It does not signify the philistine's contempt for the artist, but rather, as Leslie Stephen says, the professional's contempt for the amateur. And fundamentally Johnson's war against cant constitutes a sound protest against flattering self-deceptions, against man's desire to seem finer-grained or sweeter-natured than he is.

As for Johnson's personal faults—his bullying, his boorishness, his abusive manner when opposed—they may, while staining the brightness of his aura, light up a little the darkness of his soul. For Johnson was all his life a scarred and sick and deeply melancholy man. He could not see or hear well; he had been disfigured in infancy by scrofula; he was wracked by dropsy and asthma and gout, and tormented by sleeplessness; and he must always have inwardly suffered from an appearance that earned him such sobriquets as Polyphemus and Caliban. Such a man had only the force of mind, only the power of personality, wherewith to leave his mark on others; and, burdened with pain, was not likely to be too nice in how he did it. Then too, as many people have observed, with his blunted sight and hearing he was not very aware of his behavior, of how fiercely he glared and how furiously he bellowed. But the worst of all the maladies besetting Johnson was that profound melancholy which so often overpowered him and which, save only at intervals, he never threw off. Swift had had something like it, too—though in Swift there was great frustration of living and rancor against life—and in the end it drove Swift mad; but Johnson fought indomitably against it, and against the madness he forever feared. "I will be conquered; I will not capitulate," said Johnson on his deathbed—Johnson who elsewhere asserted that there had never been a week he would choose to live over again. He had, if anyone ever had it, character; far more than he was a moralist, he was a man. The moralist might speak in abstractions from the mind; but time and again the man spoke out, with intense feeling, from the heart. We do not easily forget such things as Johnson's comment on his marriage: "I have known what it was to have a wife, and I have known what it was *to lose a wife*"; or his comment about drunkenness: "He who makes a beast of himself, gets rid of the pain of being a *man.*"

And irascible and ill-humored as Johnson could be, he

was not ill-natured. It is almost a proof of how little real malevolence was in him that he played up his "hatreds" with humorous ostentation, making fun of Scotchmen, fulminating against Whigs. And in the very noise of such explosions there dwelt that terrific gusto which countervailed against melancholy and, along with his strength of character, saved Johnson from despair. For, sad and sick, Johnson yet loved life in every part of him, body and belly, heart and mind.

And if the boor and the bully were largely the product of his ills, they were almost the conscious product. In referring to the contretemps with Chesterfield, he acutely distinguished his pride from Chesterfield's as *defensive* pride; and so might we distinguish much of his highhandedness as defensive highhandedness. As Joseph Wood Krutch more or less remarks in his very discerning biography, Johnson had to be a bully to avoid being a butt, for the penalty of not enforcing people's rather terrified respect must have been to court their merciless derision. A stranger could only be appalled by Johnson's looks; even his most devoted admirers could barely keep a straight face at moments when this grotesque wall of flesh too grandly pontificated. Once, indeed, Henry Thrale was downright cutting about it: "There, there," he broke in, "now we have had enough for one lecture, Dr. Johnson; we will not be upon education any more till after dinner, if you please." The grotesque appearance and the pompous manner were a ludicrous combination; yet, everything considered, the manner was better suited to the appearance than any other would have been. It was sound in Johnson, who must have failed with an informal approach, to assume a magisterial one. Not that there was anything studied about it: in Johnson's bullying there was something defensive, and shaped by vanity; but his high manner, his symposiarch role, were largely born with him, concomitants of his enormous self-respect. He was by nature eminent as he was by nature odd.

But his eminence and his oddness alike made him a very lonely man, one who hungered to be loved and longed to be "normal." The craving to be loved, to be remembered, to be included, breaks out again and again, never more poignantly than in some of the later letters to Mrs. Thrale. But the less exposed pathos of his life lay in how gratified he was, not by what was extraordinary in him, but in what he fancied might seem normal. He undoubtedly took pleasure in those various displays of physical strength and health that are preserved of him—the riding to hounds, the swimming in the sea, the midnight "frisks," the boyish rolls downhill; but how much more he took pride. We smile, watching him bustle about as one of Thrale's executors; but it was not mere self-importance that made him delight in his bourgeois role; it was also the sense of being a normal man of the world. So too his light and playful manner toward young girls and pretty women masks something stronger than playfulness. Even though his marriage with a woman almost twice his age be accepted as a real love match, Johnson may have partly cherished it—a little more than he knew—as the primary experience of normal life. For his was never really a normal life; and deep down, Johnson knew it. And he knew it for what was odd no less than for what was eminent about him; beyond feeling the pangs of illness and the clutch of melancholy and the fear of madness and the terror of death, Johnson felt—more than most of us—how painfully each man lives in this world alone. His was not even a normal nature: "Have you not observed," he wrote to Mrs. Thrale, ". . . that my *genius* is always in extremes; that I am very noisy, or very silent; very gloomy, or very merry; very sour, or very kind?" With all he had to face and fight off, his was indeed a very great achievement in living. The sick man never became an invalid. The pessimist never became a cynic. The sufferer, though not free from self-pity, never ceased to feel compassion for others. The rigid moralist never turned into a puritan; no man, in fact, of such narrow views ever had broader sympathies. And few men with such turbulent natures ever showed greater self-control. As I have said elsewhere, it was a wonderful triumph of character that such a man confined his gluttony to food and repartee.

Of Johnson the talker, there can be little new to say. Other men have displayed greater wisdom in conversation, and even greater wit; but I can think of no one who has been so consistently pointed and pungent, electrical and alive; or who, by spoken words, has conveyed so much personality and character. For what he goes on being, Johnson chiefly has Boswell to thank; but not for what he was. Johnson's own age, an age very notable for conversation, considered him every bit as great a talker as we do; indeed, his talk was one of the wonders of that age. And what is finest about Johnson's talk is the sheer talk itself, not the substance, not the significance of it. On that score, we can only be delighted that Johnson was often wrongheaded in conversation, and sometimes absurd. We can only be delighted that people regarded Johnson as a sage, for he exerted himself to hold forth like a sage, and could be almost more rewarding when he pontificated than when he actually was wise. In him the power of expression was very nearly an equivalent of the power of thought—thought there could also be, on occasion, most decided power of thought. But the pith and picturesqueness, the energy and ingenuity,[1] stand out as something great in itself; and it is no wonder that Johnson's constant concern in discussion was not what arguments he should muster but which side he should take.

There can be little question, I think, that in his pronouncements Johnson was nearly as often wrong as he was right; or, which is as unsatisfactory, that he usually insisted on things being black or white, where more judicious men would allow that they were gray. Once he had unraveled (as he thought) the threads, and unknotted the kinks; once, that is, he had displayed to the full his dialectical skill, the matter was settled, the truth stood revealed. And certainly it must have seemed the truth to all but the most obstinate or perspicacious of his hearers. In talk Johnson had so superlative a gift for being pointed that it needed sharp judgment to grasp whether what he said was also to the point. Quite often it was not; Johnson's arguments could be as irrelevant as they were dazzling.

Yet we do get from his talk far more than just gymnastics or boldness or wit; we get a man with a considered view of the world,[2] a man who was enormously intelligent about many things and remarkably unillusioned about many more; and we get a downrightness that is almost as valuable as it is engaging. What answer could be better than Johnson's when asked if he would write a preface to the work of a dunce: "Yes, Sir; and *say* he was a dunce." What could be more winningly honest or generally true than: "Mrs. Montagu has dropt me. Now, Sir, there are people whom one should like very well to drop, but would not wish to be dropt by." But all this particularizing seems

---

[1] In his prose, Johnson frequently turns the concrete into the abstract, but in his talk he does the reverse, clothing most of his ideas in vivid images and metaphors.

[2] "Human life is everywhere a state, in which much is to be endured and little to be enjoyed."

of small account beside the great central fact about Johnson's talk—its sheer fascination. It is almost literally magnetic, in that it draws us to it, even where we have it by heart, over and over again.

Johnson occupied a very distinguished place in the London of his later days; but even in an age that regarded his writings as highly as his talk, that place was anything but absolute. Many important people of his time, some for sound reasons and some for snobbish ones, some from clashing temperament and some from injured vanity, could not abide him. He, who so strongly defended rank, refused to flatter the highborn and so, all too often, failed to please them. "Great lords and great ladies," he remarked, "don't like to have their mouths stopped"; and the fact is worth repeating that "only one man of hereditary title," Sir Charles Bunbury, attended Johnson's funeral. But the lords and ladies, and many people who were neither, had good reason for resenting the *way* their mouths were stopped; and Mrs. Boswell is not to be wondered at for saying she had seen many a bear led by a man, but never before a man led by a bear. We know too, though fortunately Johnson did not, that even some of the titled folk who courted him did so very much on their own terms: Lady Lucan used to suggest sending for Dr. Johnson when there was to be no other company. Late in his life he became so overbearing and ill-mannered that people refused invitations to the Thrales if they knew he was to be there. Beyond all that, we may suppose that certain people always found Johnson's ideas uncongenial and repressive; in literature as in politics and religion his thought traveled backward; and a man who loudly execrated Voltaire, Hume, and Rousseau must have seemed, to his modern-minded contemporaries, a pretty obstructive anachronism.

Yet Johnson did have a very large and distinguished circle—a fact, indeed, that is constantly flung at us as part proof of how great and conquering he was. Such "proof" has never carried as much weight with me as I daresay it should—not only because Johnson triumphs without it, but because a large part of Johnson's circle leaves me cold. Rattle off the big names how you will, they still fail, most of them, to be very enticing. They seem—for all they came together to be edified—a little smug; and simply for so coming together, a little priggish. The Literary Club, with its phalanx of bishops and bishops-to-be, shows a decided ecclesiastical tinge; and, all in all, many of Johnson's friends had a very robust sense of their own moral superiority. One of the great virtues of Johnson's strongly charged presence is that he saved various gatherings from becoming stuffy. (On the other hand, it may have been an awareness of the Great Moralist's presence that induced some of the stuffiness.) Still, it is a question how much we should have liked a good many of Johnson's friends—not only Thrale and Sir John Hawkins, Fanny Burney and Hannah More, or from the earlier days, Richardson and Savage; but even that sinuous climber and polished hypocrite Sir Joshua, even the illustrious Burke.[3] In some ways, the two most maligned of Johnson's intimates, Boswell and Mrs. Thrale, seem among the most congenial.

Mrs. Thrale was very much a society hostess and something of a lion-hunter; and in bagging Johnson, she and her husband acquired not just a monumental object for display, but someone who brought with him a whole procession of big game. As a hostess, Hetty fizzed and foamed

---

[3] Perhaps no century has produced so many distinguished or so many really interesting personalities as the eighteenth; yet among the personages who have survived, very few seem to me genuinely likable; nor are those we like necessarily those we are able to esteem.

and doubtless drew upon all those artful little insincerities that enhance the enjoyment of guests. She was a superficial woman, proud of her family connections (the more so for having married a brewer) and pleased with her social success. But at her own level she seems both attractive and amusing; her prattle must have been far more engaging than the solemn pronouncements of the *bas bleus;* and her vivacity seems as inborn as its manifestations seem occasionally contrived. In her relations with her husband, certainly it is she who gains our sympathy. She had never loved the cold authoritarian to whom she had been more or less married off; and she must have known he was constantly unfaithful to her, since she must have known he was periodically diseased. In her relations with Johnson, she was amiable and thoughtful until near the end; and near the end she behaved no more selfishly, and a good deal more politely, than he did. Their whole relationship involves as much that is fundamental in human nature as that is fine. Streatham got from Johnson the prestige of his presence, and its hostess the regard and devotion of a great man; Johnson got from Streatham all the luxury he delighted in, and that sense of home he had always craved. On the whole, the Thrales needed Johnson less than he needed them; and with the passing years Mrs. Thrale perhaps found the lion she had bagged uncomfortably leonine; yet, even in the full face of his reserving his deepest regard for her husband, she did all she could to make Johnson easy and happy. The marriage to Piozzi, so far as it concerned Hetty herself, was unexceptionable; and, as it turned out, a genuine success. The marriage, so far as it concerned Johnson, was one of those unhappy blows that cannot be condemned, that can only be regretted. For the sick and lonely old man, watching the door slowly close on what seemed to him his nearest approach to happiness, we can only be deeply sorry; but the man, wrapped up in his aches and infirmities, was decidedly querulous; in his attitude toward Piozzi he was notably unfair; and in his first rebuff of Mrs. Thrale, he was plainly insulting. To take sides in the matter would be to ignore the fact that both people were human beings. In the storybook sense, Hetty might for a year or two have held off marrying Piozzi to minister to Johnson; but that is not how people act, or can even be expected to act, in real life. In any case, her essential consideration for Johnson, and Johnson's essential greatness of heart, alike stand forth in almost the very last words that he ever addressed to her: "Whatever I can contribute to your happiness I am very ready to repay, for that kindness which soothed twenty years of a life radically wretched."

In any rapid view of Boswell, the faults must seem glaring and the man absurd. He could be an offensive toady, and then again could strut like a crow in the gutter. He not only rang the most impressive doorbells, but announced himself as a most desirable caller. And having pushed in among great men, he proceeded to ask them extremely impertinent questions. Most times he was something of a busybody, and sometimes a consummate nuisance. Anything but self-effacing when sober, he grew noisy, silly, and garrulous when drunk. Obsessed with family dignity, he had absolutely no dignity of his own; and pursuing the most ticklish enterprises, proved to be utterly wanting in tact.

Yet this man became, in varying degrees, the friend of Johnson, Reynolds, Goldsmith, Garrick, Burke, Wilkes, Paoli, Hume, Rousseau, Voltaire, of grave bishops and fine ladies and a diner-out who clearly added to the gaiety and even the solidity of countless gatherings. He was, said

Johnson, "a man whom everybody liked," and "the best
traveling companion in the world." Since what made him
a fool could hardly have made him a favorite, he must
have had very saving social virtues. Two such stand out:
good nature and high spirits. He could talk well and lead
talk on, he could make people feel he was glad to be with
them, and perhaps make them feel glad to be with one
another. The lively companion was also a pretty skillful
catalyst: he was constantly bringing people together who
he thought would like each other, or no longer *not* like
each other; and this risky and usually unwelcome maneuver for the most part succeeded. Certainly Boswell sought
in all this to indulge his curiosity and add to his prestige;
but there was present, too, a genuine benevolence. In a
world where most meddling hints at mischief, and even
the best of us get secret pleasure from seeing our friends
at odds, Boswell delighted in watching enemies bury the
hatchet. He had too in his relations with people a sympathy and sincerity that went beyond the effusive compliments he paid them. During an age when most people
were forced to be on their dignity and to care desperately
about appearances—when most people, that is, were under
a social strain—Boswell must have offered considerable,
though it was only comic, relief. What made him a fool
could hardly have made him a favorite; yet it need not
have cost him much favor. Most people do not find it
hard to like those whom they despise a little.

In solitude as in society, deep down as straight out, the
man was a tissue of contrarieties. He was both cocksure
and uncertain of himself; painfully self-searching yet comically self-deluded; a Tory in his beliefs and an anarchist
in his behavior; unable to curb any of his physical crav-
ings, yet capable of the stupendous discipline needed to
complete the *Life;* romantic about love, yet rakish about

women; an inflexible snob and a born mixer; irrepressibly gay and morbidly gloomy. "Had Boswell been invented by a novelist," Bertrand Bronson has recently written, "we should at once reject the character as an amiable monster": perhaps it is simpler to say that Boswell is a character no novelist would have the audacity to invent. Obviously, Boswell was utterly unstable; and the rush and retreat of his emotions, the surge and collapse of his ego, the veering activities, the shifting goals, the Icarian flights, the broken resolutions, the constant self-recriminations, and always the punctual re-emergence of confidence and hope, made a tangled tragicomedy of Boswell's life. No impulse went unchecked, no emotion long held sway. It was merely fatuous of Boswell to strut about the Stratford Jubilee, or dress up fit to kill when he called on Pitt or Voltaire. It was childish showing-off in him, in the audience at Drury Lane, to imitate the lowing of a cow and become so enraptured with the applause that he attempted "other animals, but with very inferior effect." It was normal rather than not, on hearing of his mother's death, to rush out to a brothel. But there were odder facets. Consider his having two friends try separately to bribe his mistress out of remaining faithful to him; consider his bidding his best friend ask the girl Boswell wanted to marry whether she didn't think the Boswells were a little mad. But if such connivings—and they include things like not writing to Johnson to see whether Johnson would write to him—spring from an almost diseased vanity and a recurring self-doubt, they also bespeak a curiosity nearly as disinterested as it is consuming. There may have been enough of the masochist in Boswell to play with fire out of an obscure wish to be burnt; but there was yet a passionate interest in psychological processes, in human reactions, in whatever provided a clue to behavior or an insight into motive. And with his powerful desire to know went a staggering perseverance to find out. What *is* stable in Boswell is the compulsion to record, to fathom, to compass his instability.

He belongs indeed with those very few beings—Pepys and Rousseau are others—in whom the fierce need to confess the truth was united with the very rare ability. Only these few men have not required some sort of mask, or not wound up striking some sort of attitude. Possibly it was Boswell's permitting himself so much play-acting and fancy dress in public, his lack of inhibitions on the social stage, that helped him not to play-act on paper. We may allow that he possessed that extreme of egoism that preferred stating what was discreditable about himself to suppressing it. Even so, there was something else, something "scientific," some compulsion in the deepest and yet least involved part of his nature that made him ferret out the truth and then hold it boldly up to the light. Anyone both so passionately self-interested and so passionately disinterested in his probing must be accounted, by his very rarity, a kind of genius. Nor need we be surprised if that kind of genius also proves to be a kind of fool, if he has no intellectual values corresponding to his temperamental virtues. Boswell is in a certain sense like Saint-Simon. Neither man had any mind worth talking about, and both men held fast to absurdly outmoded ideas about society. But both were magnificent observers of themselves as well as of others, both could consummately portray, and both were always prepared to face and confess the truth.

In his friendship with Johnson, Boswell found the most fruitful and fortunate element in his life, but it was after all only an element. Boswell saw Johnson intensively but infrequently, and even when he rattled down to London from Scotland, it was to spend much of his time with a very different sort of people. He "sallied forth like a roaring Lion after girls" from whom he all too often caught "the venereal disorder"; he drank hard and turned up at times in polite society drunk; he could seldom resist a Tyburn hanging; and on occasion he hankered as much for the company of a Wilkes as of a Johnson. It was indeed less his veneration for Johnson than his love of London and distaste for Scotland that kept driving him southward; in fact, he moved to London—against his best interests— *after* Johnson died. But Johnson did bring out the good side of the man. The two were alike in their politics and their piety, in their love of talk, in their tremendous gusto, and up to a point at least—for in Boswell it did not run very deep—their melancholy. Johnson, too, provided Boswell with an ideal to strive for, and in some sense served as a father to a man who found his own father cold and censorious. It would be quite wrong to suppose that Boswell played the hypocrite with Johnson: for though he concealed his wenching, which amounted almost to satyriasis, his desire for the good life was altogether sincere: if Hell is paved, then Boswell was padded, with good intentions. The relationship prospered rather more than less because of Johnson's flare-ups and rebuffs, for Boswell needed to have a mentor quite as much as Johnson needed to be one. As for Boswell's dissolute side, Johnson probably guessed its existence, but not its extent. But who, not knowing, could? To read Boswell's letters to Temple after reading Boswell's *Life of Johnson* is to come upon something really schizophrenic. Yet this was a remarkable schizophrene indeed, one half of him providing a supreme achievement in art, the other—in the letters, journals, and private papers—a unique and astounding revelation in psychology.

* * *

Though, for the general public, Johnson's pomposity and polysyllables still stick to him like burs, in the literary world of our time he has regained much of his old eminence as a writer. The general reaction against romanticism has helped; almost every "classical" writer is more highly regarded today that he was a generation ago. But Johnson's changed status reflects more than a change in taste. He is recognized as in many ways a distinguished and delightful writer; and has been so recognized chiefly because he has once again been read. The literary-minded have found what they had every reason to expect—good sense, keen insight, and tremendous personal force; but they have also found what may have taken them by surprise—a very full understanding of the ways of men, robust humor and droll bluntness, prose of uncommon distinction and verse of actual grandeur.

One must get used to Johnson. Parts of him are downright unreadable; but the parts that are not tend to seem better with every re-reading. The intellectual framework inside which Johnson operates is not ours; it had begun, indeed, to be outmoded while it was still current, and it is just possible to contend that the last literary age in which Johnson would have been fully at home was that of Virgil and Horace. Yet inside this framework Johnson operated with great cogency, just as inside the framework of a given style he forged something like a great one. Doubtless no one today would care to write like Johnson; but beyond that, no one could.

Johnson lacked what his century generally had: a capacity for prose that was neat yet natural, elegant yet unceremonious, and whose beauty lay not in any overpowering use of language, but in its rhythm and its tone. The best of that prose—Sterne, Goldsmith, Gray—has too much temperament and breeding to tolerate magniloquence. With this style, a sort of domesticated classical one, Johnson's has nothing in common; Johnson's, in everything but sentence structure, is the child of the seventeenth century. Drawing heavily on the Latin element in the language, it can be grave, formal, and sonorous, and shows no affinity to speech (unless it be to Johnson's own). It is a prose that when it lacks the right theme or the right inspiration can become hopelessly heavy:

> *I have discovered, by a long series of observations, that invention and elocution suffer great impediments from dense and impure vapors, and that the tenuity of a defecated air at a proper distance from the surface of the earth, accelerates the fancy, and sets at liberty those intellectual powers which were before shackled by too strong attraction, and unable to expand themselves under the pressure of a gross atmosphere.*

There is enough of this kind of thing in Johnson to explain why his style has become a byword for ponderosity. We may also condemn a side of his prose that, if easier to read, is no easier to relish—that side so overloaded with antithesis that it wears out our patience. And I would concede one thing more: that it is possible, from temperament, to dislike the way Johnson writes, even when it is vigorous or expressive in its kind. Let us take a famous passage, where Johnson almost, but not quite, parodies himself:

> *A grotto is not often the wish or pleasure of an Englishman, who has more frequent need to solicit than exclude the sun; but Pope's excavation was requisite as an entrance to his garden, and, as some men try to be proud of their defects, he extracted an ornament from an inconvenience, and vanity produced a grotto where necessity enforced a passage.*

Nobody can read that sentence without being amused at the author; but where some people will smile and turn aside, others will smile and be drawn irresistibly on. But this particular manner, though many of us would not wish it away, does not always prevail. Johnson can be downright in a way that is almost droll. Refusing to get upset over Dryden's being passed up for a fellowship at Cambridge, Johnson remarks: "Had he thought himself injured, he knew how to complain." Or, noting that a very early work of Congreve's won praise, he concludes: "I would rather praise it than read it." Again and again Johnson's elaborate style becomes thus blunt and abrupt, and the effect is delightful.

But the sesquipedalian style he could also handle with distinction; and the great paragraph which really opens his discussion of Shakespeare ("The Poet, of whose works I have undertaken the revision . . ."), or the last half-dozen pages of that Preface, or the conclusion of the Preface to the Dictionary, must take rank as great prose, though of not quite the greatest kind. Here pomposity becomes true pomp; here something Roman is wedded to something English, and sentences that are more fitly termed periods advance their meaning in a swell of sound.

If Johnson is known for anything to the present-day public, he is most likely known for *Rasselas*. Most of us "studied" it at school, and may still recall how Johnson wrote it in the evenings of one week to meet the expenses of his mother's funeral. The tale of the young prince and the old philosopher who escape from a happy, hemmed-in valley to survey the world at large was published the same year and follows much the same plan as *Candide;* but we shall look in vain for the liveliness, the malice, the headlong pace of Voltaire's masterpiece. *Rasselas* has, in fact, none of the interest or entertainment we have the right to expect of a novel. I myself can read any chapter of it with pleasure, but little more than that without fatigue. To be sure, we should not go to it seeking the rewards of a novel; what it has to offer is much sententious wisdom and much grave, even majestic, prose; and more particularly, the substance of Johnson's philosophic thought, of his settled view of life. It is a pessimistic and melancholy view, with the illusoriness—or at least the dissolution—of happiness as its constant burden: its view of life is formulated as solemnly, and much more succinctly, in the finest of Johnson's poems.

The Vanity of Human Wishes is, moreover, one of the finest poems of its kind that exists, and possibly the only extended thing of Johnson's upon which one can bestow unsullied praise. Its kind is, to be sure, by no means the highest or most magnetic form of poetry; *The Vanity of Human Wishes*, loosely rendering as it does Juvenal's Tenth Satire, is strongly didactic verse. But to it Johnson has given a certain didactic grandeur, and he has deepened it with something torn from his own experience. The famous couplets have the toll of iron bells:

> *Yet hope not life from grief or danger free,*
> *Nor think the doom of man reversed for thee . . .*

Johnson's periodical essays obtained for him high praise during his lifetime, when he was only less the author of *The Rambler* than the compiler of the Dictionary. It was chiefly in these papers, and the later *Adventurers* and *Idlers*, that Johnson won his spurs as a writer and his stature as a moralist. Johnson wished, of course, to do more in these essays than instruct and enlighten; following in the wake of the *Spectator*, he certainly at times wished to entertain; but it was not in his make-up, on such terms, to be entertaining. He had neither Addison's temperament nor Addison's touch; there was little about him of the easy, worldly depicter of manners, and even less of the genteelly whimsical humorist. Johnson in a sprightly mood is well-nigh intolerable, and Johnson trying to carve a cherrystone seems rather to be hammering a rock. Only when he comes to consider hope or friendship or fame does he seem at home with his subject: he loved the grand abstractions, and could often say something gravely witty or oracularly wise about them.

No doubt the essays have a slow, massive, glacier-like force. Yet for a number of reasons—one of them their glacier-like movement—it is impossible to read them with any real enjoyment. Many of them exhibit Johnson's style at its deadliest; nor is the style generally to be put up with for the sake of the substance. Despite many things that are keenly observed or nobly formulated, too often we fight past the polysyllables only to run head-on into platitudes. Johnson is perhaps liveliest when he writes in the strain of La Rochefoucauld, bringing home to men not how they ought to behave, but how they do:

> *Self-love is often rather arrogant than blind: it does not hide our faults from ourselves, but persuades us that they escape the notice of others.*

Johnson's account of the trip he took with Boswell to the Hebrides—his *Journey to the Western Islands*—was well summed up by Sir Walter Raleigh as the "most ceremonious of diaries." It abounds in observations and reflections that only Johnson would have made; but it is certainly never chatty, and yet hardly very solid either. Johnson saw what was to be seen, sometimes with the care of a man taking notes for a book, sometimes with the complacency of a celebrity being polite, sometimes with the attentiveness of a traveler storing up impressions; but he seldom makes *you* see it; and where the *Journey* does not seem a little perfunctory, it seems too curious or ponderous. In small stretches it is enjoyable reading, if only because the nature of the book is so delightfully ill-suited to the nature of the author; but one has only to turn to Boswell's account of the same tour to realize all that Johnson missed, and all that he mismanaged.

The Lives of the Poets, written in old age from neither want of money nor need for fame, are Johnson's most satisfying and engaging work. The story of how they came to be written you will find by turning to Boswell; the proof of how good they can be you will find by reading the *Pope.* Perhaps the first thing to be said of them is that they were better suited to Johnson's genius than anything else, save only *The Vanity of Human Wishes,* that he ever wrote. They were, indeed, exactly suited to his genius, which was that of a great man of letters rather than, in the narrow sense, of a great biographer, scholar, or critic. In the man of letters was splendidly combined a good deal of all three without providing a supreme example of any one. Johnson had at his command both language and learning, both insight and wit; he had a feeling for literature and an even stronger feeling for the literary world; he loved speculation, but equally loved facts; he was interested in poetry, but absorbed by personality; and the *Lives* offered a chance to blend his capacities in a way that best set them off. Moreover, the chance came at just the right period of his life. His perceptions were still sharp, but his approach to the world had mellowed, and he wrote less out of closeted study than out of a lifetime's knowledge. He let himself go; he moved, confidently and a little carelessly, down the long corridor of almost two centuries of poetry. Writing of Rowe's plays, he freely admitted that he had not looked at them for thirty years; and there were other things (like that early novel of Congreve's) that he would not bother to look at at all.

The *Lives* interlard biography with criticism, and remain an example of old-fashioned biography and old-fashioned criticism at its best. Boswell was to revolutionize the one field, and a host of nineteenth-century critics the other, and both fields were to be the richer for the change; but they were also to lose something, and by reading Johnson we can see just what they lost. It was a certain high firmness of touch and fixedness of limits. For Johnson as critic, the earth might still, so to speak, be flat; one never explored far places on the map; but then, one never lost one's way. He knew what he liked, and usually why he liked it; he formulated, he generalized, he summed up with the force of a master. *He* was on firm ground even when his opinions were not; and esthetically, of course, they very often were not. There are regions into which mere good sense cannot penetrate; there are gaps in taste which no amount of ingenuity can conceal; there are times when it is plainly fatal to have too little sensibility. But, as later critics have proved, there are also times when it is fatal to have too much.

That balance of qualities—of toughness and sensibility, of clear-sightedness and vision, of being equally at home on earth and in the empyrean—which is at least the theoretical mark of the greatest kind of critic, Johnson never remotely attained to; his powers are limited and too much on one side. Perhaps we may divide imperfect critics into two classes: those who fail to see everything that is there, and those who see things that aren't there at all. The one kind is apt to miss the point, the other to force it. Johnson is a good example of the first kind—a man who makes literature come to him rather than one who goes out to it, a man for whom art is rather a confirmation than an enlargement of experience. Beyond all that—if it is not anterior to all that—he was a good deal of a crustacean in his tastes; he disliked what was new or unorthodox, and was seldom equipped to assess it. Again, too much logic could defeat him: it is "logic," really, rather than prejudice, that arrives at such verdicts as the notorious one on *Lycidas*.

This is to simplify; for on scores of occasions Johnson surprises us by his largeness of grasp, or his sympathy with what seems alien to his nature. But it remains true that Johnson very often went by the rules, were they only rules of his own; and that to a certain rigidity he added a certain literal-mindedness. The moralist in him also harmed the critic, not because the moral qualities of literature can be easily overstressed, but because Johnson insisted that they be overt and didactic. Yet this, like everything else, was born of something in *him,* and not of lip-service to prevailing beliefs. It is, indeed, because Johnson is so independent-minded in his judgments that he is a traditional critic without being in the slightest degree a conventional one. He is one of the boldest critics there are; and hence, despite what seems outmoded in him, still one of the most bracing.

As a biographer, Johnson was old-fashioned in the sense that—from the standpoint of today—biography itself was. It had still to acquire more intimacy of atmosphere, more richness of texture; yet it was in Johnson's plan, as it was in his nature, to banish from biography the pious and adulatory tone that was rendering so much of it worthless. Johnson not only proposed to tell the truth about his poets, but he firmly put telling the truth above everything else. He also enriched, as well as enlivened, his biographies by his love of the vivid anecdote, the eloquent scrap or detail. Still, we must not turn to the *Lives* expecting something beautifully ordered or dramatically heightened; nor should we look for a wholly balanced treatment: Johnson, to a considerable extent, enlarged upon what interested him and excluded what did not.

The *Life of Savage* stands apart from the other *Lives:* beyond having been written some thirty-five years earlier, it is the personal memoir of a friend and the life story of a rascal. It is, indeed, not least enjoyable for setting out to be a kind of vindication and winding up, a kind of exposé. Johnson did his best by his friend: he swallowed not only Savage's claims to be the illegitimate son of a noblewoman, but even his claims to be a poet. Yet all Johnson's affection and magnanimity could not keep him from recognizing—or from reporting—a sizable amount of the truth; and we soon see, all too clearly, what sort of character Savage was. Despite its heavy writing here and there, the *Savage* is perhaps the most entertaining and flavorsome thing that Johnson ever wrote. It remains a classic study of disreputableness.

The Preface to the Shakespeare is Johnson's solidest piece of criticism. It takes an Age-of-Reason view of its subject, which comes at least as close to our own view as the long-enthroned Romantic one; whatever Johnson's limitations, he neither deifies Shakespeare nor re-creates him in his own image. To Johnson, as to us, Shakespeare was a fallible and uneven writer, and a supreme genius rather than a supreme artist. For Johnson, in fact, he was pre-eminently a "poet of Nature," someone who plucked out the universal aspects of human life, "the general passions and principles by which all minds are agitated." ("His story requires Romans or kings, but he thinks only on men.") This is praise, we may note, of Shakespeare the psychologist rather than the poet; and it is praise, once again, of what Johnson could confirm from his own experience. So too, when Johnson makes his famous defense of Shakespeare's violation of the Unities, he is prompted by a logical and not an esthetic view of art. What may possibly be lost in intensity by jumping a thousand miles or a dozen years is not investigated; and it is Johnson's common-sense conclusion that the Unities "have given more trouble to the poet than pleasure to the audience." Yet, so far as it goes, the case Johnson makes out is trenchant.

For the sublime in Shakespeare—as for the sublime generally—Johnson had real feeling; yet it would be foolish to argue that for Shakespeare's poetry as a whole—or for the poetry in relation to the psychology and the drama—Johnson had anything like a full appreciation. He was properly irritated by Shakespeare's way of defacing great scenes with curious ornament, and there is more than a trace of truth in Johnson's dictum that Shakespeare "never has six lines together without a fault." But, by and large, Johnson's responsiveness simply could not keep pace with Shakespeare's imagination, and he seems at times to have pierced through the poetry to the meaning rather than to have found the meaning *in* the poetry. It is this lack in Johnson that leads him to make the most serious, and most astonishing, of his Shakespearean blunders—the setting of Shakespeare's comedy higher than his tragedy. "His tragedy," Johnson summed up, "seems to be skill, his comedy to be instinct." But even were this so, Johnson would be ignoring the fact that Cleopatra and Iago and Lear breathe an air known to no comic character of Shakespeare's but Falstaff. Yet Johnson must have sometimes felt what he did not formulate: consider the most famous of all the Notes on Shakespeare—"He that peruses Shakespeare, looks round alarmed, and starts to find himself alone." That emotion is not born of *As You Like It* or *The Taming of the Shrew*.

Shakespeare also disturbed Johnson because he was not

explicitly moral enough; here again we may say that Johnson seems to have pierced through the poetry to the morality rather than to have found the morality *in* the poetry. It is really this objection that underlies such opinions as preferring a happy ending to *Lear:* "I cannot easily be persuaded, that . . . the audience will not always rise better pleased from the final triumph of persecuted virtue." Yet, in spite of himself, Johnson is forced to remark: "A play in which the wicked prosper, and the virtuous miscarry, may doubtless be good, because it is a just representation of the common events of human life." In Johnson's criticism, the moralist and the realist were too often at war not to tarnish the criticism; but the realist was seldom absent, however he might choose to give ground. And though Johnson may not have been the ideal critic of Shakespeare, he wrote about him with a sanity, a fearlessness, a frequent justness of perception, and a deep if partly dissembled love, that constitute a large and lasting service.

In view of Johnson's glaring faults and occasional outrageous blunders, perhaps it must always be his fate to be censured in the very act of being praised. But, after all possible deductions have been made, he is surely a great figure and something like a great force. And to read the best of his writings is to come upon a mind and character scarcely to be imagined from even the best of his talk. The lamps that gave him light were growing dimmer as he wrote, and the wild new glow in the sky was something he stubbornly refused to see; but the light he worked by recovers its brightness in the work he did, and leads us backward, but not astray.

(1947)

CHAPTER IX

Gibbon

"I was born"—so Gibbon begins his autobiography—"I was born at Putney in the county of Surrey, the 27th of April O.S., in the year 1737." Moreover, the date of his birth had a good deal to do with the tenor of his life—few people have been more the child of their age; while the family he was born into had its eighteenth-century significance also. It was an old family, but one painfully obscure further back than his grandfather's time: we may conjure up such ancient country gentlemen as we choose; what we can alone be sure of is a grandfather who grew rich as an army contractor and rose to become—as he sank by becoming— a director in the South Sea operations. With what was left to the first Edward Gibbon after the Bubble, he accumulated a second fortune, no vast part of which descended to Gibbon's father. The father—also named Edward—had received a gentleman's education and, both before and after marriage, come to indulge a gentleman's tastes. Capricious and unstable, a Tory M.P., a London alderman, he had of his wife seven children, of whom the third Edward alone survived. Mrs. Gibbon did not herself survive this final childbed; and the orphaned boy, who had been an invalid baby and continued sickly through childhood, was fortunately cared for by a most devoted maiden aunt. Having nursed young Edward at home, she presently followed him to school: when he enrolled at Westminster, Catherine Porten, both to maintain herself and look after her nephew, opened a boardinghouse near by.

At school, Gibbon showed no interest in games nor talent for friendship. He early became a bookworm—"the dynasties of Assyria and Egypt were my top and cricket ball." His aunt was his ally: they read Pope's Homer and the *Arabian Nights* together, while by himself the boy was soon reading volume after volume of the *Universal History*. He was fourteen when, paying a visit with his father, he pitched on a work dealing with the later Roman Empire, and had just become—as he puts it—"immersed in the passage of the Goths over the Danube, when the summons of the dinner bell reluctantly dragged me from my intellectual feast."

We can easily credit his account of his entering Oxford at not quite fifteen: "I arrived . . . with a stock of erudition that might have puzzled a doctor and a degree of ignorance of which a schoolboy would have been ashamed." He arrived at a time when his ignorance consorted with the place far better than his learning did: there existed at Oxford, for gentlemen commoners like himself, the most exceptional facilities for avoiding work. So far from following any regular course of study, certain undergraduates never even met their tutors, and—to judge by the life they led—might rather have been at a spa than a seat of learning. But the young Gibbon was not the less attracted to study for its making him lopsided, and he considered his fourteen months at Oxford the most wasted period of his life. There were things he much wanted to do, such as study Arabic; but his tutor promptly discouraged him, and Gibbon—bound as he was to devour books and think about them—could only, if he wasn't to be guided, explore for himself. He got deep into the Church Fathers, and then into Bossuet and the Elizabethan Jesuit, Parsons; he got in so deep, indeed, that at sixteen, with the help of a London bookseller, he was admitted a proselyte to the Catholic Church.

It was not without a certain satisfaction, an air blending mischievousness with martyrdom, that Gibbon informed his father of what he had done. As a Roman Catholic, he could not continue at Oxford; and his father, acting for once with sagacity and dispatch, decided he had better not remain in England, either. He was packed off to the house of a Protestant clergyman at Lausanne; and the sixteen-year-old boy, who had no friends there and spoke no French, whose very room displayed a strange stove rather than a fireplace, and whose penance included bad cooking, might have pondered the paradox of being cured of Catholicism by being sent to Purgatory. But matters very quickly grew better: the pastor was an understanding man who reclaimed the culprit from Romanism and rebellion by letting him gradually reclaim himself. Moreover, Gibbon soon came to enjoy Lausanne. At first he went about with a group of pleasure-loving young Englishmen: once, indeed, he lost 110 guineas at faro and was sufficiently perturbed to flee the city; though his father, on hearing of such unexpected frivolity, was sufficiently pleased to make good the debt. But inevitably—and all the more as French became his daily language—Gibbon turned toward the native life, and the intellectual life, of Lausanne. There were glimpses of Voltaire acting in one of his own comedies; there were exchanges of letters with Swiss scholars. Thus early in life, Gibbon successfully attempted an emendation in Ovid; thus early, too, he began to respond to the discipline, he began to acquire the balance, of one of the stablest of cultures. How thoroughly he responded he would make plain in the great undertaking of his life; but he perhaps made it plain much sooner, in the matter of his celebrated romance.

Celebrated the romance may surely be called, however special the reasons. When they met, both Gibbon and Suzanne Curchod were extremely young. Suzanne was a Swiss clergyman's daughter, plainly a girl of parts, plainly also one with ambitions: these included marrying outside the clergy and, if possible, above her class. How deeply Suzanne loved the short, gauche, socially desirable enough young Englishman is open to conjecture, though how deeply Gibbon loved Suzanne is open even more. Intrigued he certainly was, and smitten possibly: he swore, at any rate, "an attachment beyond the assaults of time." There is also a story of his stopping strangers at dagger point to compel their praises of Suzanne's superlative charms, a story that can just be believed because it is so out of character—because it reveals a Gibbon who protests too much. Both Gibbon and Suzanne were perhaps, with a certain real intensity, in love with love: in any case, after a number of meetings and a regular exchange of letters, they got themselves, or judged themselves, or found themselves, engaged.

The matter of getting married, however, was something else: Suzanne lacked a fortune, Gibbon his own income. And at the moment there were other complications. Gibbon's father, as it happened, had just got married himself, and Edward was now, on the eve of his twenty-first birthday, summoned home. It was an opportunity for the young lover, who, while saluting his father's marriage, might try to seal his own. His father greeted him, after five years, in the friendliest fashion, and his stepmother proved in every way kind. Between her and her stepson there indeed began a lifelong relationship of affection and esteem. She was very eager for such a relationship, and by never having children of her own—which would have cut sharply into Gibbon's inheritance—she happily brought it about. Actually his father's main reason for calling him home was to dock that inheritance himself: he offered Gibbon three hundred a year for life if he would agree to cutting off the entail. The son consented and then, in respect of Suzanne, sought his father's consent in turn. He was refused it; Mr. Gibbon could not approve his son bringing an unknown foreign girl to England, and even less his settling down in a foreign land. He did not forbid the match: he merely reminded Edward of his duties, he merely spoke of an action that would bring his father the earlier to his grave. Highly overwrought, Edward thereupon—as he wrote to Suzanne—retired for two hours to his room. When he emerged, it was to do as his father asked. "Farewell!" he wound up the letter: "I shall always remember Mlle Curchod as the worthiest and most charming of women. . . . Assure M. and Mme Curchod of my . . . regrets."

Suzanne's answer mixed self-pity with real feeling, and indignation with both. "You made up your mind in two hours!" she breaks out; but soon good sense reasserts itself and she wonders why Gibbon can't marry her with the idea of passing a few months each year in Switzerland till set free by his father's death. But Gibbon had already lowered their romance into its grave, and would in due time carve out its monstrous epitaph: "I sighed as a lover, I obeyed as a son." The result could hardly have been happier: Gibbon achieved the serene bachelor life that suited him so well, and Suzanne in due course married the great French finance minister Necker and became the mother of

Mme de Staël; became, too, a notable hostess, with Gibbon among the most famous and favored of her guests.

He, back in England at the age of twenty-one, now set about becoming an Englishman again and mapping out a career. He took rooms in London, but socially—what with a lack of exalted sponsors—things were inclined to be slow. Many of his evenings he spent at dull family parties or with "old Tories of The Cocoa Tree"; many others he passed, "while coaches were rattling through Bond Street," alone with his books. He had his books, as always: but to just what use was he to put them? In the matter of a career, the law—which his stepmother spoke of—did not tempt him in the least, nor did a suggestion of his father's, that since he spoke French like a native, he go in for diplomacy. In the matter of a career, no choice was really necessary: "I know that from my early youth," he wrote in the autobiography, "I aspired to the character of an historian." The real question was what history to write. In the next few years he chose and rejected the crusade of Richard I, the Barons' Wars, the history of the Black Prince, of Sir Philip Sidney, of Sir Walter Raleigh, of Florence under the Medici. He was plainly just glancing about; and between strolls along the corridors of history, he sat down and wrote, in French, an essay on the study of literature. By the time it got published, his quest of a theme had to be put aside. The Seven Years War was on, and largely as a gesture Gibbon and his father had obtained commissions in the South Hampshire Regiment. But in 1760 the regiment, to their surprise, was called up. Gibbon's response was at first good-humored; to be a captain of militia for a season might be rather a lark. But it was quite something else to cease, for two years and more, to be the captain of one's fate, and lead "a wandering life of military servitude." Entry after entry of the journal he kept begins "We

marched" or "We paraded" or "We halted"; while the only
thing the young scholar learned, beyond how to drill, was
how to drink. In time, however, the journal entries tend to
start off with "I read . . ."; and before he was finished
with soldiering, he had begun to resume a life of scholarship. As an officer Gibbon, though not very effective, was
fiercely efficient; and since his superiors were not, he exer-
cised on occasion real authority. But the chief value of
peregrinating the South of England, from Alton to Win-
chester, from Ringwood to Fareham, was best summed up
—as so much concerning Gibbon is best summed up—in his
own words: "The discipline and evolutions of a modern
battalion gave me a clearer notion of the Phalanx and the
Legions, and the Captain of the Hampshire Grenadiers
. . . has not been useless to the historian of the Roman
Empire."

It was not yet to Rome, however, that Gibbon hurried
as soon as his regiment was disbanded: it was to Paris.
After five years in England, he looked with longing toward
the Continent, and his father gave him the money for a
tour. In Paris—a Paris that has become peculiarly historical, a Paris of savants and *salonnières*, of *philosophes* and
Anglomaniacs—he breathed an atmosphere, he entered
into a way of life, that were at least as vital to him as those
of London and Lausanne. Moreover, it was the perfect
moment for imbibing this new element that his temperament craved, since by now it had quite banished certain
other elements it did not want. The spiritual life, early
and immaturely embarked on, had been early and unre-
gretfully cast aside: for religion Gibbon would thereafter
feel no need. The emotional life, flaring up before Gibbon
came of age, produced no second crisis; for romance Gibbon would in future sigh no more. The physical life, the

thirty months of camps and countermarches, had ended with the Peace; for action and the out-of-doors Gibbon would not even briefly pine. What now beckoned, without complication or alloy, was intellectual and social life only, the life—in the age that gave the phrase its luster—of the scholar and the gentleman.

Thanks to his French essay, to some letters of introduction, and to the prevailing Anglomania, Gibbon achieved the entree in Paris: through Mme Geoffrin he got to know Helvétius and d'Holbach; there were morning calls and evening parties; operas, dinners, duchesses, a whole enchanting milieu where the life of the *monde* and the life of the mind were one. "In a fortnight . . . I have heard more conversation worth remembering," he wrote to his stepmother, ". . . than I had done in two or three winters in London." But socially he was, for all that, pretty much an *arriviste*, and in fine company still something of a duffer: besides, if he was to enter society not just as a writer, but as a man of fashion, it would prove highly expensive. Money had to be husbanded for an Italian journey; and Gibbon husbanded it, after fourteen weeks in Paris, by revisiting Lausanne.

He was welcomed back: the scene of his adolescent recantation began ministering to his adult desires. "A holiday resort for all Europe," Lausanne offered much by way of well-bred intellectual intercourse: all sorts of cosmopolites and notabilities stopped over, summered, wintered there; there Gibbon now resumed his friendship with the scholarly young Deyverdun, began his friendship with John Holroyd, the future Lord Sheffield—they were to be the two warmest friendships of his life. There he saw Voltaire act again—"a very ranting, unnatural performance"; and mingled with some pleasant girls who, by banding together into a Société du Printemps, went freely about with young men, unchaperoned and unscathed. He saw Suzanne there, too—a governess now, who might make a most charming friend if she could be dismissed as a fiancée; yet—as things stood—*"fille dangereuse et artificielle,"* to be kept distinctly at arm's length. But the young scholar at Lausanne quite kept pace with the young worldling: thoughts of Italy were uppermost, and the matter of career, of the project that should crown it, was never far away. Burrowing for the one, studying for the other, he read on and on—books, learned journals, the first thirty-five volumes of the *Bibliothèque raisonée;* writing, at the same time, a 214-page treatise on Italian geography. His were detailed preparations indeed; and when the coming of spring "unlocked the mountains," he set forth, like a scholar knight, for Italy.

Turin first—where Gibbon, being presented to the King's daughters, "grew so very free and easy, that I drew my snuff-box, rapped it, took snuff twice"—a scandalous violation of presence-chamber etiquette. Then Milan, Genoa, Bologna, Florence—whose annals he perhaps still toyed with chronicling; then Pisa and Lucca, Leghorn and Siena; and finally, at the beginning of October—with sudden beating pulses—Rome. "From the Silvian Bridge," he wrote in his journal, "I was in a dream of antiquity." "After a sleepless night," he recalled long afterward, "I trod with lofty step the ruins of the Forum; each memorable spot where Romulus stood, or Tully spoke, or Cæsar fell, was at once present to my eye." The dream held: avoiding society, neglecting to go kiss the Pope's slipper, Gibbon inhabited the past, talked "with the dead rather than the living." The dream deepened; and suddenly, amid a concourse of images, there came what proved a moment of inspiration:

*It was at Rome, on the fifteenth of October 1764, as
I sat musing amidst the ruins of the Capitol, while the
barefooted fryars were singing Vespers in the Temple
of Jupiter, that the idea of writing the decline and fall
of the City first started to my mind.*

Commentators are careful to remind us that the friars were
singing in the Temple, not of Jupiter, but of Juno: but a
man in the moment of encountering his destiny perhaps
ought not have a too clear sense of his whereabouts.

The clock had struck; but a good many years were to tick
away before Gibbon would read—let alone write—about
Rome. In his own opinion, they turned into the least happy
years of his life—partly, no doubt, because so little got
done where so much was waiting to be; partly because full
manhood had not yet brought entire independence, while
independence itself, when it came, would at first bring
cares. After wintering in Rome and Naples, he started for
home, touched at Venice, all "ruined pictures and stinking
ditches," paused for "ten delicious days" in Paris, where
he encountered Suzanne, now Mme Necker, "as handsome
as ever" and full of affection for her former suitor. As for
Necker himself, he would each night "go to bed, and
leave me alone with his wife." "Could they," Gibbon demanded of Holroyd, "insult me more cruelly?" But now
that love had flown out of the window, lifelong friendship
might come in at the door.

Back in England, Gibbon made headway of sorts in London society when not condemned to provincial society by
visits to his father. There was work to show, too: an essay
on the sixth *Æneid;* and with Deyverdun—who came over
each year from Lausanne—a series of critiques, the *Mém-
oires Littéraires de la Grande Bretagne,* and the begin-
nings of a book about Switzerland. The chief profit from

all this was less how to write history than what language not to write it in. French was now to be abandoned for English—even if an English that had a certain air of Latin. Five more years, in any case, slipped away, during which Gibbon had but very slowly advanced "from the wish to the hope, from the hope to the design, from the design to the execution" of the *Decline and Fall*. Moreover, as his plans matured, his project itself grew larger: what was first envisaged as the decline and fall of a city broadened into that of an empire.

In 1770 when Gibbon—now thirty-three—was at last deep in his subject, his father died. From having to settle a somewhat tangled estate and remove his stepmother from Buriton to Bath, Gibbon was again diverted from his studies; but, these obligations accomplished, he was fully and permanently free. The one thing that had still impeded, that could still becloud, a scholar-worlding's life—his duty toward and dependence on his father—now vanished; and thereafter scholar and gentleman alike made notable progress.

If no vulgar climber, Gibbon had yet had to make a place for himself in London, which he did chiefly through people he met outside it—at Lausanne, in the Militia, in Rome. He became, in his own sedate, pompous, snuffbox-rapping fashion, something of a diner-out and a quite prodigious clubman. There was a Roman Club, dotted with earls and spattered with honorables; there was the old Augustan Cocoa Tree; and Boodle's and Almack's and Brook's; and White's, that great stronghold of Tory rulers; and The Literary Club, where a Tory held forth for posterity and ruled. There was finally what in those days was as much club as legislature, the House of Commons. At his fashionable clubs he could bathe in the atmosphere, however seldom he might share the activities, of the great world. Though he practiced no gallantries, he might hear the gossip about those who did; and while stopping, himself, at shilling whist, might watch others lose their own or their families' fortunes. Despite having very good friends at The Literary Club—Garrick and Sir Joshua in particular—he was not very vocal there. He and Dr. Johnson disliked each other; Johnson—whom no glass house ever deterred from throwing stones—dilated on how ugly Gibbon was; and Gibbon, speaking of Johnson, on how ursine.

In the House of Commons, where he owed his seat to a cousin, Gibbon was less vocal still. He sat, from 1774 on, for almost ten years; but though they were scarcely humdrum years, he was the most silent, as also the most steadfast, of Tories. He not only never spoke, he did not very often listen: the great speakers, he remarked, filled him with despair, the bad ones with terror. On the subject that most agitated the House—the American Revolution—Gibbon, having looked into the facts, took King George's side. He presently confessed, however, that it was easier to approve the justice of that side than the policies; and he eventually murmured that one might be better off humbled than ruined.

To be sure, Gibbon found the year 1776 momentous enough: for on February 17 was published the first volume of the *History of the Decline and Fall of the Roman Empire*. Into it had gone many years of reading and writing and polishing and recasting—the scholarly resolution, really, of a lifetime; and in the course of those years Gibbon had not simply mastered his subject, he had forged a style.

The various modes of worship which prevailed in the Roman world were all considered by the people as equally true; by the philosopher as equally false; and by the magistrate as equally useful.

It was a style that in good time would breast the Bosphorus as well as the Tiber:

> *The dissolute youth of Constantinople adopted the blue livery of disorder; the laws were silent, and the bonds of society were relaxed; creditors were compelled to resign their obligations; judges to reverse their sentence; masters to enfranchise their slaves; fathers to supply the extravagance of their children; noble matrons were prostituted to the lust of their servants; beautiful boys were torn from the arms of their parents; and wives, unless they preferred a voluntary death, were ravished in the presence of their husbands.*

Sentences had learned, as seldom before, to be endowed with majesty while being crammed with violence and overlaid with malice.

The success of the first volume was instantaneous and tremendous. "My book," wrote its author, "was on every table, and almost on every toilette." Horace Walpole hailed it with rapture; Hume's praise recompensed "the labor of ten years"; nor, said Gibbon, "was the general voice disturbed by the barking of any profane critic." Godlier critics were, to be sure, in different case. They violently attacked the even now notorious fifteenth and sixteenth chapters for being attacks, themselves, on Christianity: so much so as for Gibbon to say later that, had he foreseen the effect on "the pious, the timid, and the prudent," he would perhaps have softened the invidious chapters. But as he had not foreseen the effect, he chose instead to rebut an assailant named Davies in a *Vindication* quite as trenchant and almost as pitiless as one of A. E. Housman's floggings of his fellow classical scholars. His other assailants Gibbon took no notice of, beyond sniffing how happy he was to have helped them to worldly rewards: "I dare not boast of making Dr. Watson a Bishop; but I enjoyed the pleasure of giving a royal pension to Mr. Davies, and of collating Dr. Apthorpe to an Archiepiscopal living." Toward the Church itself he showed, in his personal life, no animus; and is said to have kept, during his later years, a Bible at his bedside.

Thereafter he was in any case an extremely famous man. "Charles Fox," he will write from Almack's, "is now at my elbow"; or from Paris: "As soon as I am dressed, I set out to dine with the Duc de Nivernois: shall go from hence to the French comedy, into the Princess de Beauvau's *loge grillée*, and am not quite determined whether I shall sup at Madame du Deffand's, Madame Necker's, or the Sardinian Embassadress's." Yet he never ceased working, though he might interrupt one kind of work for another. The second and third volumes of the *Decline and Fall* were five years appearing, partly because of Gibbon's interest in chemistry and anatomy, and his dive "into the mud of the Arian controversy." When in 1781 the two volumes did appear, there was not the furor of five years earlier; but there was not, on the other hand, the need for it. The Duke of Gloucester might respond with his famous "Another damned thick, square book—always scribble, scribble, scribble—eh! Mr. Gibbon?"; and less highborn critics might register complaint or disappointment. But the scope and solidity of Gibbon's *History* were beyond dispute, and the new books "insensibly rose in sale and reputation to a level with the first."

Seven years more were to elapse before the three final volumes appeared, by which time Gibbon would have long since quitted London for Lausanne. The move, which he never regretted, was partly a matter of money: with the fall of the North administration, Gibbon lost his seat in

Parliament and some £800 a year on the Board of Trade. The clubman and diner-out who needs must drastically retrench to squeak through in London could live in perfect comfort by removing to Lausanne. He had a deep affection for the place: he had been happy there, or at any rate young; he could live there now with immense prestige; and, most enticingly of all, could perhaps share the burdens of living with his old friend Deyverdun. *"Vous me logez, et je vous nouris,"* he wrote, after his old friend responded with joy to his feelers; and in September 1783 he returned once more to Lausanne. Thereafter the greatest historian of the age varied the writing of his history with whist and chess, strolls or calls on neighbors, and bread and cheese for supper.

Caught in this serene light, he stands forth to much his best advantage. He is a curious figure: among a few men in history no less ridiculous than sublime. On the one side, it would be hard to overpraise Gibbon's achievement, who was equally the architect of a monumentally vast and classic work and of an exquisitely proportioned Georgian existence. To be sure, he had the good judgment to get himself born in the eighteenth century—an age that encouraged its scholars to be men of the world, and that while shielding the better-born from all brusque intrusions, yet did not shut out light and air. Intolerably stilted the age could be, but it was never oppressively stuffy: its complacence was that of statues rather than churchwardens. To Gibbon's ironic temper, to his urbane, dry, skeptical set of mind, England offered much, Paris and the Continent still more. A hundred years later, and scholar and gentleman would not have been so closely or so harmoniously welded: a hundred years later Gibbon would have belonged to the Athenæum instead of Almack's, been a Regius Professor rather than sat in Parliament, overflowed with neurotic crochets rather than seignioral airs; the enormous and continuous advance of scholarship would have allowed him far less time for society, the marked deterioration of society would have doomed him to a pundit's role, or a don's. Not his personal experiences only, but his very angle of vision, would have become a great deal more provincial: he would have escaped to the Continent to be caught in the toils of German "method"; or, like his distant kinsman Lord Acton, might have whittled away his brilliance trying to cope with some sixty thousand books.

If Gibbon can't help seeming comic, the wonder is he doesn't seem more so. Extremely short, increasingly fat, extraordinarily ugly, he only stressed his shortcomings by his habit of preening himself. There is the tale of Gibbon getting down on his knees at fifty to pay romantic court to Lady Elizabeth Foster and then being too fat to get up again; servants had to be summoned and an accident invented. He was equally vain where he had more right to be. There is a tale, too, of how, having held forth in his best half oracular, half anecdotal style, he rapped the snuffbox and awaited homage, only to be quietly challenged by a mere youth in the company, one William Pitt; who, when Gibbon disdainfully retorted upon him, further argued with such success that Gibbon quit the room in prissy reproof, and at length the house in ill-hidden irritation. Again, there is the pendant to the tremendous compliment that Sheridan paid Gibbon in his great oration at the opening of the Warren Hastings trial. No parallel could be found for Hastings's crimes, Sheridan thundered, "in ancient or modern history, in the correct periods of Tacitus or the luminous page of Gibbon." Wanting a second portion of praise, Gibbon—who was present—affected deafness and asked his neighbor what Sheridan had said. "Oh," he got back, "something about your voluminous pages." He habitually conducted himself like a prelate and wrote of himself as though he were dead. Yet, having smiled, we must end by acknowledging how stupendously the man succeeded. In a way, the comic side only emphasizes his success: in other words, there *is* no pathetic side— the few small shadows derive from the sunlight in which he basked. His, moreover, is a serenity that his age, for all its reputation, seldom attained to—that age which steeped Johnson and Boswell and Gray in melancholy, which saw Swift and Smart and Cowper go mad. Gibbon represents the triumph—however large or limited it may seem in itself—of the eighteenth-century ideal. No doubt, to revive the old fling, he mistook himself at times for the Roman Empire; but so perhaps did the eighteenth century mistake itself for Gibbon.

Even that twilit flash of inspiration among the barefoot friars at Rome had to be long pondered in broad daylight before being acted upon. It was a real inspiration, moreover, because it told him, not whom for the moment he loved, but whom he should marry. The Roman Empire was a *parti* rather than a passion, which is perhaps why things so magnificently succeeded. No mere callow infatuation at the outset, it turned with time into a real union, into twenty years and more of fond, devoted, truly close companionship; and when on that June night, between the hours of eleven and twelve, he set down the last words of his *History* in a summerhouse in his garden, he felt impoverished as well as elated, widowed as well as set free. It had been an all but unparalleled alliance. To be married to the Roman Empire, even in its declining years, is a formidable exertion; but Gibbon proved more, even, than its worthy mate; he emerged its undoubted master.

On finishing the *Decline and Fall*, Gibbon himself carried the MS. of the last three volumes to London. It was

purchased for the then great sum of £4,000, and published—with a dinner to mark the occasion—on Gibbon's
fifty-first birthday. All particulars of its reception pale before the fact that it was everywhere received as a full-
fledged classic. In the 165 years since, its prestige has
hardly diminished and more probably increased. Much
has been said and must continue to be said in derogation;
but the work remains, at the very least, one of the grandest
of all *achievements*. It was most sharply attacked in the
generation after it was written—by Romantics who as
greatly disliked its style as its tone. To Shelley, Gibbon
was "cold and unimpassioned"; to Coleridge, worse even
than the language was Gibbon's using "nothing but what
may produce an effect. . . . All is scenical and, as it were,
exhibited by candlelight." Even more classical-minded
critics, even profoundly admiring ones, have deplored Gibbon's habit of sneering and his tendency to snicker. His
erudite defender and eulogist, Porson, said what a thousand others have repeated, that Gibbon's humanity never
sleeps save "when women are being ravaged or Christians
violated." And yet, on this head, there is Cardinal New-
man's characterizing Gibbon as "the only Church historian
worthy of the name who has written in English."

Doubtless Coleridge put his finger on Gibbon's great
limitation—on his being far more interested in creating
effects than discovering causes. And though that, in the
end, is only to point out his unequaled merit, clearly the
Decline and Fall is the work of a dramatist rather than a
psychologist or philosopher. A true thinker Gibbon was
not, or even an acute student of human nature. A scientific
historian he certainly was not; nor, had he been, would his
History have so triumphed over 165 years; for what scientific theory of history, or of very much else, has ever held
sway so long? The *Decline and Fall*, being art, is a presen-

tation rather than a re-enactment; it stakes its all on a theme—plainly set forth in the title—rather than a theory; it shows no interest in depth, as it possesses no equal for span. As Suzanne said, it projects across chaos a bridge joining the ancient to the modern world. It remains, too, a great feat of erudition, whether in the amassing or the disposing of its materials. If insight was blunted by prejudice or sacrificed to effect, accuracy—an accuracy that Robertson was impelled to verify and Porson was equipped to attest—was not. The inferiority of the second half of the *History* to the first, of the account of the Eastern Empire to that in the West, is partly a matter of inadequate scholarship, but much more so of temperament: to Gibbon what was Byzantine could only seem barbaric or decadent. But his book may call itself history even now when it is more than ever a triumph of literature.

His life's great work behind him, Gibbon, while ruminating new projects, began chronicling that life itself. He wrote no finished version, merely six sketches out of which, after his death, Lord Sheffield wove the autobiography that bears his name and, better than the *Decline and Fall*, asserts and glorifies his manner. Gibbon had, in a sense, not so much a life to record as a way of living it. Even those elements that smack of drama or hint at tragedy—expulsion and exile, stepmother and blighted romance—far from leaving scars, seem almost a vindication of the eighteenth-century precept that "whatever is, is right." Yet if few lives have been, in a way, more undramatic, few have been better dramatized. Gibbon's fateful moment at Rome vibrates almost as memorably as Cæsar's a few miles north of it; and not Hector taking leave of his family, or Mary Queen of Scots of the world, catches the light more vividly than Gibbon bidding his *History* adieu.

There is little for any biographer to add beyond where

the autobiographer leaves off. Deyverdun died; but Gibbon obtained a life tenure on the house they shared and continued in the old way of living. The Bastille fell; but though the French Revolution shocked Gibbon, it scarcely discommoded him: indeed, by bringing the Neckers and other congenial spirits as refugees to Lausanne, it really brightened his existence. English friends also came to Lausanne, among them the Sheffields. Their sharp-eyed daughter found Gibbon's circle deadly dull, and thought their flattery "the only advantage this place can have over England for him."

He talked much of an English visit; but the Revolution had made travel rather hazardous; and the visit kept being put off. The death, however, of Lady Sheffield in April 1793 prompted Gibbon to return at once, to bring any comfort he could to his most intimate friend. But it was the friend who must soon think of Gibbon: back in England he took ill. A hypercele, or swelling of the left testicle, that had been diagnosed as far back as his militia days and been totally disregarded ever since, now grew acute. Operations afforded temporary relief; there were even intervals of dining out and of driving to Bath and Apthorp and Sheffield Place. But there could be no cure; and Gibbon died in London on the 16th of January 1794 at the age of fifty-six.

(1953)

CHAPTER X

Byron's Don Juan

Sooner or later Byron will enjoy a decided vogue again. He will never, of course, be so famous as he once was—he once, after all, intoxicated all England and half of Europe. He carried a sable and self-conscious melancholy to its farthest height; he turned pose into poetry. A dashing hero with some of the glossiest attributes of a villain, he was first swooned over and then hissed, the greatest social success and the greatest social scandal of his age. The whole thing has something excessive about it; there are writers whose careers are an affront to realism, an offense against art. Disraeli's, for example, is too flashy; Beckford's too opulent; Byron's too lurid. Anyone with blood so blue ought not to have blood so black—not kings' and madmen's both. If one is a lord and romantically handsome, need one also walk with a limp? Byron inherited a dank, half-ruined abbey where it was only decent to drink wine from a skull; he could ride like a streak; he swam the Hellespont. He hated and cursed and sobbed over his mother; committed incest with his sister; snarled on his wedding day at his wife. For love of him, titled ladies stabbed themselves with scissors; for love turned hate-wise, had him burned in effigy.

After a life of pleasure and excess, he died in squalor fighting for the independence of Greece. And amid all this fame and obloquy, this dandyism and violence, the Lady Carolines and Lady Oxfords and Countess Guicciolis, Byron, before dying at thirty-six, constantly wrote letters, insatiably wrote verse.

It is all too purple for any self-respecting story-teller, let alone real life. That it happens to be true may be the most fantastic part of all, but is not much my reason for recapitulating it here. My chief reason is that for any even brief discussion of *Don Juan* it happens to be immensely revelant. I don't mean in any strictly factual sense; I mean that only someone with the endowments for living so privileged and tempestuous and superbly exuberant a life could have written so worldly and torrential and superbly exuberant a poem. *Don Juan* is not an example of literature compensating for life, of the romantic imagination fleeing mean streets for fairyland. *Don Juan*, to be sure, gallops with imagination; shoots the very rapids of romance. But on that side it hardly bounds more swiftly than Byron's own life did: while, from another side, it is crammed with knowledge of highborn sin and folly, with intimate understanding of the great world. To create Haidée and hymn the isles of Greece it was doubtless enough for Byron to be a poet. But to portray a Donna Julia or Lady Adeline, to move through ballrooms and glide up staircases with so much assurance, Byron needed also to be a peer.

Don Juan is not autobiographical: Byron set down here something better than autobiography, he set down himself. Here at last, after so many studied twitchings of his mantle, here amid a hundred extravagances and excrescences, in a rush of words, a pell-mell of impressions, here where the operatic tumbles sheerly into the farcical, where the beetles of mockery kill the flowers of romance, stands revealed the whole unruly man. *Childe Harold* is in large part Byronism, but *Don Juan* is Byron.

Don Juan is also one of the most staggering performances in literature. So far as I know, there is nothing truly like it—for one thing because no one more of an artist would have dreamed of doing it as Byron did, while no one less of a genius could have contrived to do it at all. In its obstreperous magic, its aristocratic vulgarity, in the eloquence of its praise and far greater eloquence of its abuse, there is such swagger as even Byron never elsewhere attempted; but also such power as he never elsewhere achieved. What he did in *Don Juan* was, fortunately, not portray but express himself.

Than Byron there is in general no stagier actor in our literary history; but the immensely rewarding thing in *Don Juan* is that Byron altogether eschews the leading role, the center of the stage. In return, it is true, he insists on being almost everything else connected with the production: now dramatist and now drama critic; now heckler, now prompter, now minor actor muttering brash asides; frequently stealing a scene, unblushingly interrupting the show. Hence what we get is as much production as play, as much rehearsal as performance, as much brilliant confusion as clear sense of design. And for Byron it is all wonderfully in keeping and wonderfully liberating: he has found his happiest calling—not actor but showman.

This exchange—of posturing for showmanship—works tremendous good: instead of a personal desire to attract attention, there is the professional ability to command it. And, indeed, filled as it is with such antics and interruptions as no formal work of art could endure, *Don Juan* is most accurately called a show. Nor are we merely hanging on to a metaphor; nothing else—not satire, not epic—so truthfully describes *Don Juan* (which is as often comic as satiric, and less epic than picaresque). Nothing except a show dare be so explosive in its energy, so filled with fireworks and gaudy trimmings, so played in the very lap of the audience; can contain such tossed-off insults, such haphazard profundities. And one of its most showmanlike qualities is that, though episode after episode may be treated tongue in cheek, the episodes themselves are never thrown away, never whittled down to a mere satiric point. Juan's intrigue with Donna Julia is almost as good Boccaccio as it is Byron; the storm and the shipwreck have their quota of excitement, the harem scenes their quota of indecency. Byron deals in meaningless wars but not sham battles; in too lush Mediterranean scenes, perhaps, but never painted backdrops. And writing of Juan and Haidée he can, of course, be genuinely romantic, and chronicle a romance that is genuinely tender and moving:

> *Alas! they were so young, so beautiful*
> *So lonely, loving, helpless . . .*

It is the one haunting episode in the poem, its innocence and ecstasy staining our memories more deeply than all the cynicism and worldliness. Nor do the digressions and asides in *Don Juan* come through as mere random frivolities: they not only lend variety, comic vigor, and change of pace, but often help to create suspense: the retardation of Haidée's father's entrance, for example, is managed to excellent effect. For all its waywardness, the story-telling in *Don Juan* is seldom flabby.

But it is for its satire, in the end, or at any rate its elements of laughter, that *Don Juan* must really be praised: for the spectacle it makes of high life, the farce it makes of pretension. Its wars bring nothing about; its lovers (save only Haidée) are all untrue. Juan—an acceptable *jeune premier*, but the least interesting thing in the poem, a merely acquiescent rake, an insipid grandee—is exposed, now in chains, now in triumph, to all the best barbaric society, the most sumptuous misrule, in Europe. But since there's no place, for the satirist, like home, Juan is brought at last—and just when the story needs a complete change of air—to England. In England, Byron's vision narrows but intensifies, his coloring is soberer but his brushwork more expert; we pass out of a world of swashbuckling and opéra bouffe into that of Congreve and Pope. There is no longer any stalking strange beasts through exotic forests with barbaric weapons, but a stiff ride with the hounds after hypocrites and snobs; a long day on the moors bagging philistines and pharisees; a large coaching-party clattering at the heels of politics. The subject being the most nearly "civilized" one in the book, the treatment is, with justice, the most nearly savage: yet the slashing at morals is maintained at the level of manners, with a wonderful accumulation of detail; it is Byron seeking heavy damages for exile, perhaps, but not cheap revenge; and it concludes, in mid-air, on a wild high note of farce.

A powerfully charged, helter-skelter production, indeed: exhibiting that ebullient gaiety so often twin-brothered by loneliness; that peculiarly magnanimous love of liberty of one who takes inordinate pride in rank; that over-emphasis on sex of one never quite at ease with women: the production of a poet in whom two centuries meet with a great clang but no very deep hostility; the performance of someone versed in English and European and Eastern ways who, if he was in Shelley's words the Pilgrim of Eternity, was also, in Mr. Wilson Knight's, our only cosmopolitan poet.

As with anything so recklessly creative, *Don Juan* has its share of unconscious confession, curious oscillation, odd twistings and turnings. Yet I do not think it superficial to suggest that what the poem *is* enormously outdistances anything it may mean. The critical malady of our age is an indifference to sheer creativeness as a thing—of power and of pleasure—in itself. In its itch to correlate and laminate and explain, current criticism has half lost the instinct to respond and enjoy. Worse, in its obsession over what makes the clock tick, it all too often fails to notice whether it tells the right time. Most great books, it is true, are complex and not lightly mastered; they need to be unraveled and explained. But with something like *Don Juan,* the overwhelming thing is to pitch in, to participate. For you cannot explain inexhaustible energy and high spirits; you can only explain them away. And you lose out if you so concentrate on the targets in *Don Juan* that you only half appreciate the hits; if you care more for Byron's motives than his manner; if you persist in making a laboratory of an amusement park. The motives, to be sure, aren't to be brushed aside; the targets, after 125 years, are still there to shoot at. But what is most exhilarating in *Don Juan* is not so much the satire as what might be called the satiricalness. Obviously what makes any great satirist is much less the occasion for scoffing than the disposition to scoff; for the true satirist, opportunity, so far from knocking only once, knocks all day long. In themselves, ruling classes may or may not be always rotten; but for satire, obviously, they are always ripe. Furthermore, there is about *Don Juan* too great a love of battle for its own sake for us to identify each sideswipe as a blow against tyranny or time-serving, against this vice or that. All the same, the man who wrote *Don Juan* was very far, at bottom, from being either a cynic or a trifler: its cascading poetry, its tumultuous energy cannot consort with the merely cynical and small; and amid the impudences and extravagancies, there sounds again and again the war-cry of the intransigent

rebel. Though Byron himself, as Mr. Quennell has remarked, abandoned Juan for Greece out of a "haunting
death-wish," *Don Juan* is a very dazzling exhibition of the
life-force.

It is difficult, again, to find anything resembling a level
of achievement in *Don Juan*, for it dashes up and down
the whole ladder of comedy like a monkey. It shows none
of the instinct for tone of a satirist like Pope. Pope, for the
most part, confines himself to the rapier and the poisoned
dart; but Byron (though he worshipped and at times resembles Pope) grasps hold of any weapon, sharp or blunt,
subtle or crude; and not guns, swords, arrows only, but
stones thrown at windows, firecrackers tossed under chairs,
and occasionally a massive field piece, as in the onslaughts
against Southey and Wellington. *Don Juan* mingles the
wit of the salon with the horseplay of the schoolroom,
sensational rhymes with impossible ones, all varieties of
facetious nonsense, insult, abuse, pleasantry, unpleasantry.
Now it is the buxom widows at the battle of Ismail who
wonder despondently why the ravishing hasn't begun;
now

> *Guests hot and dishes cold . . .*

or

> *He was the mildest-mannered man*
> *That ever scuttled ship or cut a throat . . .*

or

> *And whispering "I will ne'er consent," consented . . .*

or

> *So for a good old-gentlemanly vice*
> *I think I must take up with avarice . . .*

But it is the profusion, succession, accumulation of jibes,
jokes, comments, epithets, apostrophes, the rhymes and
running fire throughout sixteen cantos and some sixteen

thousand lines that make *Don Juan* the most tumbling and impromptu of epics.

A portrait of a civilization, *Don Juan* is also a kind of pastiche of one. It is immensely "literary"—crammed with poetic tags, critical and biographical tidbits, historical and mythological allusions. In his turning—to sharpen his satire or brighten his narrative—to history, literature, all the compass-points of culture, Byron is like Pope, and achieves a like glitter. For satiric purposes, *Don Juan* is even more a parade and parody of quotations than *The Waste Land;* while it is a virtual anthology of worldly wit and wisdom— Pope and Horace, Chesterfield and Montaigne, Johnson and Swift.

> *In her first passion woman loves her lover:*
> *In all the others, all she loves is love.*

> *And if I laugh at any mortal thing,*
> *'Tis that I may not weep.*

Byron has made both these sentiments his endlessly quoted own; but the first of them, of course, is pure La Rochefoucauld; the second, pure Beaumarchais. And of what is entirely Byron's own in *Don Juan,* how startlingly much has passed even beyond common speech into rank cliché: *"Man's love is of man's life . . .";* *"But words are things . . ."* and so on; even *"Stranger than fiction,"* even—though I fear fortuitously—*"Sweet Adeline."*

We come last to the fact that *Don Juan* is a poem, which is perhaps the most crucial fact of all. Three things, it seems to me, save *Don Juan,* with its prodigious breakneck energy, from coming to grief, from skidding or careening off the road. Byron's great comic sense, which checks his impulse to rant, proves a stout wall on one side; his feeling for tradition, his sensibility for the highbred, the historic, the classical, walls him in on the other. But it is the requirements of verse itself, of rhyme and meter and stanzaic form, that keep a smooth road under him. By virtue of these things indeed, Byron—for all his antics and vulgarities—is an aristocratic poet. As to how decisive such qualities can be, we need only turn to the most democratic of poets, Whitman, who lacked the first quality, never fully acquired the second, and almost wholly rejected the third; and may see how much more impurely and wastefully his genius operated. Byron's sense of the past, of the poetry of history, is much more evident in *Childe Harold*, yet certainly not missing here:

> *I've stood upon Achilles' tomb*
> *And heard Troy doubted: Time will doubt of Rome.*

But it is the actual versification, the use of rhyme, meter, touches of poetic diction, stanzaic form, that lifts and liquefies *Don Juan*, that helps give it the "beauty" that Shelley noted. Of immense value is the heightening power of the verse, the regularity that goes with the rush, giving it not an eccentric but a dramatic speed. Or consider the splendid exordiums to so many of the cantos, with their sense not of breaking new ground but of instantly getting *off* the ground: for this, too, we have the élan of the verse to thank.

To perceive the difference—and distance—from prose, we have only to compare *Don Juan* to the long work in English that, all in all, it perhaps most resembles—*Tom Jones*. Certainly both works are in their way first-rate. Both, again, are epical: the one a panoramic entertainment with all England for its stage; the other a kaleidoscopic spectacle, with all Europe. In both the well-placed hero is a youthful rake who comes to know one pure love and countless varieties of lust. In both, the pre-eminent aim is an elaborate satiric survey of manners: in both the author's strongest hate and most frequent target is hypocrisy. In both, conventional morality is regarded with scorn: Fielding and Byron alike forgive many "sins" and castigate many "virtues." Fielding and Byron alike, moreover, deliberately and unceasingly obtrude themselves, interlarding their story with personal comments and confessions, curtain speeches and familiar essays, parodies, denunciations, every variety of obiter dictum. And yet . . . well, I have actually, and understandably, never seen the two compared. For it is somehow like comparing a solid with a liquid, a side of beef with a great bowlful of rum punch, a stagecoach with an Indian canoe—prose, in short, with poetry. As poetry, *Don Juan* is disfigured by some slipshod verses and some ghastly rhymes; it is blunted by Byron's sometimes being too busy with satiric weapons to care enough about artistic tools. But as poetry, Byron's masterpiece remains curiously true to itself: it sails off into highfalutin now and then, or nose dives toward bathos, but it never merely dodders into prose.

(1949)

PART
II

CHAPTER XI

Some Notes on Comedy

COMEDY is not just a happy as opposed to an unhappy ending, but a way of surveying life so that happy endings must prevail. But it is not to be confused, on that account, with optimism, any more than a happy ending is to be confused with happiness. Comedy is much more reasonably associated with pessimism—with at any rate a belief in the smallness that survives as against the greatness that is scarred or destroyed. In mortal affairs it is tragedy, like forgiveness, that seems divine; and comedy, like error, that is human.

One might perhaps begin by talking about comedy in its philosophic sense, as an attitude toward life, rather than as a mere technical aspect of the theater. One might begin, in other words, by speaking of the comedy that unites such writers and writings as Lucian and Aristophanes, the *Decameron* and *Candide*, Congreve and Peacock and Sterne, *Pride and Prejudice* and *Le Bourgeois Gentilhomme*, rather than of the comedy that is the official label for such diverse plays as *Measure for Measure* and *The Man of Mode*, or *All's Well That Ends Well* and *The Importance of Being Earnest*, or *The Misanthrope* and *Private Lives*. For obviously—despite immense differences—the same spirit animates an Aristophanes and a Jane Austen; whereas a vastly different spirit separates *Measure for Measure* from *The Importance of Being Earnest*. *Measure for Measure*, we feel, is not really comedy; and *The Misanthrope*, again, is something more than comedy. But coarse as Aristophanes can be and genteel as Jane Austen, broadly as Aristophanes can clown and exquisitely as Jane Austen can annihilate, the two have much the same vision of life, much the same eye for its absurdities. They have in full measure the comic point of view, as other writers have the tragic point of view. In the theater, comedy and tragedy are forms that can be used with some purity. Much Restoration comedy was indeed written with some purity. Today, when the theater is debased by the naturalistic drama, when the drama itself is three parts play to seven parts production, when the only comedy that most playwrights try for is standing-room comedy—today very little in the theater really expresses the comic sense of life. Far from probing, it seldom even honestly paints the surface. And the real trouble is not that the contemporary stage aims at artifice, but that it professes to aim at naturalness. It was one of the real virtues of the Restoration stage that it never sought—and never managed—to be "natural." It lied its head off about a good many of the appurtenances of life, but it managed to capture a surprising amount of the thing itself; and even its lies squared with the partial truth that life is a masquerade.

Comedy appeals to the laughter, which is in part at least the malice, in us; for comedy is concerned with human imperfection, with people's failure to measure up either to the world's or to their own conception of excellence. All tragedy is idealistic and says in effect, "The pity of it"— that owing to this fault of circumstance or that flaw of character, a man who is essentially good does evil, a man who is essentially great is toppled from the heights. But all comedy tends to be skeptical and says in effect, "The absurdity of it"—that in spite of his fine talk or noble resolutions, a man is the mere creature of pettiness and vanity and folly. Tragedy is always lamenting the Achilles tendon, the destructive flaw in man; but comedy, in a sense, is always looking for it. Not cheaply, out of malevolence or cynicism; but rather because even at his greatest, man offers some touch of the fatuous and small, just as a murderer, even at his cleverest, usually makes some fatal slip. In tragedy men aspire to more than they can achieve; in comedy they pretend to more.

The difference, again, between the two is the very question of difference. A great tragic hero—an Œdipus or Lear —strikes us as tremendously far removed from common humanity. But comedy, stripping off the war-paint and the feathers, the college degrees or the military medals, shows how very like at bottom the hero is to everybody else. Tragedy cannot flourish without giving its characters a kind of aura of poetry, or idealism, or doom; comedy scarcely functions till the aura has been dispelled. And as it thrives on a revelation of the true rather than the trumped-up motive, as it is in one way sustained by imposture, so in another it is sustained by incongruity. Here is the celebrated philosopher cursing the universe because he has mislaid a book. Here are all those who, like King Canute, would bid the clock go backward or the waves stand still. Here is not only the cheat, but the victim who but for his own dishonest desires could never be cheated.

Comedy, in brief, is criticism. If through laughing at

others we purge ourselves of certain spiteful and ungenerous instincts—as through tragedy we achieve a higher and more publicized catharsis—that is not quite the whole of it. Comedy need not be hostile to idealism; it need only show how far human beings fall short of the ideal. The higher comedy mounts, the airier and more brilliant its forms, the more are we aware of man's capacity for being foolish or self-deluded or complacent; in the very highest comedy, such as the finale of Mozart's *Marriage of Figaro,* we are in a very paradise of self-deceptions and misunderstandings and cross-purposes. At the heart of high comedy there is always a strain of melancholy, as round the edges there is all gaiety and ebullience and glitter; and Schiller was perhaps right in regarding high comedy as the greatest of all literary forms.

Comedy is criticism, then, because it exposes human beings for what they are in contrast to what they profess to be. How much idealism, it asks, shall we find entirely free from self-love? How much beneficence is born of guilt, how much affection is produced by flattery? At its most severe, doubtless, comedy is not just skeptical but cynical; and asks many of the same questions, returning many of the same answers, as that prince—or at any rate duke—of cynics, La Rochefoucauld. "Pride," La Rochefoucauld remarked, "does not wish to owe, and vanity does not wish to pay." Or again: "To establish oneself in the world, one does all one can to seem established there." Of these and many similar maxims, a play or story might easily be written; from each much cold and worldly comedy, or harsh and worldly farce, might be contrived. But comedy need not be so harsh, and seldom is: though it can be harsher still, can be—as in Ben Jonson—gloating and sardonic. But always it is the enemy, not of virtue or idealism, but of hypocrisy and pretense; and what it does in literature is very much, I suppose, what experience does for most of us in life: it knocks the bloom off the peach, the gilt off the gingerbread.

But though the comic spirit is, in Meredith's phrase, "humanely malign," it is also kindly and even companionable, in the sense that it brings men together as fellow fools and sinners, and is not only criticism but understanding. Comedy is always jarring us with the evidence that we are no better than other people, and always comforting us with the knowledge that most other people are no better than we are. It makes us more critical, but it leaves us more tolerant; and to that extent it performs a very notable social function. Its whole character, indeed—quite aside from that point—is rather social than individual.

The social basis rests in the very subject-matter of comedy—in all that has to do with one's life as part of a group; with one's wish to charm or persuade or deceive or dazzle others. Thus no exhibitionist can exist in solitude, no hypocrite or poseur can work without an audience. There are indeed so many social situations that engender comedy that many of them are notably hackneyed. There are all kinds of classic family jokes—the mother-in-law joke preeminently; but equally the rich-uncle theme, or the country cousin, or the visiting relative who forgets to leave, or the one that proffers advice, or the one that prophesies disaster. Right in the home there is the precocious brat or the moping adolescent; there are countless varieties of comic servants; and there is finally the question, though it perhaps belongs in a different category, of who heads the family—the husband or the wife.

The idea of husband and wife more likely belongs with the social aspects of sex, with the War between the Sexes as it is fought out in the drawing-room. As a purely sexual conflict, this war would not be social; but by the same token it would not be comedy. The question whether man really makes the decisions—including the decision to marry —or is merely permitted to think he does, is, whatever the answer, thoroughly social in nature. Or there is the business of how men and women perform in society for one another's benefit: being the fearless protector or the clinging vine, the woman who always understands or the man who is never understood. We have social comedy again when we pit one nationality as well as one sex against another, when the American puritan is ensnared by a Continental siren, or when the suitor is German and humorless and the besought one is French and amused. There is still another social aspect when we add a third person to the situation, a mistress as well as a wife, or a lover as well as a husband; or—for the situation need not be illicit, it need only be triangular—when the wife's old beau or the husband's old flame reappears on the scene. Or there is the man who does not know which of two sisters, or two heiresses, or two widows to marry; or the girl which of a half-dozen suitors.

Comedy, indeed, must gain admittance into any part of the world—including prisons and sickrooms and funerals —where people are thrown together. Any institution involving hierarchies and rivalries—for example, a university—is a perfect hotbed of it. There will be everybody's relation to the President or the President's wife; or the President's relation to the President's wife; or to his trustees; all the struggles for precedence and the problems of protocol; the progressives on the faculty and the die-hards; the wives who can't help looking dowdy, the wives who suppose they look chic. For obviously any institution, whether a college or a department store, an artist colony or a country club, provides a cross-section of social types and traits, and brings us face to face with a hundred things out of which comedy is distilled: ambition and pride, arrogance and obsequiousness; a too slavish following or a too emphatic flouting of convention; all the stratagems men use in order to outwit or get their way.

And of course comedy becomes purely social in that best-known and perhaps best-liked of all its higher forms—the comedy of manners. Here we have hardly less than a picture of society itself; here the men and women are but parts of a general whole, and what survives—if we have it from the past—is likely to be known as the Restoration Scene, or Regency London, or Victorian Family Life. Here the drawing-room is not merely the setting of the play or novel, but the subject and even the hero; here enter all the prejudices, the traditions, the taboos, the aspirations, the absurdities, the snobberies, of a group. The group, to constitute itself one, must partake of a common background and accept a similar view of life: though there will usually exist some outsider, some rebel, some nonconformist who, as the case may be, is ringing the doorbell or shattering the windowpanes; trying desperately to get in or desperately to get out; bending the knee or thumbing his nose. Or the comedy of manners will contrast one social milieu with another—the urban and the rustic, the capital and the provinces, Philistia and Bohemia, America and Europe. And in the comedy of manners, ignorance of good form has much the same value that, in straight drama, ignorance of some vital fact has.

And with ignorance of one kind or another we begin coming close to the very mainspring of comedy, or at any rate of comedy in action. For most comedy is born of ignorance or false knowledge; is based on misunderstanding. (Obviously not knowing the truth—though here one might add "until it is too late"—applies to much tragedy also.) At the level of ordinary farce or romantic comedy, the lovers are estranged until a quarter of eleven because the young man misunderstood why the young lady was walking with Sir Robert in the garden. At a higher level, it will not be mere circumstance or coincidence, but qualities of character that block the way. Envy proves an obstruction, or arrogance; or a too great tendency to be suspicious or to take offense. In *Pride and Prejudice* the very title makes this clear. In Jane Austen's finest novel, *Emma*, there is every variety of misunderstanding, but the greatest misunderstanding of all, and the one that leads to so many of the others, is Emma's concerning her own nature. Emma —so highhanded and so wrongheaded, so often reasonable and so seldom right—is herself a wonderfully modulated comic character. And what matters is not so much the realistic consequences of her mistakes as the assured and benevolent air with which she commits them. And now moving higher still, to Meredith's *The Egoist,* we see self-deluded character constituting, really, the whole book. Sir Willoughby Patterne is the supreme example of self-centeredness in literature—the man who, in his absorption with the creature he is and the role he plays and the impression he makes, can care about nobody else. He tramples on the emotions and even the liberties of all who come his way, only cherishing such people so far as they cherish or pay homage to him. He is stunned by what seems to him *their* selfishness when, appalled by his, they walk out or turn away. And as we watch Meredith's great demonstration of human egoism, as we see with what comic flourishes and farcical leaps and wild extravagant motions it proceeds—as we smile and even laugh—we become increasingly uncomfortable. The more monstrous Sir Willoughby seems, the more we realize that in some sense this man is ourselves. If no one ever misunderstood his own nature worse, no one has ever pointed a moral better.

Comedy at its greatest is criticism indeed; is nothing less, in fact, than a form of moral enlightenment.

The Egoist is sometimes declared to be comedy in name only, to be at bottom tragic. I would myself disagree— Meredith carries his theme to so extreme a length as to transform his hero from a man into a sort of sublime caricature, and gives him a purely comic intensity, an intensity quite disproportionate to what it is intense about. If just this is the "tragedy" of most human beings, it must yet serve to expose rather than exalt them; otherwise what shall we call genuine tragedy when we encounter it? Malvolio in *Twelfth Night,* who has also been looked upon as tragic, comes somewhat closer to being so. For pretension with him does partake a little of aspiration; his vanity, moreover, is stung because he is a servant, and stimulated by the mischievousness of others. But Malvolio, like Sir Willoughby, is really too trivial for tragedy, as he is also too priggish. What happens to him seems painful rather than tragic; it is not quite our modern idea of fun.

And this brings up the point that though comedy has its permanent subject-matter and even its body of laws, it is liable, like everything else, to changes in fashion and taste, to differences of sensibility. One generation's pleasure is the next generation's embarrassment: much that the Victorians shuddered at merely makes us laugh, much that they laughed at might well make us shudder. One always reacts—and quite fortunately—from the vantage-point of one's own age; and it is probably a mistake, and certainly a waste of breath, to be arrogant or snobbish or moral about what amuses or does not amuse one: we may fancy we are less callous than our grandfathers and only be less callous about different things. The cuckold was clearly, in Restoration comedy, a figure to hoot at. Simply for being cuckolded we do not today find a man so comic, or even comic at all: though the moment we add an extra element to his role, such as his elation over cuckolding others, he becomes a comic figure for us. To what exent sex itself is a comic theme must naturally vary with the morality of a particular age: there are times when it seems shocking for a man ever to have a mistress; there are times when it seems even more shocking for a man never to have one. Right in the same age, what is considered virtue by the parson may be termed repression by the psychiatrist; and in such an age, which is usually one of moral transition, we may well find conflicting comedy values. The pendulum-swing of taste always makes it hard for people to know what they really like: if they are in revolt against gentility, they are likely to confuse what is funny with what is merely bold or obscene; if they are converts to gentility, they will be too much outraged by the indecent to inquire whether it is funny. There is nothing at which the Comic Spirit must smile more than our fickle and inconstant notions as to what constitutes comedy. We need not always look back to Shakespeare's drearier clowns as an instance of how tastes change: sometimes we need only attend a revival of what convulsed us ten years before.

(1950)

CHAPTER XII

Shaw

SHAW was not simply the longest-lived of modern writers and in some degree the most many-sided; he was also in a sense the most challenging and disruptive. No other writer, as a result, has been the subject of so much criticism and so much near-nonsense. In an effort to understand what Shaw "meant," a whole battery of journalists, a whole army of pundits have sadly misunderstood what he was. Some of them have wrestled in solemn social-worker fashion with Shaw as though he were entirely a writer of textbooks and tracts; some, at the other extreme, have tried to make Shaw's irreverence and iconoclasm the engine of their own craving to startle or demolish. But neither through ignoring what was most Shavian nor through trying to outdo it did much worth saying about Shaw get said. And even the wisest of Shaw's critics cannot always have known how far Shaw's showmanship concealed his serious intentions, how far it coincided with them, and how far it concealed the lack of any.

But, in whatever spirit and from whatever side, it has been notably easy to write about Shaw. Any man with a specialty or a mania must somewhere have found Shaw adverting to it; any man with a grievance must have found in Shaw an antagonist or ally; whatever a man's politics, or his God, or his denial of one, Shaw—early or late—must have had his say about it. For on however outmoded or ill-reasoned or cantankerous a basis, Shaw's collected works constitute a sort of encyclopedia. Shaw has greeted an end-less succession of events with a twenty-one-gun salute—his little innovation being to take lethal aim as well. He not only took all human activity for his province, but strongly suggested that nothing superhuman was alien to him, either—he swept heaven clean of charm, drastically low-ered the temperature of hell, brought back the dead, land-scaped and peopled the future. No matter what one's field or one's foible—God or Devil, O'Leary or John Bull, prize-fighters or soldiers or poets, armament-makers or brothel-keepers, Shakespeare or Wagner, phonetics or marriage or divorce, slums or drama critics, war or revolution—Shaw may serve as a pretext for writing about it, or it as a pre-text for writing about Shaw.

But exactly as his work supplies something for almost everyone to write about, it embraces too many things for any one person to write about with sufficient authority. Whoever would deal definitively with Shaw must go well beyond the writer of plays or of prefaces, the critic of plays or of music, must plunge into Marx and cross over to Ire-land and turn back to Lamarck, must buy himself an atlas and burrow deep in history, must know medicine and law, the Church and many churches, the whole arena of poli-tics, half the arcana of science, plus much miscellaneous knowledge and very much curious lore. Even where Shaw is shallow or fanciful or mistaken, the critic who would pronounce judgment cannot be. Hence the most we can really hope for is that anyone who would write with some breadth about Shaw should be a man of letters with an informed concern for ideas; should offer a literary man's verdict of Shaw's talent and a knowledgeable, however disputable, version of Shaw's "thought." No one can write comprehensively of Shaw as just a literary or dramatic critic: for again and again one must stop and explain, or digress and co-ordinate, or go after the facts and compare. And the difficulty isn't just how much Shaw wrote about, it is how consistently—or inconsistently—he wrote about it, in how dedicated or mischievous a spirit, with how controversial a slant, how contradictory an aim: so that one is dealing with shock tactics as well as principles, with the man who wrote for Hearst as well as for posterity, with *poseur* no less than puritan, thinker and thought-processor too, and with in some ways the most bourgeois as well as the most anti-bourgeois writer of his time.

All the same, if we are to isolate and honor what remains most vital and Shavian about Shaw, we must neglect the role he assumed most vividly in his own time for the role he more and more occupies in ours; we must care less about how informed or inflammatory or even intelligent he was in favor of how supple and witty and articulate he remains. Like Shakespeare he filled his plays with historical characters, like Ibsen with social ideas, and as with them it only matters now how creatively he went about it: the problem of *Ghosts* no longer presses, the first act of *Ghosts* is a marvel of exposition still. To be sure, from the real place he occupies in history Shaw's treatment of issues and ideas has a more than usual historical interest; due tribute must be paid to such of his "thinking" as proved fruitful, or to such leadership as actually led somewhere. But equally where Shaw seemed most sound or most mistaken, his thinking side has, for our day, been too much stressed; not because of how often Shaw may have been wrong or right, but because his true genius and—as it happened—his real job lay elsewhere. Most of all and most triumphantly of all, Shaw was a showman of ideas. If it is true that intellectually he was something more, perhaps it is also unfortunate that he was; for what counts less has blurred what easily bulks largest. By a showman of ideas, I mean something big-scaled as well as admirable, I mean someone who, at his weakest, made a fashion show of all the contending issues of his age; and who, at his most trenchant, made a superb military spectacle where those issues crossed swords and drew blood and often killed one another off. His were, in many cases, sham battles and arbitrary victories and defeats: but such was his staging of them, he attracted the whole civilized world to the battlefield. This is not to deny how serious, how astute, how learned Shaw could be. There is much solid matter indeed to Shaw's encyclopedia, as there is much to Dr. Johnson's *Dictionary;* but its value will rest more and more on what is Shavian about it, as with the *Dictionary* it is what is Johnsonian that counts. Shaw's delineation of ancient Egypt or modern England is, for vividness and bias alike, of a piece with Johnson's definition of lexicographer or excise.

So long as we have a Shaw in the role of showman, dramatist, virtuoso, entertainer; so long as his chief function is rather to exhilarate than to enlighten the audience, it matters much less how often he contradicts himself, how glaringly his demonstrations nullify each other, or even how wantonly he betrays the scruples of a lifetime for the gratification of the moment. And what for me clinches the fact that Shaw is above all a showman of ideas—equally in terms of classification as of achievement—is that his is so very much more a triumph of method than of meaning—that again and again we can admire the approach while resisting, while rejecting, the arguments. T. S. Eliot once raised the point how far one can enjoy a writer whose ideas antagonize one: I don't know that he answered it, or that it is safely answerable; but the answer may well be, to the degree that he is an engaging showman. (With the pure work of art, something different—something like a willing suspension of disbelief—is involved.) In any case, write though he did on a hundred subjects, with cogency very often, with real conviction as often as not, Shaw yet never wrote so as to fuse all his contentions, reconcile all his contradictions, make some innermost quality of self light up the whole. He wears no heraldic armband, neither the *Que sçais-je* of a Montaigne wise enough to doubt his own wisdom, nor the *cor laceratum* of Swift, in lifelong explosion for what deep down refused to explode, nor the *Écrasez l'infame* of Voltaire, divided by passion from Shaw however joined to him by wit and prankishness. Of dialectics, again, Dr. Johnson, like Shaw, often made a mere game, playing brusquely and unfairly to win; but the dialectics was one thing, the view of life another. When we speak of Dr. Johnson as a humane reactionary, the two words are ultimately not a contradiction but a coalescence, for to Johnson the Tory scheme of things was really at one with the tragic sense of life: inequality must needs be acquiesced in as a principle since it could not be escaped as a fact. But despite how many things Shaw espoused and militantly fought for, or exposed and fought militantly against, just where do we pierce to the heart of the matter? We all know G. B. S.; but what, precisely, is the GBessence? Possibly no symbolic heart exists because no human heart declares itself; how much gayer is a Johnson or a Mozart or a Keats for his streak of melancholy. But we no sooner seize on the gaiety of Shaw's mind than we become aware of the gaunt puritanism of his body; we no sooner respond to his anti-bourgeois laughter than we are conscious of his curiously bourgeois art. He ridicules Ireland by way of England, England by way of Ireland, he turns waggish in the pulpit, injects purpose into his pranks. Plumping for reason, he dissolves in mysticism; whooping up socialism, he lets his eye stray toward the Strong Man and worldly power. Such dazzling contradictions go far to explain Shaw's success as dramatist, but tend also to point up his untrustworthiness of mind. To put it mildly, it is all much too confusing, it is as though what one's doctor prescribed as a sedative should also prove an emetic. Were Shaw's the pervasive skepticism that frowns on all absolutes and is mistrustful of all systems, were his even the feeling that every human benefit has its price, we should know where and in what excellent company we stood. But in spite of his laughter, Shaw does deal in absolutes; in spite of snarling them up in paradoxes, he does offer solutions; and we have accordingly to reconcile a constructive program with a nihilist technique. And superbly as laughter can demolish, or paradox reinterpret, neither thing can be systematically constructive. Shaw's *modus operandi* becomes too much an end in itself; the penalty, perhaps, of diverting all who watch you is converting none of them. It is the showmanship that drapes itself in sacerdotal robes, that chants and swings incense and utters solemn proclamations—whether after Wagner's fashion, or Stanislavsky's, or Mr. Eliot's—that acquires not just audiences, but followers. The really costly thing with Shaw was not how many other people he made light of, but that—and never more than when he swaggered—he so decidedly made light of himself.

Yet we must always bear in mind two things. A man born with a genius for juggling—whether colored balls or controversial ideas—can hardly escape the role of performer, can hardly avoid ending up on the stage. So much for what Shaw was; as for what he in some measure failed to be, as for his final lack of philosophic wholeness and weight, the very thing that made him in one sense more than man—the free, volatile, unvindictive, dazzlingly gymnastic play of mind—left him not a complete man as well. He rather reversed the usual human order: in him, the animal spirits and sensual enjoyments that keep other men zestful and young were soberly dislodged or puritanically suppressed; while the philosophic doubts, the worries over the world, the concern for the good life that turn other men into split and neurotic personalities were for Shaw a source of invigoration and release. The effect, if extraordinary, is also just a little monstrous, as of someone not created but invented, as of someone marvelously, miraculously . . . two-dimensional.

The masks, the pranks, the poses were in their way, of course, psychologically necessary as well as professionally shrewd. Shaw—as he himself confessed and Bertrand Russell and others quickly noted—was by nature a painfully shy man; one who compensated in print for a lack of ease in ordinary conversation; one who went still further, and made of himself not just a dramatic figure but an almost fictional one. It doesn't matter that part of the fiction consisted in speaking the truth. Shaw's habitual joshing, moreover, bespoke not a mocking mind or witty tongue alone: the habitual josher is oftenest someone who finds the unselfconscious give-and-take of human intercourse a strain. His joshing, on the personal side, represents a kind of avoidance of conversation, while on the intellectual side it is a way, among one's inferiors, of not having to talk drivel or talk down. Something faintly mysterious, because faintly monstrous, surrounds this man in whom the mind bulks so large and the body so blatantly dwindles; whose

puritan view of sex may rather signify a sexual difficulty
"solved" by puritanism. But the more palpable and, I
would think, serious personal difficulty was social and economic, and derives from the shabby-genteel family background, from the indigently transplanted Irishman, from
the father who drank and the mother forced to work.
Shaw solved the thing magnificently as a writer, but the
emotions it begot he never wholly mastered or outgrew.
He was one of those to whom birth wouldn't have mattered
in the slightest had he only been really wellborn; he was a
snob not for something he was but for something he wasn't.
One thinks, if for only a moment, of Swift. Shaw, like
Swift, resented his ambiguous social position, and took
more than good care of his money. Like Swift again, Shaw
was fascinated by men of power, and oddly evasive about
women and love. But the likenesses only emphasize, in
the end, the contrast between one of the most perfectly
managed and one of the most tragically mishandled of all
careers; between a self-regulated and smooth-functioning
life and one that, deeply fissured within, ended in madness. For want of a brooding and melancholy streak,
Shaw's work fails of a kind of beauty inherent in much
of the finest art; but the absence of it in Shaw himself left
the showman free to shuffle his masks at will and achieve
the most unlikely roles: a Savonarola who should twinkle
while he thundered; a puritan man-of-the-world who, in
the most Jaegerish of garments, attained to the jauntiest of
styles. Consider merely the beard—by which Shaw instantly attracted attention and permanently concealed his
face; by which he contrived to look flatteringly male and
engagingly Mephistophelian; and by which, most of all,
through seeming to part with it, he permanently preserved
his youth.

· · ·

In our time there have been some very good things written about Shaw, and some very good names indeed among the writers. Yet what stands forth glaringly is the extent to which Shaw has *not* been written about—that is to say, by the most influential of our serious critics. Though often touching on Shaw, Mr. Eliot has made no attempt to traverse him; nor, so far as I know, has a Leavis, a Blackmur, a Tate, a Trilling, a Ransom, a Winters—the list, if it is not to be lengthy, can only be suggestive. And it is of real interest to ask why so many fashionable and formidable critics have passed Shaw by, even though the answer, up to a point, seems clear enough. For one thing, of course, Shaw lived too long and, save here and there, his later work—a full twenty years of it—had almost in common decency to be ignored. More integrally, Shaw in his "art" was the kind of bourgeois writer who would antagonize today's higher criticism, and in his tactics was the kind of anti-bourgeois writer who would perhaps antagonize it even more. And not only, of course, is Shaw's method sharply didactic; his concern is not with humanity but with society. He goes at slums in terms of slum-clearance, at brothels in terms of capitalist profiteers, at marriage in terms of crippling divorce laws, at the early Christians in pointed contrast to the later ones. His Cæsar or his Joan is not, thanks to the creative imagination, more richly complex than in history's pages; rather each is brilliantly simplified and straightened out, each his own most eloquent spokesman. Thus not only art in the final reckoning, but life itself at the very outset, is too much cut to measure; everything functions mechanically, nothing breathes. Worse still, there is the fact that Shaw, whether a poet of sorts or no poet at all or Mr. Eliot's poet strangled at birth, quite lacks the kind of poetic sensibility that prevails today. And indeed, even after scraping away all that is *not*

Shaw's view of Shakespeare, his insistence on the banality of Shakespeare's thinking really constitutes a misapprehension of Shakespeare's art. It is part of Shakespeare's greatness as a *creative writer* that he avoided Shaw's mistake, that he preferred poetic truism to scientific truth; that with such a writer ripeness is all, and ratiocination, in the end, is nothing. Shaw is indeed least poetic where he tries hardest to be. Marchbanks is most a monster for being even less of a poet than of a normal human being; he is quite inept when he tries to talk like Shelley and only forceful when he begins to talk like Shaw. And when Shaw himself aspires to poetry, as with the March winds and frisking lambs of *Saint Joan,* his rank failure is all too notorious.

As many critics would find no sense of poetry in Shaw, so would they find no awareness of evil; of a troubled, darkly religious vision of life; of the lost, or damned, or guilt-gnawed, or salvation-seeking soul. There are no bad people, no black-hearted, God-hounded evildoers in Shaw; there are only corrupt classes or intolerable social conditions or vicious laws. (Shaw's failure to understand personal wickedness is a real deficiency.) And we have finally to reckon with the fact that serious modern criticism has shown, quite understandably, little interest in the theater, for there has been little there to interest it. Thus, for many critics, if there has been no incentive to discuss Shaw's own achievement as a playwright, there has equally been no need to examine his influence—or even his lack of influence—on playwriting.

But though one can well understand why so many critics have failed to write about Shaw, one yet can wish that they had, or that they would. They might nail all that on the one hand is frivolous and on the other hand tractarian, all that is bloodless or bogus or mongrel or out-of-date, and contrive a sharp new formulation of where he failed or fell short. But they might also conclude that, in violation of his own tenets quite as much as theirs, Shaw achieved magnificent effects; that with his verve and energy he is, time and again, nothing less than irresistible; that for sheer articulateness and wit, he is in modern times all but unmatched. No one can dismiss Shaw's talent; one can at most deplore what Shaw did with it.

(1952)

CHAPTER XIII

Chekhov: The Four Plays

CHEKHOV, among modern playwrights, is as clearly the truest artist as Shaw has been the greatest intellectual force. It is amusing and possibly instructive that both men have triumphed by disregarding the usual rules and gambits of their trade—Chekhov by showing, for one thing, that feeling can create more intensity than drama; Shaw by showing that talk can prove as enlivening as action. Yet the point in these matters is less that Chekhov and Shaw were right than that they were geniuses. Both have been widely imitated with harrowing results.

Chekhov's very special effects derive from his individual methods; and we cannot assign his plays to convenient categories. In a conventional sense, they are not easily called comedies: in any large and classic sense they are even less easily called tragic. But what they can be called least happily of all is dramas. Chekhov was too delicate an artist to create the kind of drama that goes with prose; the kind of play that has dominated the serious stage since

Ibsen. In a sense, as I said above, Chekhov substituted feeling for drama. His method, which is doubtless characterized in the textbooks as "lyrical naturalism" or something of the sort, has been oftener appropriated by writers of drama than of comedy—for Chekhov is associated with frustration and neurosis, subjects that are eyed too earnestly in a theater that lacks true perspective. But Chekhov, who had true perspective, called most of his plays comedies; and their humor, their comic sense, may well be the decisive thing about them. It is certainly the solder without which the plays would become either too soft or too hard. They perhaps lack the form of classic comedy, though they have that form as much as any other. But they do have the perspective and proportion that only humor can supply: the word that possibly comes last to mind about Chekhov is yet the most important—his extraordinary sanity.

Chekhov called *The Seagull* a comedy—which may shed some light on his conception of tragedy. Tragedy, for Chekhov, seemed a matter not of death, but of death-in-life; not of violence or disaster, but of attrition and decay. It consisted not in losing something, but in having never had it, having never dreamed or desired it. We must understand this, not as a means of personally defining tragedy or comedy, but as part of any approach to Chekhov, and in particular to the common belief that his characters are futilitarians. They are in a sense almost the opposite; the point is not that they cease to care about life, but that they have no ability to cope with it. It is much less that they would not than that they cannot; it is not that they have too little faith in the future, but that they have, fecklessly, too much. They are inefficient people who drift rather than act, but for whom it is pleasant to drift and to put off deci-

sions till it is too late to decide. They are thus comic in
the degree that they are "poetic"; they are thus lovable in
the same sense that they are exasperating. They lack the
stature or purposefulness to be tragic, and they often have
sensibilities too quickly responsive to constitute genuinely
serious feelings. But, beyond that, there is Chekhov's
fatherly, family-doctorish attitude toward his people, his
humorous, tolerant nature, but keen, sharp, unsentimental
eye; all this brings a certain spirit of comedy into all his
plays—even the first one, which ends in violent death.

But whatever *The Seagull* be called, it is a good starting-
point for studying Chekhov's achievement. The triangle
story, which in other hands might have become—all by itself—an agitated, darkly dramatic play, is made part of a
large picture; of a group of people who represent, and
faintly misrepresent, a way of life. It may thus denote, with
Kostya and Nina, individual tragedy; it provides, notwith-
standing, a sense of social comedy. It is almost like saying
that youth is tragic but life is not—a remark not made at
youth's expense.

In any case, a sort of balance is struck by telling the
story of Kostya and Nina and Trigorin against the background of a provincial, middle-aged, largely self-centered
society, with which it frequently merges. For Arkadina is
at once Kostya's mother and Trigorin's mistress; and just
as Kostya loves Nina and Nina loves Trigorin, so Mascha
loves Kostya, so the schoolmaster loves Mascha and Mascha's mother loves the doctor. But the play has to do with
more than love and the pangs of love, it has to do with
talent and temperament, with the artist's vanity and ego;
with Trigorin and Kostya as writers and Arkadina and Nina
as actresses, not to mention Sorin, who would have liked
to write, or Shamreyeff, who is forever chattering about

the theater. *The Seagull* thus has to do with people's ambitions for themselves no less than with their love for
others; and, again, with young people and older people;
and city people and provincial people; and poor people and
people of means; and successful people and failures and
has-beens: with a good deal of life, in fact, and of what
mars or makes for happiness in life. But it is also set in a
certain time and place; it is the first, though the least typi-
cal and definable, of Chekhov's pictures of a certain kind
of Russian society.

It is not entirely Chekhovian—for one reason, because
it is chiefly concerned with people who do something:
artists and professional people rather than landowners and
drifters; for another reason, because it is in some degree
concerned with people who do something about themselves. More than in the later plays, they make decisions,
they act, rather than merely daydream or let themselves
be acted upon. Perhaps a key fact about them is that they
refuse to do something about other people. Trigorin is
only the more irresponsible and morally lax for visualizing
in story form what proves to be his own selfish treatment
of Nina (treatment involving, besides, disloyalty toward
Mme Trepleff); while Mme Trepleff, vain and posturing,
has neither affection nor sense of obligation toward her
son. Chekhov wrote a little more overtly as a moralist in
The Seagull than he would write thereafter; precisely as
many of his characters, here, are more recognizable (and
"international") types than most later ones. If this is true
of Trigorin and Mme Trepleff, it is no less true of Kostya
and Nina. Kostya as much suggests nineteenth-century
Weltschmerz, even Wertherism, as he does Russian melancholy; and Nina is the young girl, so common in late-nine-
teenth-century fiction, who breaks romantically with the

conventions, who is almost fated to have an interesting older man ruin her life, and whose emotions are not so much false as a couple of sizes too large for her.

But though the subject-matter does not seem entirely Chekhovian or even Russian, and the two young people seem almost fictional today in their period intensities, in tone and method *The Seagull* already suggests Chekhov in marked degree. The method was, for its own day, truly revolutionary; even in ours, despite how familiar it has become, it keeps an admirable economy and a sly expressiveness. Take, for one example, how Chekhov reveals his characters not engaged in true communal talk, but pursuing their own line of thought and seizing on whatever in the conversation provides an opening for their own concerns. Shamreyeff must always be reminiscing about the theater of long ago; Mme Trepleff must always be reverting to the theater in terms of herself. This distortion and discontinuity in the dialogue is a fine device for showing what the characters are really thinking about, and hence for characterizing them. And if it has that kind of psychological value, it has often a dramatic value too, of expressing the apartness and solitariness of people, never more *seul-à-seul* than when *vis-à-vis:* it conveys both the tireless ego, too self-centered to reach out, and the lonely heart, always yearning to be reached. Such dialogue, however scrappy and elliptical, yet constitutes a marvelous sort of notation.

The mood and coloring are often Chekhovian too, though less distinctively than in the plays to come. Chekhov has imported here a certain rather stagy sadness; and the fact that to some degree he mocks it, that he is satirizing certain poses and self-pities, doesn't altogether redeem what he does or make it seem quite his own. It comes off as a mixture of satire and sentiment, rather than as that blend of comedy and pathos that emerges later. One doubts whether in a later play Nina would be so classically seduced and thrust aside, or Kostya would so theatrically commit suicide. We should have a surer sense of how much they really suffered, and of how much they merely dramatized the situation. Here Chekhov has not yet fully achieved his capacity for being at once so compassionate and so unsparing toward his people: his humor is a little harsher than at his best, which is to say that it is less often humor than satire. Consider the third-act scene between Arkadina and Trigorin, then compare it with the perhaps overrated, yet irresistible speech of Trigorin when he ruefully visualizes his fate as a writer.

The Seagull is a special kind of play; it is about writers, and hence about what Chekhov thought of writers, and even thought of himself. To the degree that the play concerns artists, it a little less concerns human beings as such; and to the degree that it concerns artists of a particular period and place, it is even more special, and now quite dated. There are more special elements, more subjective and traditional elements in *The Seagull* than in any succeeding play; in artistry, and for me in appeal, it lags behind any succeeding play. It constitutes, rather, the place where Chekhov found himself on the stage, but still owed a good deal to others, and was inferior to the precise degree that he was indebted.

With *Uncle Vanya,* all sense of indebtedness, of identification with received forms of playwriting, vanishes. *Uncle Vanya* is pure Chekhov. Conceivably it is the purest— though not the best or deepest—Chekhov of the four plays. It lacks the poetry of circumstance, the deep-throated symbolism of *The Cherry Orchard,* as, too, the poignancy and profound humaneness of *The Three Sisters.* The cello note was to come later. But just because there is more sense of prose about *Vanya,* there is more emotion that seems direct and less that seems distilled; and more disposition to show human beings capable of very ordinary irritations and resentments. The two later plays have an aura that *Uncle Vanya* lacks and is the poorer for lacking; but simply for lacking it, *Vanya* has a more life-sized sense of truth. In certain ways it is all very Russian, in others not Russian at all. There are Professors and Vanyas everywhere, and everywhere households and families quite disrupted by visitors like the Professor and Yelena.

The small, largely unemphatic story is ample for what Chekhov feels about his people and about life; and the misleadingly mild, casual method (the only drama in the play is muffed, the only climax proves anticlimatic) is a triumph of selection and suggestion. The so-called well-made play drops out of sight here in favor of a better-made one: better-made because it nowhere seems made at all. Rather than form, it has fluidity: there is no sturdy bone-structure on which flesh is laid, simply something—not so bony as to be rigid nor so fleshy as to seem soft—that is alive.

Chekhov's method, so successful with him and so celebrated because of him, is not to be indiscriminately praised. At its best—and it is only at its best in Chekhov himself—it achieves an evocativeness, a truthfulness, a sensibility great enough to compensate for a certain lack of vigor, a certain lack of the sharp rhythm and movement that are natural to drama. Moreover, it is a method that not only requires great tact and talent in the playwright if it is to succeed; it requires almost equal tact and talent in the director and actors if it is to succeed on the stage. Or to succeed, at any rate, on Chekhov's own terms on the stage. It is possible in some sense to succeed with Chekhov by sentimentalizing him, as with Chopin by sentimentalizing him. Indeed, we seldom get a Chekhov, any more than a Chopin, who isn't in some degree sentimentalized, or at least robbed of fiber and guts: Chekhov and Chopin are equally regarded as creators of "mood." Because Chekhov has so completely fleshed his bones, many people seem to feel that he works without any.

But Chekhov's method is dangerous for more than the obvious reasons—of being hard to do justice to in the theater, of lending itself to the soft and the prettified. On this last score, it is less the method that impinges than the man: it is Chekhov's own sensibility that is so easy to strum and twang, and to mistake for something wistfully "Russian." The *method* is dangerous because its fluidity can become sheer formlessness. By relying on something internal and poetic rather than on something external and dramatic, the method extends a strong invitation to be sloppy or arty, or vague or self-indulgent. The playwright can shirk the mechanics of the job, or convert what in Chekhov is eloquent detail into mere naturalistic embroidery. Indeed, what is atmosphere in Chekhov is in lesser writers simply fog; what with Chekhov is merciless exposure is with lesser writers mere impressionism. We can be eternally grateful to Chekhov for liberating the theater from rigid rules; nor need we blame him personally for seeming to suggest that the theater can function with no rules at all. In a sense, of course, there never are rules in art; there are only risks. But since great risks don't often succeed, and succeed only then in the hands of great writers, most established rules do matter. To be sure, the tight, well-made play has the great drawback of seldom carrying conviction. But the looser, less contrived one has often a great drawback, too—of forfeiting the audience's attention. And in terms of audience response, though neither reaction is healthy, it is perhaps better to suspect what goes on than to sleep through it.

Chekhov himself, however, never took unfair advantage of his method: he was a very careful no less than a very subtle workman; and though he refused to write plays that went like a straight road between two high fences, he did set out lamp posts and signposts along a road that constantly dipped and curved. There are, for a most obvious example, certain leitmotivs of theme and speech in his plays. To the extent that such remarks may identify or characterize people and let us know what obsesses them, they are simply in the tradition of the comedy of humors. But in Chekhov the effect will often be more resonant; the repeats—sometimes coming at long intervals—have an extra dramatic or nostalgic or comic value. They don't merely reiterate, they reinterpret; they don't simply characterize, they begin to reflect on character. The same statement may have become a quite different statement, yet be the more incisive or poignant for being the same. Chekhov of course achieves many of his effects, not through normal dramatic methods of continuity or forward movement, but through deliberate discontinuity, digression, *contrast*. His talent for dramatic contrast is proof of his innate feeling for the stage: Chekhov's plays furnish the most telling oppositions of atmosphere—daytime and nighttime, bright weather and gloomy, indoors and outdoors, autumn and spring. Thanks to this kind of talent, Chekhov need not make his plays move in a straight line, need not chronicle every journey between two points. He does something not only more economical but more evocative. He plumps us down at the destination, and immediately we ourselves journey back to the starting-place. His whole art, of course, is one of evocation, of making the part suggest the whole, the detail imply the design, the moment communicate the lifetime. And because his people are so much given to reverie and regret, the evocative mood often kindles an elegiac one. But by no means always: Chekhov can just as expressively evoke weakness, shallowness, selfishness, insularity; dry bones as well as fluttering hearts; and flagrant self-pity as well as stabbing pathos. We must always beware of playwrights who move with catlike tread. They are apt to be far deadlier at bagging their prey than are those who brandish the big stick.

With *Uncle Vanya*, in any case—though the play is a reworking of an early one that Chekhov had laid aside—Chekhov has established both his own mood and method, has found his feet. The story, on the surface, is just such a minor, dun-colored one as might bring out Chekhov's gift for contrasting lives that look flat and unimportant with loss so personally intense as to seem very important indeed. Here is a pompous, pedantic, third-rate Professor, for the greater glory of whom a daughter and a brother-in-law have sacrificed themselves for years. Here is the Professor's shallow, pretty, flirtatious second wife, who toys and trifles with the love that two men better than her husband feel for her. Here is Vanya, a man of sensibilities and perhaps of parts, who might have been somebody but for his blind faith in the Professor; here is Dr. Astov, able and understanding, who might, at some other time and place, have been much more than a provincial G.P. Vanya is the victim of a third-rate man, Astov of a third-rate culture; both are frustrated by a commonplace attractive woman. Vanya, at length disillusioned by the Professor and angered by the man's plan to rob him of the roof he has slaved under, tries to shoot him, but fails. And so, at the end, the Professor (in a forgiving mood) goes away with his wife; Vanya and Sonya go back to working for him; and Astov, who cannot return Sonya's love for him, goes away too.

The play conveys a sense of lives wasted not through spinelessness and blunted purpose, but wasted rather through lack of perception and force of circumstance. Vanya, Sonya, Astov aren't simple weaklings, they are victims—though we must ask whether, had they shown more fiber, they could have been victimized. We grant Vanya's superiority over the Professor, yet are not quite sure that he is a superior man. We sympathize with Astov, yet wonder how much his fate represents something in life, and how much something in him. And Sonya, at the end—movingly as she pictures the life to come, exaltedly as she cries out: "We shall rest!"—though we need not doubt that she has faith, we cannot doubt her need for consolation.

In truth, it is just because all this lies in a middle zone where not character only, nor yet circumstance either, is decisive, that *Uncle Vanya* is so convincing and moving. We cannot feel that Vanya and Sonya and Astov were at all doomed to what came to pass; plainly they helped along their fate; and plainly, by now, when Vanya cannot handle a gun or Astov refuse a glass, it is past mending. These people can still be oddly passionate—but about what might have been. And yet, though nothing about it was inevitable, nothing was self-willed either. Vanya was deluded, and Sonya daughterly; and Astov worked with a doctor's strange, almost professionally induced selflessness. Doubtless they were indecisive people—the sort who take refuge in chores, who find gratification in sacrifice; but they were not fools or misfits, and they had too great rather than too little sense of obligation. They are people, moreover, who have worked very hard.

But together with the sense of pointlessly sacrificed lives, there is the sense of wonderfully life-sized people. Vanya and Astov are the sort we meet often and particularly sympathize with—far better than ordinary, far less than distinguished. They are more than just part of existence, they are part—though its merest walk-ons— of civilization. Their roles, which they muff but for which they may also be miscast, are familiar and recurrent ones. They are by no means all alike, they are not a type but a tribe. Nor again do they hurtle to disaster; they merely coast to negation. They have no tragic flaw, they display rather a sad sense of wear and blur; and something comic, too—the ineffectualness, perhaps, of their "superiority." They lack those traits of character that compel things to happen. Vanya waters his selfishness with self-pity, and so becomes a duffer and, as Astov says, a bit of a crank. And yet they *are* superior, and deserve better of life. There is something deeply Chekhovian in people just their size, with just their shortcomings. Lesser writers are content to portray such people "sympathetically"—and all the more for portraying them as failures. But Chekhov shows, too, how life has coarsened *them;* has made them cranky, sarcastic, even callous; Chekhov shows their very virtues rubbed thin and full of spots. Indeed, if we look closely, if we really listen for a moment (with due allowance for who is speaking), we grasp how unamiable and ill-adjusted is the whole household life:

> *It's dreadful in this house [says Yelena to Vanya]. Your mother hates everything except her pamphlets and the Professor; the Professor is irritated, he does not trust me and is afraid of you; Sonya is angry with her father, angry with me, and hasn't spoken to me for a fortnight; you hate my husband and show open contempt for your mother.*

Those people—happily, they grow fewer—who think of Chekhov only in terms of autumn leaves and samovars and longings for Moscow forget this grubbier side of his work.

(189)

But the point is that with these characters in *Vanya,* indeed with Chekhov's characters everywhere, justice seasons mercy. Chekhov does not acquit his people, he pardons them. And where he cannot pardon, he will smile rather than scold. The Professor in the end, is not so much found guilty as made ridiculous. He is a horror, a man who can take advantage of people and spoil their lives; but a sort of unconscious hypocrite, genuinely surprised to find he has taken advantage of anyone; and feeling genuinely misused, himself, what with advancing years and a very painful gout. He is even comic to the people around him. "You talk of your age," says his wife, "as though we were responsible for it." But before Chekhov rounds off the Professor as the idiotic character that in planetary terms he clearly is, he lets us know what he is like in household terms as well. And if everything else were lost, the second-act curtain of *Vanya* would be proof enough how special and great was Chekhov's genius for the stage. What playwright has said so much as Chekhov does here with exactly two words, with Sonya's "We mustn't"? This is the catlike tread, the small whisper, *in excelsis.*

It is with *The Three Sisters* that the mood of Chekhov deepens and the cello note is heard. *Uncle Vanya* and *The Three Sisters* are unmistakably by the same hand: the difference between them is much less that one is better than the other than that it is richer, that it invokes more complex responses, that it provides a more evident catharsis. I say catharsis, though I mean nothing very Aristotelian by it, or even that in any classical sense *The Three Sisters* is tragedy. Its people are too small for tragedy, even where they are not too comic. The tragic quality comes rather from something in life itself. To the extent that these people are romantics, are given to daydreams, to wearing black, to yearning for Moscow, to crying for the moon; to the extent that they can't come to terms with the life around them, can neither accept nor rebel, they are the stuff of comedy, perhaps even of satire. But to the extent that theirs is not the fate of daydreamers or self-dramatizers alone, but of all people who feel and care, who love and snatch at happiness, and hardly know why they are suddenly grown old—to that extent, they spell out the tragic nature of existence. These people may of themselves be escaping from reality; but reality, Chekhov makes us feel, can be as bewildering as any dream.

We spend four acts in the household of the Prozorovs, of three sisters and a brother, children of an army officer who had commanded a garrison in a provincial town. Now that the father is dead, the children long to go back to Moscow, their original home; to move from a provincial to a metropolitan world, a world they remember as excitingly brilliant and gay. "In Moscow," says Andrei, "you sit in a large room at a restaurant; you know no one and no one knows you, and at the same time you don't feel a stranger. But here you know everyone and everyone knows you and yet you are a stranger."

It all looks bright enough at the outset: Andrei seems a promising scholar; Olga, the oldest daughter, is level-headed and hard-working; Irina, the youngest, is full of romantic hopes, but has a real *joie de vivre* to match them; and though Mascha is married to a fool of a high-school teacher whom she doesn't love, she seems the mooning type that enjoys unhappiness, and is actually dissatisfied rather than unhappy. They are people—sensitive and well-bred—who belong in Moscow, and there seems no reason why events shouldn't prosper for them.

And, indeed, nothing very tragic or unforeseeable intervenes. Andrei merely marries a vulgar minx who takes to bossing the household and to proving unfaithful; and Andrei doesn't amount to much and loses at gambling; and Mascha has a rather fragmentary and desperate love affair with a married officer; and Irina can't bring herself to accept the good, decent, homely young Baron who loves her; and the talk of going to Moscow becomes, in time, mere phrase-making. The tragedy really lies in the fact that nothing tragic happens, that this is a world where clocks tick on and on and never chime. What yesterday one turned away from, one can face today and will be resigned to tomorrow. Irina at length can agree to marry the Baron, and theirs will be a contented life enough.

They all still long for Moscow, but till they are wrenched out of it, are hardly aware how endurable and even comfortable they find their groove. All at once the garrison officers who have been such pleasant company are transferred, and on the eve of his marriage the Baron is killed in a duel. Yet even this, in any personal sense, is not tragic, for Irina doesn't love the Baron, nor Mascha, really, her officer. But life and the promise of life have miscarried: small, trivial, unforeseeable things have with time made great and irreparable changes; there is a sense of vanishment and loss, of vanishment and loss unexplained. "What," Andrei cries, "has become of my past?"

Uncle Vanya conveys a sense of waste; *The Three Sisters* a sense of loss. We judge *Vanya*, to a certain extent, in realistic terms; we understand what happened and how easily it happened, but it never quite needed to happen. In *The Three Sisters* the circumstances are, by realistic standards, immaterial: nothing here, either, needed to happen; but our viewpoint here is not realistic, it is philosophical. This, we say, is what becomes of people, this is what it means to be a human being, to be young and then suddenly find that you are old. Life has dripped away, as it were, in a kind of slow leak. The scene has remained un-changed, but the light now is in the west. In *Vanya* we somehow feel that the better people were misled, and lives mismanaged. But in *The Three Sisters* it is life, we feel, that is misleading, the world that is mismanaged, and we can do little but submit. And the terrible pathos of these sisters' lives is born of the scanty, blunted, miserably mi-nor drama; of the slow vanishing of their dreams and hopes. If that all but discredited word *heartbreaking* is anywhere valid in modern literature, surely it is for the closing pages here, as the three sisters stand side by side and the gay, confident, lighthearted music of the depart-ing garrison dies away in the distance. Only for these three women would life seem to have stopped; there is music in the next street; gaiety, romance, happiness in the next town. And how they themselves long for life!

For me, *The Three Sisters* is the finest of Chekhov's plays—the finest play, indeed, in the whole modern theater. Many people would give the first place to *The Cherry Or-chard,* and I should like to say something of *The Cherry Orchard* before making a comparative claim for my choice. But for some things in *The Three Sisters* an absolute claim is to be made: for, to name one, the poetry of loss (loss is poetic where waste is not) that suffuses it. For, again, the poetry of longing; the almost Virgilian sense of

Tendebantque manus ripæ ulterioris amore.

But what counts equally with *The Three Sisters* is its uni-versality. The people may be Russian, of the military or professional or landowning classes; one of them may be killed in something today so outmoded as a duel; they may have name days, they may call one another Andrei Ser-geyevitch or Olga Sergeyevna. But what happens to them is what happens to people everywhere; is not this man's or

that man's life, but life itself. We don't identify ourselves
with these people in terms of local manners or particular
social situations: the kinship is just the other way round,
quite beyond accidents of time and place, or even of face
and fortune. On Chekhov's part, it is not just that he has
touched very deep chords of feeling, but that he has portrayed human beings with an awareness of their own
depths. This is a play in which people, however sadly
frustrated, aspire to the very end. Ronald Peacock has said
that there are no "moral problems" in Chekhov as there are
in Ibsen, but that there is everywhere moral aspiration.
We might say that though in Chekhov there are people
who lack souls, there are none with dead souls; none in
whom the fire of longing has quite gone out, none without
some last bright particle, a particle all the sadder for being
the very last. And dreadful as the soul can be in inferior
writing, in Chekhov it helps give his plays their intensity.
The refusal of his characters to be defeated inside their
own hearts, though the hearts have suffered the darkest
of defeats; the insistence of his characters that though
they have reached an end of happiness or hope, it cannot
be the end—this, if the final pathos, is yet the saving af-
firmation of their lives.

Yet it is not at all a question of their being gallant, of
anything chin-up about them: this is not a matter of preserving moral appearances, of refusing to go to pieces. It
is almost as if, just because these people lack conventional
will power, they possess some sustaining inner strength.
On the other hand, we must guard against taking the
popular view of Chekhov's characters, which sees them—
as individuals—unable, even unwilling, to cope with existence; and which sees them collectively as a doomed,
fiberless leisure class whose days are numbered. This isn't
to say that some of them aren't feckless or frivolous; that

Nina in *The Seagull* and Mascha in *The Three Sisters* aren't arrant romantics; or that *The Cherry Orchard* isn't overtly concerned with pleasure-loving, irresponsible aristocrats. But it is rather unfortunate that most notions of Chekhov derive from *The Cherry Orchard* because—important and expressive though the play may be—*The Cherry Orchard* isn't Chekhov. It alone is concerned with the collapse of a leisure class: elsewhere in Chekhov we are more often only concerned with people at leisure. Dr. Astov in *Vanya* may take a look at the Professor's gout, or Olga in *The Three Sisters* grade some examination papers; but we are overwhelmingly treated to people not at work—to officers, teachers, doctors, writers, stewards in their off-hours; worse still, we meet most of these people when they have become resigned to their lots, or regretful about them. Hence we may have an impression of people who do not work, or of people who do not want to. But in actual fact very few of Chekhov's characters are aristocrats, very few were ever affluent. True, Irina says in *The Three Sisters:* "We come of people who despised work"; but the truth is that most of Chekhov's characters do work—many of them hard, quite a number of them well. Astov works hard and well despite how uncongenial he finds his surroundings; Olga works hard and successfully despite how drab she finds her provincial life; Irina works, and the Baron seems not at all afraid to work. Indeed, a majority of Chekhov's characters work: it is only that so few of them work with any relish.

That Chekhov was aware of this want of relish, and aware that it expressed something decisive in Russian life, could scarcely be plainer. That the three sisters' yearning for Moscow was not merely romantic or nostalgic, I would also think true: between life in the great cities and life in provincial towns there must have been a really staggering difference. Provincial town life, in a country with so small a middle class, must have been peculiarly drab and shut-in. In the three plays we have so far considered, never once have we encountered a merchant or manufacturer or banker: how, along bourgeois lines, *could* one easily make one's way? So that while in *The Cherry Orchard* Chekhov was concerned with the dying out of a landed aristocracy, elsewhere he deals with a middle class that hardly yet seems born. Doubtless we are to understand that these military men and would-be professors and petty landowners hold themselves too high for trade. But most of them are in fact too cultivated to need to be tradesmen. We cannot quarrel with Andrei, in *The Three Sisters*, for wishing to be a professor; nor, since he failed to become one, can we suppose he would have come off better making stoves. And Andrei is perhaps the only out-and-out failure in the whole gallery. The Professor in *Vanya* is a fraud, but not an outright failure; Mascha's husband in *The Three Sisters* is a fool, but no failure at all. The satire at his expense is obvious enough: at the same time he poses an irony at the expense of all the others, for, cuckold and idiot though he is, he is much the happiest character in the play.

Chekhov's principal characters are no more mewing weaklings than Hamlet is. Nor, though Chekhov's plays have always a social texture, is he chiefly concerned with showing society hastening toward destruction, and pointing toward the revolution that was historically to come. Chekhov saw a society that lacked health and initiative and could not endure as it was; but he was content to picture what he saw as an artist, for its own sake: he never wrote as propagandist or prophet, or as today's type of "social-minded" playwright. He was an affirmative playwright, he had—in spite of everything—hopes for the human race; he desired change quite as much as he sniffed its coming, but that is something else. Certain of his characters might, of course, themselves be visionaries. The Baron might say very prophetically:

> *The time is at hand, an avalanche is moving down upon us, a mighty clearing storm . . . will soon blow the laziness, the indifference, the distaste for work out of our society. . . . In another twenty-five or thirty years everyone will have to work. Everyone!*

But the Baron is not Chekhov; nor, for that matter, were the Baron's visions the same on Tuesdays as on Fridays. Elsewhere he says:

> *Not only in two or three hundred years but in a million years life will be just the same; it does not change, it remains stationary, following its own laws which we have nothing to do with.*

I stress this, not just because Chekhov during a social-minded period was propagandized into a propagandist and endowed with the kind of social purpose he never possessed; but also, and much more importantly, because that was to make him out a smaller and less distinctive writer. It is not with the social pressures of living that he is ultimately concerned, but with the very stuff of life itself.

The peculiar fragance of *The Cherry Orchard* is caught in the very title. The play seems as much valedictory as exposé. The old order crumbleth: here stands revealed the rotting away, the death, the suicide of a class. Chekhov reveals it with strokes as incisive as those of the ax on the cherry trees; his picture of almost exultantly helpless, almost defiantly lax aristocrats is implacable. But his play is acid dissolved in the most ravishing perfume, and for most of us the gallantries of these people remain as vivid as the follies. Moreover, *The Cherry Orchard* is as specific as it is fragrant. It has a clear theme, the rotting away of a class; and, in the Ranevsky estate, a definite framework. It is often thought to be the most Chekhovian of the four plays; it is perhaps only the most Russian. For though all aristocracies that have run to seed may have points in common, Mme Ranevsky and her brother have exceedingly Russian traits as well as patrician ones. Their way of life is a matter of class, but their response to life seems a matter of race. One can't imagine similar French or English landowners retaining, among so much that is rotten, so much purity of sentiment. For their tears, however futile, are not just boozy and self-pitying. Even Mme Ranevsky's foolish, often outrageous generosity isn't merely that of a woman who does not—and will not—understand the value of money; it is equally that of a woman who refuses to put a value on money. However degraded her pleasures, they bespeak a kind of spontaneous participation in life; they go with something that, if it shows an utter lack of responsibility, shows an equal lack of calculation. We see Mme Ranevsky lacking all restraint and quite deaf to reason; we cannot mistake the kind of life she has led in Paris, or how much more sordid a life she will lead now the estate has been sold. We cannot but know, too, how much harm and suffering she brings upon others. And yet —much more than any comparable French or English woman—she has redeeming graces and certain generosities of spirit. Nor are we touched only by her plight; we are touched by the woman herself. It is, I suppose, a characteristic of really uncalculated highborn living that though it spreads poison, it sheds perfume as well. It remains a kind of charming chimera; the trouble is, it is far too dangerous and expensive a reality. (This is not merely to "pity the plumage but forget the dying bird.") We may strip Mme Ranevsky morally naked, we may display her all socially tarnished, but she has still something it is not merely snobbish or romantic to respond to.

Her brother, on the other hand, emerges quite as God and fifty-one years of doing nothing have made him, and as not just an incorrigible wastrel, but as an utter fool. He and his neighbor, Semyonov-Pistchik, represent the real breakdown of the aristocracy: for as a woman of her time and class, Mme Ranevsky might be supposed naturally fluttering and giddy and unable to take thought.

It is the measure of Chekhov's sensibility and art that while this is a merciless exposé, it has never the tone of a moralist or the narrowness of a tract. The truth is enough for Chekhov always. He will not blink the truth to spare people, but neither will he brandish it to punish them. No writer, in his moral evaluations, could be less doctrinaire, less smug, less holier-than-thou; at times, indeed, we might wish he would more fully enclose what he writes about inside a point of view. Yet much oftener we can be grateful for an approach so disinterested and uninvolved. When Chekhov is finished with his aristocrats in *The Cherry Orchard* there is nothing more to be said; there is only, in Chekhov's view, something more to be said for them. Thus Chekhov grants the old order at least something aromatic and charming; thus he implies that these people's own grave sins have preserved them from sins of an opposite kind. At least they are not crass or philistine, nor do they sit coldly in judgment. Chekhov will stress their virtues at the expense of a Lopahin—though Lopahin, we are made to see, has as much decency as Mme Ranevsky, and infinitely more virtue. Chekhov plays one type or class against another, not—after the fashion of the propagandist—to show a disparity in vice or virtue between the two, but to show rather how many virtues and vices they both have. Temperamentally, Chekhov would feel no desire to *attack* the aristocracy, but he would know in any case that there was no need; exposing it would be more than enough. A doctor does not read a doomed patient a lecture; and Chekhov was a doctor.

Chekhov's humor, Chekhov's comic sense—the two are not quite the same thing—not only pervade his work, but help decisively to characterize it. His was the kind of humor that inspires benignity and breadth of understanding; he knew how deeply people crave love and attention and position; how hard it is to forgo pleasure, or resist temptation, or rise above self-interest; how easy it is to rationalize one's desires or shut one's eyes to the truth. Without such humor, his lynx-eyed perceptiveness must have mercilessly condemned the human nature it never failed to see through. At is was, Chekhov showed that to err is human, not criminal; he found it impossible to treat of villains, for he saw no one as villainous. His humor pleads for human nature, as his comic sense deflates it. His comic sense is death on pedantry, pomposity, all grandiose thinking: no one is easier than Chekhov on human weakness, but no one is harder on human pretense. As there are no villains in his plays (for one thing, his characters are generally too weak to be villainous), so there are no heroes; he equally avoids the dark pits of evil and the white peaks of heroism. Mistakes and injustices abound, but as part of the temperate zone of life. At the end of *The Cherry Orchard,* old Firs is left behind (quite conceivably, to die) in the deserted house: but though this is just the thing a Mme Ranevsky would do, it is the last thing on earth she would mean to do—an outrageously thoughtless woman, she is not in the least a heartless one.

And while we are on the subject of Firs being left behind, I must agree with William Gerhardi that this final touch, though effective and even revealing, is a little pat. And that may constitute, in turn, the moment for comparing *The Cherry Orchard* with *The Three Sisters*. For, to begin not at the beginning but at the end, how far beyond the sharpest effects of theater, beyond even the most graphic symbolism, has *The Three Sisters* got; with what a simple chord that is yet a cathedral swell of music does it conclude. The end of *The Cherry Orchard* completes a journey, rounds off a social theme: the King is dead (in fact, he poisoned himself), long live the King. Chekhov has made an unchallengeable demonstration, has been truthful and at the same time touching. I mean this for high praise, and, after all that has been said of *The Cherry Orchard's* charm and fragrance, need say no more now. But, however universalizing it may be at moments, the play more often has to do with something quite passing and particular. Chekhov has put his subject-matter to the most delicate and revealing use, but the play yet shares its subject-matter's limitations. For it is concerned not only with a dying class, but with a particular country and a specific period.

On the other hand *The Three Sisters*, when it reaches its end, is under such emotional pressure as derives from much more than the lives of three women. By then it doesn't matter how flawed or limited or foolish three such women may be, or how far superior one may be to another. They have lost all particularity; they have passed —with enough awareness and emotion—through enough experience to bear the look of humanity itself. They have come out nowhere, and perhaps would have got nowhere even had they got to Moscow; and now, when most lost and bewildered, they console themselves with wispy and watery hopes. Just so human beings reveal their weakness. Just so human beings summon up their strength.

But such emotional pressure as is released at the end of *The Three Sisters* could only accumulate in a play that was building, with great variety of materials, toward an intense unity of effect. There are many kinds of people in *The Three Sisters:* it overflows a family, cuts across a class. The Baron is an aristocrat, Andrei's wife a rank upstart; between these two are all grades of military and professional people. But where *The Cherry Orchard,* within a smaller group, stresses the distinction between old and young, where it makes a contrast of old and new, *The Three Sisters* blends all its voices, even the rasping ones like Andrei's wife; the people are united by life itself, as it rises and falls, stirs and subsides; and are perhaps most united by the sense of separation. Upon the three sisters, at the end, descends the particular desolation of having been left behind; but those who are marching away to such brave, jaunty music are merely being moved about, toward a destination that is not home, a mode of existence that is not happiness.

What saves all this from being merely bleak or depressing is, of course, the lyric note which is the offset, in Chekhov, to his naturalism. It makes life seem sad but not ugly, and frustration painful but not meaningless. As I have said, there is something Virgilian, something of the *lacrimæ rerum,* about it: but in Chekhov the emotion is felt by the characters themselves as well as by the author and reader. They accept the very life that fails them from a sense that there is importance about the thing itself; and though they often cannot face reality, from inner experience they almost never shrink.

· · ·

Chekhov broke away from a half-century of one kind of theater; he has perhaps bequeathed us, not always advantageously, a half-century of another kind. His methods can be very dangerous; they all too plainly require not less talent than other methods, but more. Chekhov's style —intensely selective, wonderfully modulated, sidelong rather than frontal—proceeds out of Chekhov's own very personal genius; it runs counter, on the whole, to the genius of the stage. Even Chekhov himself tends to lack vigor, which means that inferior writers attempting his methods can easily seem spineless and thin. Their naturalism is drabber and more commonplace than his, and they douse it with a lyricism that seems sentimental or purely decorative. But the separate qualities in Chekhov create a whole much greater than the sum of its parts. For Chekhov's naturalism is aerated by his lyricism, as his lyricism is domesticated by his humor. Without the lyricism, the plays would lack their peculiar compassionateness; without the humor, they would reek of self-pity. Without the lyricism, the plays by now might seem drearily dated; without the humor, they might seem comically "Russian." Chekhov began, always, with the fact. But he gave it vibrancy by touching it with feeling. Yet he knew better than to be swamped by feeling; knew better, even, than to make life seem more tragic at a cost of becoming less truthful. His humor is rudder as his lyricism is sail. At times he merges personal suffering with the tragic current of life itself, but at other times he makes equally plain that our subjective moans have far less than cosmic meaning. Always, as he deals with people who have lost their sense of proportion, he relentlessly maintains his own. His people, as I have said, are never heroes. But however absurd their pretensions, however bungled their chances or their very lives, they escape the gross, fatty, bovine death of drab philistine living. There is still, somewhere, a far-off glimpse or quickened breath; or a groping awareness of

> *Effort and expectation and desire*
> *And something evermore about to be.*

(1950)

CHAPTER XIV

The Education of Henry Adams

FOUR generations after one member of the Adams family helped compose the Declaration of Independence, another sat down and wrote a book declaring it null and void. So rapidly had events come to pass that it required just a century and a quarter to demolish America's greatest act of faith with her most withering words of denial. Between John Adams and his great-grandson Henry lay the total wreck of a dream. The disaster had robbed Henry Adams not only of his illusions but equally of his usefulness; the thing that had come about was beyond Henry Adams's ability to cope with or fight against or repair; he, who had burned to participate in American life, was reduced to becoming its stern and dissident historian. Hence, to confess his own failure, and to reveal the far greater failure that had brought his own about, and to fail (as he thought) in confessing it, Adams sat down and wrote the *Education*.

The *Education* found its most responsive readers in those years following the World War when they too had reason to believe that American life had failed them; and to every American intellectual who still retained inside him vestiges of the American moralist, Adams's grim citation of a century's crimes and blunders helped explain the plight of the modern world. The demonstration seemed Euclidean enough to justify the bitterly ironic tone which overhung it: for here was Henry Adams, supremely well born, talented, eager, thoughtful, industrious, confessing that every ideal he owned had been traduced; insisting that the world of action had been impossible to enter, and the world of thought powerless to give hope. Only chaos, explosion, cataclysm loomed ahead. A sensitive person was better out of life; in it, a Henry Adams could only by turns shudder and grow brutally cynical.

The book which reached these conclusions remains an important document of American intellectual and moral inquiry, if only because not a dozen Americans of any period were intellectually and morally of a stature to produce it. It is predicated of very nearly a first-rate mind and something like a first-rate experience. If the mind fails us, it is chiefly from not being purposeful enough; if the experience, it is from being largely of one kind. Adams came to know everything within the reach of the cultivated man of the world, everything to be had of drawing-rooms and libraries, colleges and clubs, churches and ruins, senates and courts; but, though such contact was capable of a thousand variations, its bounds were immovably fixed. Henry Adams was an aristocrat, and a peculiarly modern aristocrat: the tame and squeamish product of London or Boston, quite unlike his spacious Renaissance ancestor for whom privilege meant an extension, not a curtailment, of adventures.

This is palpable everywhere through the *Education;* but something else about Henry Adams is palpable in its very title. Adams self-consciously sought to channel his experiences and to convert them into education. The attitude is praiseworthy enough, but at the outset it is interesting to note what produced it. What first of all produced it, we may suppose, was his Puritan background, quivering with moral earnestness: a background which, moreover, if it served as a spur to education, served equally as a backstop; and which, if it accounts during four generations for the Adams strength, accounts no less for its want of suppleness. But the Puritan impulse coincided perfectly with something else which caused Adams to treat life as education: the nineteenth-century crusade for progress and enlightenment. The nineteenth century seemed to think that if man only knew enough, and remained a "moral" animal, he could reform and stabilize the world. The belief was hardly one which Adams, as he grew older, was encouraged to share; but the atmosphere that produced it was one he never outgrew. It was a moral as well as an intellectual impulse that caused him to plunge headlong into the flood of science and philosophy that engulfed his age; it was some desperate faith in pure knowledge, which even a highly ironic temperament could not extinguish, that turned Henry Adams into a lifelong student. True enough, it was difficult for him to make something systematic and cosmic of all he studied. The result, in that line, was never much more than brilliant dilettantism; but it saved Adams, if not from disillusionment, then from disintegration.

If the *Education* were no more than a worldling's reminiscences and a student's recapitulations, all tied together with philosophical ribbons, we might praise its prose and wit and acknowledge its intellectual expressiveness of an era; but we should put it among the memorials, and not the textbooks, of American experience. But the *Education* is a grand-scale study of maladjustment, of the failure of an exceptional personality to mesh with a prodigious civilization: posing, with one gesture, the problem of the man and his times. The problem of each, by the time Adams's autobiography was made public, had grown greater and more acute; so that in the decade following Adams's death the *Education* had a significance that it only partly had in his lifetime and that there is small likelihood it will ever have again.

Like most serious autobiographies, the *Education* is an attempt, not to record a man's life, but to explain it. It is the work, at bottom, of one who set out both to judge and to justify himself. This dual intention is significant, even though what Adams attempted to justify was failure. We may take the liberty of supposing that this dual intention was embodied very simply: Adams judged himself by asking a question, and justified himself by returning an answer. Why—he asks in effect—should someone who started off with every opportunity, and with faith and eagerness, have ended up with so little achieved, dissentient and in utter flight? Because, he answers, the world he had set out to serve had been seized by forces he would not accept for master; and nothing better remained than to try to understand those forces and inveigh against them.

The *Education* is, then, a perfectly *conscious* study of frustration and deflected purpose; of the failure of a superior man to find the right place, or any tolerable place, in a civilization growing ever more corrupt, rapacious, and vulgar. No one ever wrote a more deliberate apologia of his life than Henry Adams. I shall have much to say later concerning the make-up of the particular man, concerning his blunders and prejudices, his distaste for enduring his situation, his predisposition to abandon it. But all that has a psychological importance, not a philosophical one; it delimits, but does not destroy, the real meaning of his book. What gives the *Education* its lasting value, what made a generation of futilitarians clasp it to their breasts, is the validity of the predicament regardless of the shortcomings of the man. For if not Henry Adams, then another, or many others, were paralyzed by the terms of that struggle in which he was so centrally engaged. Confronted by the greed of a banking civilization, the crookedness of boss-rule politics, the vulgarity of a parvenu culture, the cynicism of an exploitative ruling class, the middle-class intellectual was pretty well doomed either to suffer or succumb or escape. At the best, if his convictions had real fiber, he might die fighting the reformer's luckless battle; more likely he would accept the situation, as John Hay did, and wax fat off the spoils; or flee it and accept its more graceful counterpart elsewhere, as did Henry James; or take to excoriating it, aware that his mockery was the sign of his weakness, as Adams felt driven to do.

There appeared, in any case, to be no lasting adjustment that could be called an honest one. The superior man might, by the world's standards, succeed or fail; it hardly mattered, since he could not remain whole. No doubt he best avoided contamination by going into retirement; but then he was not fully alive, and then he had abandoned his responsibilities. If he remained in action, he might deceive himself into thinking that he was fighting the good fight by opposing specific men, by championing specific measures; but if he remained in action and refused to deceive himself, he knew he had for enemy the whole huge mass of things. And unless one was an incorrigible idealist or a convinced revolutionary, that was a task leading to dislocation and despair. Henry Adams, very early, became too pessimistic and cynical to go on being a participant. He chose, instead, a place on the sidelines, and from there set about recording the minutes of all the unsavory transactions of America's public life. The picture of such proceedings which Adams drew, or at least suggested, in the *Education* is a final one. For not only were its revelations damning, but its sources were unimpeachable. It was the indictment of a supremely placed worldling who had listened at the most private keyholes, who had been told—or allowed to guess—the secrets of those who worked behind the scenes. Scarcely anyone else who did so little knew so much. Adams's indictment stands: the great documentary merit of the *Education* is its demonstration of what nineteenth-century America had become, and by what process, and on what terms.

The philosophical merit, which once seemed a merit so much greater, is by no means so great. For the intellectuals of the twenties, the *Education* was an epic after their own hearts. *Epic* is no idly used word; the scale and severity of the book are important. In one sense, the most misleading thing about it is its impressiveness. Written with much of the formality that Gibbon used in his *Memoirs,* it comes at the reader with so magisterial an air that halfway through it he grants it the confidence reserved for an attested masterpiece. The Adams manner confers on the Adams apologia a definite extrinsic weight. There is the sense of a large mind and an imposing personality; there is the sense—unimpaired by the irony of the book—of deep purpose and high seriousness. Henry Adams, who lived his life in a minor key, took every precaution to write about it in a major one. The *Education* is a completely full-dress performance.

The 1920's could use such an authoritative approach. The 1920's could bend the knee before a master who celebrated their own misgivings and disappointments. He ennobled their dilemma. He gave dignity to their frustration. For theirs was the individualist's dilemma, and for them the idea of integrity involved the idea of withdrawal; environment, to them, defeated the artist, as participation corrupted the thinker. Their dilemma, too, sprang from personal weakness no less than from social disorder. The *Education* gave to the 1920's, not the signal to fight, but the leave to withdraw, by revealing how a better man had got waylaid and misplaced, had been passed up and slurred over and left to go unsung; for surely there is something in the tone of the *Education* that suggests as not the least of the nineteenth century's blunders its failure to recognize the worth of Henry Adams. On its lowest level, there is an immense amount of self-pity in Adams's book. On their lowest level, there was an immense amount of self-pity in the futilitarians of the twenties. Deep called unto deep.

But at another level there was something in the *Education* to make it one of the justly pivotal books of its era. It may express futility, but its tone is not wholly negative; there is something affirmative in it. And what it affirms is a toughness of mind, a quality of searching, weighing, testing, of coming to clear-eyed conclusions about the nature of things. Above all, it sets forth a mind and morality that spurned the optimistic and opportunistic formulas, from Emerson's down, that had made of American life such a shallow, shifty, spurious thing. At least the *idea* of education which Adams, solitary and recusant, imposed upon himself was an exemplary idea. What Adams signifies at his best is unadulterated and grown-up thinking. This was something that his pupils of the twenties, groping backward in American letters—stumbling over the confusions of the Transcendentalists, the rampant Americanism that mars the democratic fervor in Whitman—could not easily find elsewhere. No wonder, then, that they thought they had found more than they actually did.

. . .

For, impressive as the *Education* is, and definitive as is its mood, it somehow is not profound. It befits very few of us to condescend to Adams on the score of his cultural background, his political knowledge, his cerebral weight; but the fact remains that it is not for his "discoveries," or his clarifications of the human struggle, that we can seek him out. Those celebrated later chapters of the *Education*— "The Dynamo and the Virgin," "A Dynamic Theory of History" [1]—are superb intellectual exercises, but it is hard to believe that they offer a synthesis which is more than personally brilliant and picturesque. When Adams looked to the past, for example, it was originally in search of perspective. He set about contrasting twelfth-century "unity" with twentieth-century "multiplicity," and the contrast is striking. But to what end? He conceived the earlier age as the better one, but must have known that it was impossible to return to it. The structure of twelfth-century life has no application in ours; the old wheels went round from a social force that had become inoperative and spent. Yet, more and more in the manner of an escapist, Adams tried to go back; there came to be more than an esthete's interest in his medieval studies, in the long twilit mystic spell of Chartres. Coldly judged, does not one pamper one's maladjustment by pining for what one cannot have?

There was nothing shallow about Adams's inquiry into human culture, either in its feeling or in its facts; but it failed to produce any profound philosophy of life, even a profound skepticism. Adams knew too much, he knew (or thought he knew) too well whither things were drifting, he had—too arrogantly—a disbelief that any good could come of it, ultimately to profit from his career of "education." The philosophy he did evolve is understandable

---

[1] For which he was mainly indebted to his brother Brooks.

enough, and one must grant that there was a basis in experience for it. But it comes to no more than the pessimism of one who sees the world being ruined, and the cynicism of one who gives up trying to reclaim it. And in Adams there was also an uglier cynicism, of sitting back and watching the world, with a not unmalign satisfaction, go to hell. The motif of effort and education which carefully governs Adams's autobiography tends to obscure this uglier cynicism; but from a reading of the *Letters* one knows that it was there, and one sees how, after a time, the moralist in Adams gave up being in any sense a crusader and became a merely captious and querulous censor.

A crusader in the old Adams style Henry never was at any time. In John and John Quincy Adams there was little of Hamlet and much of Cœur-de-Lion; there was the impulse, scarcely questioned, to act. Henry never had that impulse. At the very outset of his career, he thought rather of being induced to enter politics—thought of his dignity as soon as his duty. The silver-platter method failed, and in a way Henry would have no other. It was not simply that he was as proud as he was ambitious, or as squeamish as he was moral; it was that for a lifelong career in opposition the work was too grubby, too dispiriting, too harsh, the odds against winning were too fantastically high. The reformer who would take on so forbidding a task needed to be something of a fanatic; and, after all, Henry Adams was from the beginning the most sensitive of intellectuals, the most cultivated of worldlings.

It would be absurd to imagine such a man becoming a John Brown, a William Lloyd Garrison, a Debs. But it would surely not be absurd to imagine such a man becoming a Matthew Arnold. Each was born in the shadow of a

name outstanding for earnestness, each was by temperament the reverse of a democrat, and each grew up to find
a place waiting for him in that world where society and
intellect, art and politics meet. There may have been a decisive difference in the fact that Arnold had a living to
earn and Adams did not. But Arnold was not self-indulgent
and Adams was; so that Arnold became the embattled foe
of what seemed to him the powers of darkness, and Adams
merely their bitter and acidulous historian. (It only counts
against Adams the more that he understood the issues in
a far wider sense than Arnold understood them.) There
was something in Adams which, though it might have
borne the arduousness of high public office, balked at the
indignities of Arnold's private campaigning. By Adams's
strongly developed eighteenth-century standards of worldliness, Arnold was doubtless a little plodding, a little
ridiculous. He called Arnold the most honest man he knew,
but he was never driven to accept the burdens of such an
honesty. It was his Chesterfieldian sensibilities that largely
ruined Adams; that turned him into a man who thought
one way and lived another.

For he lived, during many years, in elegant and patrician
retirement, choosing for his intimates the Hays, Cabot
Lodges, Theodore Roosevelts for whom morally he had no
respect; traveling *en prince;* entertaining *en connaisseur;*
parading in his letters a calculated snobbery that sneered
at Stevenson's indigent bohemianism, that instantly seized
on Kipling's social second-rateness, that inveighed half to
the point of mania against the Jews. He said of himself that
he "should have been a Marxist," and knew, overwhelmingly, that he could never have been one. The whole story
is told, I think, by Adams's reactions to English upper-
class life. With his mind he saw all too well its hypocrisy,

insularity, complacence; but temperamentally the sweetest air he ever breathed was that of London dinner-parties and English country-houses.

The present moment is not congenial, and not disposed to be fair, to the *Education*. The book compels respect for a sense of weight behind, not in, it. It suggests tragedy; but it is not—at least on the terms it set out to be—tragic, because the author chose the less costly form of defeat, and the less noble. Impotence, to Adams, was preferable to mutilation. Psychologically—by which I mean that were Henry Adams the problem of a novelist—his life followed a convincing pattern. But in real life, an ultimate failure of character is not to be excused by being accounted for; nor does a lifetime of self-analysis compensate for a failure to see things through morally. If a crude capitalist era "crushed" Adams, it was as much from being enervated by the fruits of it as from being poisoned by its roots. Was Adams willing—was he ever willing—to lose just part of the world to gain his own soul? It is just possible to say yes; but if so, Adams's reason was purely pride.

However great the merits of the *Education*, its "method" can already be seen to have failed. Culture and education are of the highest importance—according to some philosophies, the very end of living. But for Henry Adams they were clearly intended to be a means, carrying him forward to a better understanding and fulfillment of his obligations. Instead they produced in him the indecision of a Hamlet; they became a kind of luxury, a kind of solace, and a kind of escape. It may be that Adams has taught us more in autobiography than he could have in action. It is at least certain that he has warned us more unforgettably. For it is not through confusing the mind by overloading it; it is not through dissent without protest, or humanism without humanity, that the beleaguered intellectual can fulfill himself, or the world he views with horror be put right.

(1939)

CHAPTER XV

Lytton Strachey

I⊤ is very understandable that, for last year's Rede Lecture at Cambridge, Max Beerhohm should have chosen to speak about Lytton Strachey. The two men are far from unlike in temperament; the epigram that Wilde coined for one of them—"The gods have bestowed on Max the gift of eternal old age"—might have been better applied to the other. And the two men are very much alike in their approach to literature as, above everything else, an art. Max's lecture, indeed, is the most graceful of tributes from one very literary man to another. What Max appreciates most in Strachey is his manner, his artistry, his prose; they are the things we should most expect him to appreciate; very likely they are the things that are most to be appreciated. But, like many other graceful tributes, Max's lecture is not very searching criticism; and, like much else in Max's writing, it tells more about the author than the subject. But it comes at a good moment, since Strachey was never more neglected; and even its too genial desire to praise serves a good purpose. For the reaction against Strachey—though it was clearly inevitable and in large part sound—has gone too far. I think he will be honorably remembered again, though he will be remembered on other, and smaller, grounds than those on which he was first acclaimed.

Strachey's work already dates, for it embodied an attitude more congenial to its own moment than convincing in ours; an attitude, moreover, that became almost tawdrily fashionable. Yet to call Strachey a debunker is—as Max remarks—not only vulgar but silly: Strachey looked for much more than the feet of clay. Indeed, it was rather less the feet of clay than the Achilles tendon that absorbed him; less what was ignoble in people than what was petty or provincial or absurd; and he often—as with those last words on Manning's hat or Creighton's black bag—forced the note. He was a little too eager to show that a great deal of history's size and brawn was only excess fat. This, I think, arose less from any positive desire to debunk than from a temperamental necessity to question. Strachey was a natural skeptic; but he became much more of one, and a shallower one, because at bottom he was also a romantic. He was half afraid not to be skeptical, for when he forgot to be, he too often soared off into hyperbole and now and then even sank into gush.

Though Strachey won his real recognition as a biographer, he was essentially a man of letters who could almost be said to have seen life in terms of literature. It is one of his fascinations that he treated biography as less a branch of history than an outer province of fiction. His subjects, shaped with a novelist's art, cry out to be imaginary: if only he could take a few real liberties with them, how incomparably glittering or delightful or unbearable they would be! Had Albert not been real, Strachey might have portrayed him as the greatest of all prigs; had Bacon never existed, he might have become the most brilliantly devious of all self-seekers. Even as it was, Strachey went so far as to forget that Dr. Arnold *had been* real; and when the true Elizabeth eluded him, he trumped up something that might pass for her. Victoria, to be sure, with her royal manner and schoolgirl's mind, offered a contrast too piquant to need much tampering with, which may be why she emerges as Strachey's masterpiece. Many of his other characters suffer from more than a sense of the fictional. For Strachey did not handle them fictionally in the one way that might have vindicated his method—that of penetrating to unsuspected depths. On the contrary, while pretending to make people more complex than they seemed, he often made them simpler. The most notorious example of this is Queen Elizabeth. Her shilly-shallying, instead of being probed to its origins, is made the equivalent of the woman herself, and she winds up much like Indecision in a morality play. I think there was an excessive taste for melodrama in Strachey—it is fairly common to over-civilized minds; at any rate, he too often saw people in a theatrical light and wrote about them in a rhetorical manner.

Strachey's claims as a biographer must rest on *Eminent Victorians* and *Queen Victoria*, for *Elizabeth and Essex* is pretty clearly an ornate failure. For its own time *Eminent Victorians*—and not merely because it came first—was more valuable than *Queen Victoria*; in our time it seems less successful. Its indictment of Victorian values—values, most of them, that did not perish with Victoria; values, some of them, that will only perish with the race—is still a powerful one. Everything narrow, stupid, rigid, muddled, snobbish, scheming, brutal in the official British character was somehow brought to light; in the moral rather than strictly documentary sense, *Eminent Victorians* ranks among the most telling of modern exposés. But, like too many exposés, the moral tone is superior to the factual evidence.

After all, if you plan to submerge a whole society by means of four human beings, you have to put weights on all four to make them drag so much else down with them. Toward Dr. Arnold, Strachey lacked a sense of justice; toward Florence Nightingale, a sense of proportion. Perhaps none of the four, except Manning, counts greatly for himself; it is what stands behind and around and above them that Strachey is really firing at. And as a weapon of combat, *Eminent Victorians* was admirable. It hit hard, and afterward things were not quite the same. Certainly biographies were not. A school of genuine debunkers arose who confused Strachey's faults—not least, his impulse toward malice—with his virtues, and hastened his decline.

Queen Victoria, created in a more relaxed and temperate mood, has certainly less bite than *Eminent Victorians*, and very probably less seriousness. It has the tone of comedy rather than of cold irony. Its exasperating but hardly dangerous heroine can more safely be rendered justice, and justice demanded a certain liking and admiration. The meaning of the events of Victoria's reign is seldom probed; but it could not be if Victoria was to dominate, for it was only society Victoria dominated, not affairs. Yet within limits—and perhaps because there are limits—*Queen Victoria* is a well-nigh perfect biography. Its morality is held in suspension, which makes in the long run for better art. There is a touch of brassiness about *Eminent Victorians*. *Queen Victoria* is less weighty, but the metal is purer.

Leaning far more, as a biographer, toward the man of letters than toward the historian, Strachey provides no feeling of mass or scope. In *Eminent Victorians*, it is true, much is successfully implied in little. But the great forces and conflicts of history he did not respond to, and perhaps did not fully understand. Too much of history dwindles, with him, into melodrama, tableau, *vanitas,* or a mere joke. His selective method could be deadly; his command of irony accomplished more, at times, than any accumulation of facts could have done, or perhaps any power of analysis. But there remains, for all that, an imperfect insight into large events and *really* eminent men; and a certain want of positive values. Strachey disliked the reactionary, yet he never truly emerges as a liberal. He makes fun of the old-fashioned, yet he is certainly no modern. He judges the nineteenth century rather by the standards of the eighteenth than of his own. Furthermore, his skeptical nature rejected any real idea of progress. He was "enlightened" in the frosty, urbane eighteenth-century sense of the word, which meant rather to deprecate the weaknesses and evils of mankind than suppose they could be cured. All reformers, to Strachey, were apt to be a little funny; all revolutionaries a little mad; and prigs, whatever their virtues, more unendurable than knaves. The point of view has its artistic advantages, but for understanding and interpreting life it is over-civilized—too fastidious and quirky, and not sufficiently humane. Strachey's was a highly cultivated attitude of *ne quid nimis* and *nil admirari,* with a smile at life that hinted a shrug. That is one reason why he appealed so greatly to a postwar generation; another is that, for all his destructiveness, he never attacked the generation's own defenses.

Strachey's happy hunting ground was, of course, the eighteenth century: the Augustan way of life, the classical virtues, are what he most admired, and in a sense most romanticized. He recognized, as who would not, the personal faults of the Augustans. He understood, too, the price —in breadth of experience—that a Walpole or Mme du Deffand paid for what he got. But he did not think the price too high. The eighteenth century delights the artist in almost all of us, but repels the human being; Strachey, however, saw the period almost entirely artistically, and so became romantic about it. He even copied its tendency to snigger. What he could not acquire was its prose style; as the child of the nineteenth century or at most of the Gibbonian eighteenth, Strachey liked rhetoric and high language far too well. He could be insufferably highflown in a way that would have made Gray or Walpole wince. On the other hand, the best of his short pieces—which rank with the best of his work—spring from his intense feeling for the eighteenth-century way of life; and his strong classical sense led him to write, long before the reaction against romanticism, his tonic essays on Racine and Stendhal.

I do not think that Strachey was a notably good critic. He could appreciate genuinely, and a little more eclectically than we might imagine; he could demolish stupidity, pedantry, incompetence; he could raise some very interesting points. But the critic in him lay too close to the bookworm and too far away from the psychologist and real man of the world. He is too literary to be a first-rate judge of literature.

It would not be easy to maintain that Strachey will be a figure of any lasting importance. Yet there is a different view to be taken of him, the view that Beerbohm—without formulating it—takes in his lecture. Uncritical as the lecture is—doubtless tact made it ignore what taste would have made it condemn—it yet reminds us, as we need to be reminded, of the sheer pleasure that Strachey provides. For all its faults, the style *is* both a commanding and a brilliant one. The narrative gift is remarkably fine; the architectural sense remarkably sure. A little like Macaulay before him, Strachey made, as it were, a good story of everything he wrote; he might be vulgar, or shallow, or high-pitched, or misleading; but he was never dull. The lively, cultivated, often distinguished pleasure he knew how to provide need only be assessed at its true value; it certainly need not be spurned.

(1943)

CHAPTER XVI

Max Beerbohm

WE shall shortly celebrate a notable occasion: Sir Max
Beerbohm's seventy-fifth birthday. But a not unnotable
one is already at hand: Sir Max's first book in nearly twenty
years. And if one would survey the career of a distinguished writer, a book, I think, provides a sounder start-
ing-point than a birthday. To find oneself criticized in the
very act of being congratulated must be a pretty dampen-
ing experience—much as though a writer should discover,
on opening a beautifully wrapped birthday present, that
someone had sent him a grammar.

Mainly on the Air, furthermore, though it unfortunately
does not crown Sir Max's career, considerably illuminates
it. It reveals, quite as much as anything he has ever written, the kind of writer he is, and the kind of man. Indeed,
it pretty sharply reveals that he is seventy-five. This is not
because it shows an old man's infirmities, but because it
overflows with an old man's recollections, an old man's
harking back to the loves and landmarks of his youth.
Max,[1] God knows, has never not been a period writer. But

[1] Alone among writers, he was universally referred to by his first
name. Yet the "Max" never denoted familiarity or even, primarily, affec-

always, in reading him before, one felt not so much a gulf between past and present as that Max had made time stand still—that Victoria, or at any rate Edward VII, had not ceased to reign, and world wars not been fought or waistcoats changed fashion. Max was still, somehow, a dandy of the nineties, a worldling of the 1900's; reading him, we saw him framed eternally against a background of *fin-de-siècle* Piccadilly, as Keats's youth is young forever on his Grecian urn. When, in an essay on Strachey a year or two back, Max protested—with as much fervor as an urbane Tory would permit himself—against the Century of the Common Man, what surprised you was not that he saw red at (and in) the phrase, but that he should ever have heard of it. He had seemed out of earshot of it by at least a generation.

But now we find that Max has not been living, placidly oblivious of the present, in a *fin-de-siècle* dream. He is too constantly jarred by the present not to be most uncomfortably aware of it. All the things Max loves—elegance, urbanity, a quill-pen leisureliness, the pleasure to be had of little things, the noiseless flick and delayed smart of irony —are not much valued in our day. All the things he hates —noise, speed, garishness, ugliness, Americanization—are ubiquitous and, as he might say, regnant. Again and again he can only shudder at what he sees, and sigh for what has vanished. But the sigh is really far more significant than the shudder. For one feels it is not so much that the present is all wrong for Sir Max—though of course it is—as that the past is all-important. Each of his complaints is fundamentally a comparison. One suspects that Max was already retrospective in his cradle, and downright reminiscent in

tion; it was a kind of badge of his uniqueness. One referred to him by his first name much as one does to a king—which may be why it now comes hard to demote him to a knight.

his crib. And now Max is really, however ironically, the elderly gentleman who sits in his Tory club-window shaking his head at everything he observes in the street. Very often he is soundly protesting against vulgarity; but surely sometimes he is protesting against life. Yet this is not just Max turned elderly—he has always been someone who preferred a style of living to life itself.

On the literary side, *Mainly on the Air* is pretty slight, even for its author, much of it having been composed, as the book's title indicates, for BBC broadcasts. Yet I have found a second reading of the book more satisfying than a first: one starts off keenly disappointed because so little comes even close to Max's best; then gratefully accepts these pieces for what they are—still rather bright, still unmistakably Beerbohm. Their very titles supply their text —"London Revisited," "Music Halls of My Youth," "The Top Hat," "Advertisements," "Speed." But the best thing in the book, the thing most in the old, happy, essayist vein is "Fenestralia," where Max considers the role that windows have played in literature and history. It is a true carved cherrystone, and not from a sour cherry. Possibly the next best thing in the book, the amusing "T. Fenning Dodsworth," is not quite a stranger; it was published, in this country at least, as part of *A Variety of Things*. But we may look upon it, surely, as one more link with the past.

And the past is most of all the nineties. The nineties stamped Max and sent him forth as their most engaging ambassador. It does not matter in the end that what Max wrote in the nineties is very far from his best work. It is simply that as the child of esthetic dandyism he never— however often he chose to treat it with a smile—ceased to cling to it. It was his achievement to commemorate an attitude by lightly mocking it, and to emerge from a period of much ill-fated trifling as the perfect trifler.

"The perfect trifler" may seem a slighting way to describe the man who has conceivably written the finest familiar essays in the English language. But I think the phrase fairly suggests, on the most honorable terms, the scale of Sir Max's work and its quite unregrettable lack of "significance." For it does lack significance, in the sense that Peacock and Congreve, not to speak of Rabelais or Molière, possess it. Max—though he once confessed himself "no book lover"—is palpably, impenitently bookish. Very likely, as he has often declared, he turns to books only when he is unable to be with people. It does not matter. Sir Max is as literary as a quotation from Horace. It is never life itself, only the cultivated, the artistic, the aristocratic life, that he savors or satirizes; and when he savors it is not to make converts, any more than when he satirizes it is really to protest. His work exists simply to give pleasure of the most delicate kind—simply to distill all that we mean by temperament into something characterized by all that we mean by style.

His sheer spoofing aside, most of Sir Max's work may be summed up as the manipulation of a personality. He began manipulating it when it was not yet formed, and when his style, whatever its merits, was still a little absurd. He began impudently; not with the callow impudence of youth, but as a precocious and sort of parthenogenic man of the world. The art that reveals art came before its most celebrated opposite, if indeed the opposite ever quite came at all; the fun in Max lies not in wondering about his dexterity but in watching it. He is acrobat, not conjurer. At the start, however, he was not entirely deft: in *The Works* and *More* the cleverness is fatiguing, the personality obtrusive, the matter quite often thin. (Even something successful like "Diminuendo" or "An Infamous Brigade" is rather a *jeu d'esprit* than a true essay.) Just as Maltby, in *Seven Men*, sat up all night breaking in his new suits in rotation, so was Max, much earlier, breaking in his mannerisms and effects.

What is cardinal to the manipulation of a personality is a completely expressive style; and that, despite an instinctive finesse, came late. Max's style, being mannered, never needed perfect naturalness; but it did need perfect ease. And as late as *Yet Again* and *Zuleika Dobson* there is too often a slight strain in the writing, as there is a slight stretching in the contents. It was the many years that separate *Yet Again* from *And Even Now* that brought perfection. Finally everything came right: the proportions, the tone, the touch that is both intimate and reserved, the *un*exhibitionistic wit, and the Tory point of view that is worn, not as in too young a man, outrageously; nor defiantly, as in too insecure a one. Above all, the personality has found a prose that exactly suits it. It is a personality raised out of life into art, and one that while seeming to confide continues to elude one. There is the pleasantest sort of frankness; the greatest willingness to confess to all one's prejudices, predilections, oddities. But *is* this Max Beerbohm—or is it merely Max being sly? Has he told the truth or had his little joke; revealed a man or trumped one up? Is this autobiography or art, or both?

It is, at any rate, something remarkably engaging. For a certain kind of reader, the small habits and hankerings of this blameless exquisite can be as fascinating as all the demonic and outrageous and unsanctified adventures of a Byron or Jack London. That, whether or not it projects a real person, is proof of real personality. Perhaps in the factual sense we have never been given the true Max

Beerbohm. Artistically it makes no difference—though it is my own guess that Max has usually been altogether candid, exploiting the worldling's knowledge that the truth is the last thing people ever believe.

But beyond the question of fact or fabrication lies the *effect* of personality through style; the juggling, so to speak, of the first person singular. It is probably the most ticklish problem that can confront a writer. Many very distinguished writers—Thomas Mann is perhaps the latest —have failed abysmally in talking about themselves. There is the Scylla of egotism, which must be skirted without crashing against the Charybdis of mousiness. There is the danger of striking a pose, which must again not be circumvented at the cost of a priggish earnestness. Moreover, a writer using the first person must seem neither too familiar nor too aloof; neither smug, again, nor obsequious. There is finally the peril, the besetting peril for the familiar essayist, of coyness. And though Max escapes all the other pitfalls, at times even he becomes rather coy. Yet the redeeming thing is that he does not become so oftener, particularly as his style can be very irritating. Even his mature style trades too freely in inversions, in Latinisms and archaisms, in double negatives, in "do but" and "averse from" and "belike" and "how great soever"—becoming precious, conspicuous, waxen; and I suppose one is riled the more from knowing that Max indulges in all these mannerisms with a quiet smile, with an implied "Of course I know the risks I am taking, the effects I am creating—do you take me for a fool?"

It is personality that animates Max's work, but form and finish that will go far toward preserving it. The essays are not simply serpentine excursions in personality; they are real essays, often perfect essays, that explore a subject without seeming to exhaust it, that move suavely and wittily from point to point, till they reach a sound resting-place and stop. They breathe culture, but never down your neck; they are as light, but certainly not as colorless, as air; they are as beckoning and satisfying as his own Golden Drugget. One sometimes wonders just why Sir Max's best essays so completely transcend everyone else's in our time, and one seems to find the answer in their tone. Somehow the most noticeably precious of our writers is also the most genially conversational; he chats with us as Chesterton never did, as Shaw—for all his greatness—never could. He shows the reader every courtesy, but his greatest concern is for the essay form itself—which shall remain an essay and never become a dissertation, an impromptu, or even an out-and-out memoir.

To achieve that tone a writer must definitely possess a temperament. A mind, no matter how bright or agile, is not enough; not even if a sense of fun and a sense of humor go with it. We are back again, no doubt, in the realm of personality, but with some differences; for personality is not temperament, as many writers who had the one without the other—Milton, say, or Macaulay—will prove. It was well for Max to come of age in the nineties, for with all its faults and extravagances that was the last period in which temperament was highly prized or could wholly prosper. It was the last time that a man could play his own tune in his own house, and not against the chords, and frequently the clangor, of the outside world. It was the last time that the eighteenth century—which for all its sense of form reveled in attractive eccentricity—had any decisive influence. Behind Max stands, quite plainly, Yorick. Since the nineties certain writers have had "sensibility"—a word suggesting the frustration of temperament rather more than the fulfillment—and certain others have had "manner"; but temperament in the purest, most unobstructed sense they have for the most part lacked.

It took Max a long time to master his tune; for all his finest essays are to be found in *And Even Now* (1920). Here is "No. 2 the Pines," that glowing memoir of Swinburne which is saved by its impish touches and sly sidelights from being too reverent. Here is that perfect trifle "A Clergyman." Here, again, is "Hosts and Guests," the model and despair of anyone who would write an essay that is exactly, supremely, an essay. Here, indeed, with very few exceptions, is one good thing after another. Yet, before turning away from Max's essays, one ought to note how in all periods they exhibit—though in late periods most keenly—his wit. That wit was pretty enough in the nineties, when Max could remark that "theatrical reminiscence is the most awful weapon in the armory of old age. I am sure that much of the respect which we pay to an elderly man is due to our suspicion that he could avenge any slight by describing the late Charles Matthews in *Cool as a Cucumber*." But later Max's wit became deeply wedded to his style, as in the inimitable last sentence of "Hosts and Guests."

Sir Max's only novel is not a great favorite of mine. *Zuleika Dobson* contains delightful things, and excellent judges of literature—E. M. Forster for one—have praised it highly. But for me *Zuleika* is unsteadily poised between fantasy and satire, when indeed it is anything more than a classicist's picnic or an Oxford family joke. As to form, perhaps it might better have been a long novelette: stretched into a novel, it has to be elaborate to avoid seeming thin, and it doesn't avoid seeming thin. As to content, the story it tells does not altogether come off. Possibly I lack the delicate imagination that is needed to enter with a whole heart into Sir Max's conspiracy. But possibly the author himself lacked the robust imagination that is needed to make something of this kind really succeed. In satiric fantasy the author must somehow, with a bold maneuver, steal (rather than woo) the reader's credulity; and however great Sir Max's finesse, it is not finesse—and certainly not archness—that a story like *Zuleika* most needs; it is high spirits, lively turns, audacity. And that is just what it frequently lacks. I can't help thinking that the only character in the book whom Sir Max wrote about with real wickedness of understanding was the Duke of Dorset. And the chill, haughty, impervious Duke, though a delightful character for a book that might then have been called *Eight Men*, is not at all the best character for a book needing gusto and energy. (It could be part of the joke that *Zuleika* lacks these things precisely because Oxford lacks them; but if so, that is carrying the joke, artistically, rather far.) The Duke is a superb subject for satiric portraiture, but a doubtful hero for an extravagant plot.

And, for all its skill, there is also a slight crudeness about *Zuleika* and a slight unpalatability. Max, by failing to dissolve the real in the fantastic, cannot make the drownings, when they come, quite matters of disembodied comedy. And this is as good a place as any (since in *Zuleika* we meet the Rhodes scholar Abimelech V. Oover) to touch upon Max's treatment of America and Americans. His aversion, real or assumed, for America would trouble me very little if it did not so consistently coarsen his touch. Certainly nothing lends itself more to burlesque than a certain type of Rhodes scholar. But Abimelech is a burlesque of a burlesque—or rather a parody of a parody, since it is his lingo that chiefly matters. How the greatest parodist alive could have gone so startlingly wrong with the American language is not easily explained.

For Sir Max is by all odds the greatest parodist, as he is the greatest essayist, of our time; and the best things in *A Christmas Garland* are almost beyond praise. The parody of Henry James, for example, is not only a wonderful take-off of the style ("the scarred, the poor dear woebegone and so very beguilingly *not* refractory mirror of the moment"); but the subject-matter—two tots worriedly debating whether they should inspect their Christmas stockings—is, as a travesty of a Jamesian predicament, little short of inspired. And the take-off of George Moore contains perhaps the finest single touch in all parody, when the all-too-Gallic and posturing Moore, seized with "strange thoughts that I cannot express in English," turns Pater's description of the Mona Lisa into French. To be quite perfect, there should be one or two mistakes in the French; though possibly there are.

If one persists in asking oneself why Max's treatment of Abimelech falls so flat, the answer may well lie in the less effective of the *Christmas Garland* pieces. All Max's finest parodies are at the expense of writers he loves or appreciates: "One can't really understand what one doesn't love, and one can't make good fun without real understanding," Maltby tells Max in *Seven Men*, though it might better be Max telling Maltby. The parodies of Wells, say, or Kipling, are extremely clever; but they fall short of the piece on Gosse or James because they are conceived in antipathy. Max bludgeons Wells, but somehow Wells escapes only bruised; but he kills James, in the sense that each man kills the thing he loves.

If Max partly failed with his one novel, he brilliantly succeeded with that other work of fiction, *Seven Men*. These stories make up a book almost as original as it is captivating. In "Enoch Soames" and "Maltby and Braxton" Max has spoofed the literary temperament of the nineties, and of more than the nineties—its affectations and insane vanities, its snobbery and emulousness—with superb skill. In these tales Max found his perfect material, reviving with precision and nostalgia a real world of real people, and then, through fantasy, standing it squarely on its head. "Enoch Soames" is a fine yarn into the bargain. I feel sure that on June 3, 1997 there will be many Maxists posted, in a high state of tension, about the Reading Room of the British Museum; I shall be ninety-two, but I hope to be there myself. And in "Savonarola Brown" Max has woven Shakespeare and seventh-rateness into imperishable nonsense.

Sir Max's theater criticism doubtless suffers from the fact that its author was never deeply drawn to the theater, or powerfully held by it. No one could have been less stage-struck than that reviewer, who confessed he was bored by the play he saw on his tenth birthday. But his critical approach has, besides a certain personal charm, a certain solid usefulness. By not surrendering easily to the theater's "glamour," Max was saved from swallowing a lot of its silliness. He saw the stage for what it was and largely still is: the least impressive, the least adult of contemporary arts. He never, like Shaw, attacked it frontally; he just slowly undermined its pretensions by quietly underlining its stupidities. I suspect that, in the perspective of half a century, we get a sounder estimate of the English theater of his time from Max than we do from his more knowledgeable and responsive colleagues Walkley and Archer. To be sure, Max's temperament led him into errors and inadequacies. He underrated Gorki, for example, and overrated Maeterlinck. There is again no gusto in his criticism; but there is much unprofessional shrewdness, there is fairly much professional observation, there is mild wit and—mixed blessing—an essayist's emphasis on form.

Max was not an outstandingly good critic; nor, like Shaw, so superb a journalist and electrical a personality that he himself still holds up where his subject-matter doesn't; but he wrote the sort of antiseptic criticism that, by not succumbing to the moment's emotionalism, has more than the moment's value.

As to Sir Max's general "place" in literature, one can more easily dispute how high it is than how permanent. Of all the writers of their time, it is men like Max and A. E. Housman—men who in their minor way frequently achieved perfection—that we can feel surest will be read with pleasure for many generations to come. They cared more for art than for life, for art, moreover, that has shapeliness rather than size; and the preference greatly limits them in stature. But it should also preserve them in time, in the sense that enamel outwears flesh. In terms of posterity, perfection is much less of a gamble than greatness. How big Max's audience will be a generation, or a century, hence is indeed something else again. Max was always caviar; probably he always will be. But a dozen of his essays and two or three of his stories should survive as long as there is a civilized point of view.

(1947)

CHAPTER XVII

H. L. Mencken

AT a first night a year or two ago I found myself seated in front of Mencken and Nathan; and thought how, had this happened twenty years before, I should have been half out of my seat to hear what those two dragons were talking about. And at once it struck me that I still would like to hear, so that I at once proceeded to eavesdrop. And what those two dragons were talking about, or rather what Mencken was talking to Nathan about, was—wallpaper.

Twenty years before, it would have been as great a shock to find Mencken talking of wallpaper as to find, say, Calvin Coolidge talking at all. But a year or so ago, though still an unlikely topic, wallpaper seemed a charming and not unsuitable one. For this once fiercest of dragons holding forth on the tamest of subjects had himself, with the passing of years, come to seem tame; had himself come to seem decorative. He might still, like a sort of old-fashioned fire engine, symbolize clangor and commotion, but he no longer could stir them up. In a sense he belonged so vividly to the past that he was compelled to exist less as a man than a memory.

Certainly no one just like him, either for personal bite

or as cultural yeast, has quite arisen since. Since Mencken, no one with so keen an eye for the follies of American life has had also so sharp a tongue. Since Mencken, indeed, there has come about a sort of division or bifurcation of Mencken's labors, the neatly fenced critical highroad climbing toward the chill uplands of the Eliots, the journalistic lowroad dropping to the swampland of the Peglers. Mencken was superlatively the right man for the job, but he almost certainly arrived at the right moment. Not only did he open up shop with almost no competition from pollsters and syndicated critics and nationally hooked-up commentators: even more, in the years following World War I, he had for customers Americans with a lot of newly acquired money and emotions—Americans who wanted to reach out rather than dig down for culture, to overturn rather than investigate morality; who desired to feel superior in ten lessons; who craved, above all, to be amused while being instructed. Mencken, between what he was born with in the way of style and personality, and what he borrowed from a Nietzsche or a Huneker or a Shaw, could offer, at will, considerable food for thought, unlimited opportunities for laughter. Hence in no time a vast number of people were following him with delight, while (what proved even better for business) a vast number of others were recoiling from him in horror.

It was an extraordinary show that he put on, in issue after issue of *The Smart Set*, in volume after volume of *Prejudices*. And it was also a vigorous crusade—or at any rate crusade-in-reverse; for of course Mencken had come not so much to win recruits as deserters; had contrived to make every American *less* pious, less patriotic, less proud of his heritage; to insist that almost without exception newspapers distort and books misinform; that professors are pedants, politicians are crooks, doctors, quacks, preachers hypocritical time-servers, farmers puritanical oafs; that the American picture of things doesn't exist and democracy doesn't work. Mencken did not pretend to know, or attempt to find out, the remedy: at reform he not merely threw up his hands but wrinkled his nose. The wise course was to stand apart and survey so grotesque and degraded a scene with faintly rueful amusement. Let the few superior souls—and the reader was always made to feel he was one of them—enjoy what satisfactions they could in their role of the civilized minority.

Always a fine, gaudy exhibit and often a scorching indictment, Mencken's operation covered enormous ground —became a kind of Ill-Will Tour of the American mind. To be sure, it so much disparaged the sights that you might have imagined it discouraged the sightseeing; but no, it merely set forth the right irreverent terms for travel. And though, in conducting the tour, Mencken relied chiefly on picturesque abuse, he was by no means lacking in acumen. He introduced a great many plausible comments, he let fall a whole lot of home-hitting cracks, and now and again spoke such genuine wisdom as "Injustice is relatively easy to bear; what stings is justice."

From out all this, moreover, there emerge solid and even definitive things—and not simply such things as the valuable spadework for Dreiser or the wonderful obit of Bryan. On a much larger scale, Mencken laid on the counter the whole stock-in-trade of our culture; caused us to test the quality and examine the price-tags on everything displayed. America was in a mood to change, and would have changed with Mencken or without him. All the same, he more than anyone else made America conscious and hence critical of itself; he more than anyone else, despite his own trick photography, revealed the face of America minus the false whiskers and the hair-dye. He made plain that charlatanry was America's leading profession; that to the Puritan, nothing is pure; that a democracy is at times a mob and freedom of expression at times a misfortune. He exposed half our national heroes; and orated about them as they died off, much less as though they were being mourned in death than tried for murder. In his debunking, Mencken revealed a gimlet eye for the pretentious, the counterfeit, the absurd; no one has shown up quackery with keener relish or more notable results. And for doing all this, Mencken had a brilliantly right style—vivid, daring, now and then bullying, and always a little unscrupulous. Though his method, with its pile-up of "learned" examples and irrelevancies, is journalistic and expansive, the prose itself is compact. The vocabulary is large and resourceful, even though the most trademarked parts of it —the "Rev. Dr.," the "bos taurus," the synonyms for twaddle—have naturally grown stale. But the Menckenisms can be picked off like burs from a coat, and the coat is good sturdy worsted still, and far from threadbare. And the breezy showmanship, the brazen circus air, plainly saved the crusader-in-reverse from becoming a yapping bore or common scold: although, following Mencken's lead in never taking anything quite seriously, most readers never took Mencken himself so. He never built or even blueprinted anything of much value; he was simply the accomplished and enthusiastic foreman of a wrecking-crew— and *what* a crew, as Sinclair Lewis and others came to join it. Far less can be said for Mencken as a sort of rough-and-ready *arbiter elegantiarum.* He made the mistake of whooping up the Cabells and the Hergesheimers, who had themselves made the mistake of becoming sophisticated without becoming fully mature; though it was much more, I think, their point of view than their dainty ways that Mencken found congenial. He himself typified not French wines but good German beer; a rowdy masculine gaiety with more nose-thumbing than eyebrow-raising to it; a ribaldry as much of the body as the mind; an attitude in which the knowledge that All Is Vanity was mingled with the principle that Nothing Is Sacred: such was Mencken during the twenties, when his stock, like so very many others, hit its all-time high.

Now, with the publication of *A Mencken Chrestomathy*, we can hardly not inquire where that stock stands today. The new volume, with its quarter-million words taken from Mencken's shelf-full of out-of-print books, is a sound and varied selection that still makes lively reading. Reading it, you perhaps more quickly seize the chance to relive an era, to raise people and ideas from the dead and the dustheap, than to revaluate Mencken. Yet all this may well affect our revaluation, in the sense that, having flourished as a critic and satirist of the period, Mencken may preeminently survive as its memoralist. Doubtless Mencken's greatest monument will be in the field where he himself has displayed the greatest talent—the field of language. *The American Language* and its two *Supplements* are much his solidest work. He might, I think, have done better by relying less on communications sent to Hollins Street and going oftener where the American language holds sway; and at times he assigns too much weight to obvious nonce-words or facetious coinages. But he has consolidated an immense amount of material with great care and skill, while all the time providing the sprightliest of reading-matter.

About life he has been less exacting than about language; particularly as critic. His judicial sessions are enjoyable courtroom comedies enough, but we far too often not simply quarrel with Mencken's verdicts; we distrust the evidence. For, like most journalists and virtually all

jesters, Mencken maneuvered and embroidered, unduly
limelighted or unfairly veiled the facts. To keep the show
going, he not only became more and more of a showman,
but cared less and less about who sat in the audience. And
his tone, of course, could be enormously misleading. It was
not so much that, employing the methods of a bomb-
thrower, he half concealed the prejudices of a Bourbon;
nor so much, again, that he was almost as leery of anything
newfangled as he was scornful of anything old. What was
much shoddier is that while so skeptical in theory, in practice he was always so knowing; inscribing *Que sçais-je?* on
his shield, slamming out Q.E.D. with his pen; and indeed
going on from being opinionated, as he ought to have been,
to suggesting omniscience, as no man ought.

As a campaigner he was of incalculable value. In the
vital sense, he both launched and led the fight against Puritanism and gentility; he really cried down snoopers and
bluenoses and lavender-and-old-lacers, and spoke up for
(and printed) those who dissented and protested and
pioneered. And for doing this he must always have an important place in the development of our culture. In the
end, however, his represents a campaign for freedom of
speech rather than real excellence of writing. For so soon
as something not immediate but ultimate was at stake, he
might all too readily misapprehend and betray. In the end,
of what use was it to oust Hopkinson Smith in favor of
E. W. Howe, if he could suppose that Henry James
"would have been vastly improved as a novelist by a few
whiffs from the Chicago stockyards" (no doubt Blake
should have joined a country club); if he could blandly
link Jane Austen with Hannah More; if he could adjudge
Dr. Johnson "the first Rotarian"? As for music, a field to
which he devotes more space in the *Chrestomathy* than to
quackery or morals, he can speak with a sneer of the nine-

teenth century producing "a whole horde of Tchaikow-skys . . . Debussys . . . Verdis" (how nice if it had!); can refer to the "naïve idiom" of Mozart (the finale of *Figaro,* shall we say?); can remark of Haydn in relation to Beethoven that it is "like pitting a gazelle against a bull" (a good moment to remember Swinburne's separating the great in art into gods and giants). Mencken had, besides—like so many of his fellow critics since—the need, in raising one thing up, to pull another down: thus praise of *Heart of Darkness* requires condemnation of *King Lear.* And, like so many of his fellow scoffers, Strachey for instance, when Mencken *doesn't* scoff he is terribly likely to gush.

The truth is that, in his tastes and his esthetics alike, Mencken was often glaringly philistine. Art, in the purest sense, fed nothing in his nature and wholly eluded his grasp; at times he seems to suggest that the "sanity" of art is much the same as common sense. But at least one great trouble with his criticism is that he wouldn't confine it to what really interested or affected him, that he felt called upon to express an opinion about everything—so that many of his snidest judgments are largely snap judgments, and he is most intolerant when least informed. All this left its mark; Mencken helped father the manysided, encyclopedic commentator of today—the type that, professing doubt, serves up dogma, and setting forth to expose other people, reveals the bluffer in himself.

Nor is Mencken's thinking measurably superior to his taste. His exalting Junkerdom at the expense of democracy; his denunciation of things like birth-control and universal education; his defense of things like capital punishment and war, label him an almost cantankerous reactionary. The real point of it, indeed, is less how reactionary Mencken proved to be than how responsible. He was very largely irresponsible; he must stand condemned not for being

a pessimist about progress, but for being a cynic; not
for being glum about the incorrigible blunderings of mankind, but for being, all too often, gleeful. Civilized mi-
norities are all very well; but they have, or should have,
work to do. The aristocracies that thoughtful conserva-
tives like Burke have believed in were to legislate and labor
quite strenuously for the good of others; they were to be
the chief actors in a very weighty drama. Mencken's fine
folk were only to be spectators at a loutish farce—which, it
was surely on the cards, would become either too monot-
onous to endure or too obstreperous to control. After 1929,
in any case, it played to empty houses.

. Not unnaturally, Mencken was slain in his own crusade.
He pointed the way to something better than himself; he
was not the big city, he was only the train that took you
there. But if only briefly instructive, he was for the longest
time enjoyable; and if he perished quickly as a god, for
years and years he persisted as the devil. Actually the hate
he aroused was one of his best achievements; whatever
else, he could always be proud of his enemies. There is
some virtue, too, in the fact that one was liberated from
benighted dogmas without becoming enslaved all over
again to Mencken; the danger with greater liberators is
just such an enslavement.

Though Mencken sinfully abused his role, the role itself
was culturally a needed one. Something is gained when a
man writes pungently and powerfully enough to interest
every class of reader; something is gained, again, when a
man raises all the right questions, whether or not he re-
turns the wrong answers. Mencken's real function was not
to shed light, but remove dust. Even so, he did help tear
down a few dangerously obstructive walls before turning
his attention to wallpaper.

(1949)

CHAPTER XVIII

Virginia Woolf as Critic

AT the same moment we are given a posthumous book by Virginia Woolf and two books about her.[1] Of the two, Mr. Forster's, originally a Cambridge lecture, is the brief memoir of a friend, charming yet candid, full of sharp comments and animating touches, but too short to say all it might; that of Mr. Daiches is the interpretation of a critic, painstaking, sometimes penetrating, and too long for what there is to say. Virginia Woolf's own book, like the two *Common Readers,* is made up mainly of critical essays, and coming when it does, perhaps serves to emphasize what Mr. Forster and Mr. Daiches tend to slight—the importance of Virginia Woolf's criticism in the general body of her work. Mr. Forster gives but two or three sentences to her criticism, and Mr. Daiches a dozen of his 157 pages. The fact is easily explained: Virginia Woolf nowhere al-

---

[1] "The Death of the Moth and Other Essays," by Virginia Woolf; "Virginia Woolf," by E. M. Forster; and "Virginia Woolf," by David Daiches.

tered the face of criticism as she did the face of the novel, she extended no critical frontiers, she attracted no critical disciples. All the same, Mr. Forster's and Mr. Daiches's relative allotment of space may not be posterity's, for Mrs. Woolf forged her criticism into something quite as distinctive as her novels, and the best of it may well survive everything else she wrote except *To the Lighthouse* and *Mrs. Dalloway,* and may conceivably survive them.

Which is all the more interesting, seeing that, in addition to being no critical innovator, Virginia Woolf was in one sense really no critic. At least her real strength did not lie in any remarkable powers of mind, any systematic principles of criticism. In fifty pages of any first-rank critic we shall find more inseminating ideas than in all three volumes of Mrs. Woolf. Where we do find a purely critical perception, it is likely to seem neither new nor old, and we are likely to value it for its pertinence rather than its originality, or for the light it throws on Virginia Woolf. Thus she says of Euripides: "To understand him it is not so necessary to understand Greek as to understand poetry"; or of the Elizabethans: "The Elizabethans bore us because they suffocate our imaginations rather than set them to work"; or of Sterne: "Sterne, from fear of coarseness, is forced into indecency." These are things, we feel, that beyond any question Virginia Woolf discovered for herself, but we feel too that they say more succinctly what someone else has said first.

With rare exceptions ("Modern Fiction," "How It Strikes a Contemporary," "Mr. Bennett and Mrs. Brown"—all of them more or less critical defenses of her creative methods), Mrs. Woolf is hardly more a suggestive critic than she is a systematic one. She seldom reacts to literature in a purely critical way: to the writing of her own time she reacted as a writer; to the literature of the past she responded, for the most part, as a reader. She was in the one case more combative than critical, and in the other more appreciative. What seems best in her approach to the classics is a superb responsiveness: she had fine imagination and extraordinary sensibility; she was a born reader and could assimilate effortlessly, but she was also a very cultivated reader, and could correlate and compare.

Having both an esthetic and a historical sense, she was capable of really informed appreciation; but having an artistic gift also, she chose not merely to record an author's quality but to reproduce it in a form, a framework, of her own. What she distills is much less the meaning of a writer or a period than the temperament, the savor, the personality: she is a kind of highly skillful portrait-painter who catches the style of her model while imposing a style of her own. We shall not learn from her just what the Greeks or the Elizabethans, Montaigne or Chaucer, signify, but we do know how they look. She reveals them, with beautiful clarity, in a mirror: it is for others to peer down at them through a miscroscope. Accordingly her best work, most of which will be found in the first *Common Reader,* has about it a real charm of artistry. One reads it a little less for profit than for pleasure, for its freshness, its shapeliness, its sensitiveness, for its language, its wit, its sense of poetry. The poet in Virginia Woolf constantly pleads for a hearing in these essays, as in her novels it ultimately insists on being heard.

After the first *Common Reader* the language becomes a little too fine; the style, at moments, tends to inflate the contents. For, like too many other writers, Virginia Woolf began to evolve something approaching a formula; she lost the secret of her earlier distinction as soon as she discovered in what it lay. What had once been highly individual begins to seem, in *The Second Common Reader,* merely professional. There is less submerged poetry and more protruding rhetoric. The particular insights become fewer, the generalizations and analogies more frequent. Virginia Woolf is not so much writing about what she has read as reading something in order to write about it. A note even of cleverness has crept into it. On one page of an essay on Hazlitt a painfully smart sentence crops up, and on the next page a curiously flat one. There is something overwritten about the essay on Hardy. Mrs. Woolf still writes extremely well, but one feels that she has no desire to write differently. There is no sense here of trying to break the mold, to alter the pattern, as there always was in her fiction.

The Death of the Moth reveals a further decline, though some of it must be judged as early work and some as in not quite final form. But additional polish would hardly have given additional weight. Here, to be sure, are many things that give pleasure. Here is urbane and witty writing on urbane and witty writers—Gibbon, Walpole, Mme de Sévigné. Here are quick flashes of insight: Strachey, says Mrs. Woolf, succeeded with *Queen Victoria* because he respected biography as a craft, and failed at *Elizabeth and Essex* because he tried to make it into an art. "The phrase," she says of George Moore, "came before the emotion." Here are pointed, though sometimes rather shallow and even querulous, comments, as this one concerning modern poetry: "The poet is much less interested in what we have in common than in what he has apart." Here, indeed, is a good deal of the old skill. And yet there is far too much emptiness and inadequacy—nothing, for example, could be more disappointing than the essays on Henry James. Too many of these pieces are book reviews, lectures, *jeux d'esprit,* made-to-order things that disappoint even as they divert us. The style, moreover, is full of horrible Stracheyan flourishes.

> *And then we turn to the book again, and to our amazement we find that the rocking-horse has left the ground; we are mounted on a winged steed; we are sweeping in wide circles through the air and below us Europe unfolds; the ages change and pass; a miracle has taken place.*

Tradition, which hampered Virginia Woolf in fiction, greatly helped her in criticism, but only up to a certain point. She was at home in the past, and happy there; she accepted what the classics had to give without quarrel, sometimes without challenge; feasted off them, time and again envied the terms on which the old writers could write—with a sense of their age and their audience behind them. Aware—heavily aware, as a novelist—that all this had broken down in her own age of flux, she was possibly a little undiscerning and literary about the past, a little too fascinated with its décor and not quite enough concerned with its large outlines. For acute as her historical sense clearly was, it pre-eminently reflected the student of manners; she was most at home, after all, in the eighteenth century. What almost equally drew her to the past, however, were its echoing corridors, its grace of distance, its poetry. Both these interests reveal that intense literary feeling which was so distinctive and valuable a part of Virginia Woolf, and which she could embody in entirely consonant prose. This is what she could do best, and what she could do better than anyone else of her time. She will survive, not as a critic, but as a literary essayist recording the adventures of a soul among congenial masterpieces. For on the whole she did not approach—modern authors excepted—what she could not in some real sense enjoy. Her taste in the classics were surprisingly catholic, and her range, at first glance, seems amazingly broad. Yet the writers who are most downright, and masculine, and central in their approach to life—a Fielding or a Balzac—she for the most part left untouched. (They fathered, of course, the contemporary fiction that she most disliked.) Her own approach was at once more subterranean and aerial, and invincibly, almost defiantly, feminine.

(1942)

CHAPTER XIX

Pundits and Philistines

THIS, as everyone knows, is the age of the specialist, when you consult one doctor about the left elbow and another about the right. Where elbows are concerned, there is doubtless much to be said for it; even so, one wonders whether the doctor has perspective; whether he understands, say, the elbow in relation to the arm. For everywhere there is a growing lack of perspective; the tendency everywhere is to specialize, to narrow the field, to cultivate—and eventually over-cultivate—one's garden.

Take current criticism at its higher levels; much of it, surely, suggests not the roving mind of criticism but the burrowing methods of scholarship. Once upon a time criticism boasted a good many superior, even rather noble, hacks: doubtless the Saintsburys read too much, wrote too much to order, failed at times to see the forest for the trees—but they kept a great body of good literature in circulation, they made it seem important or alluring. Today criticism runs to pedants who can't see the trees, even, for the branches. Any cultural diversity is scouted today; culture itself is giving way to education. But the merely educated man may very well, like the cynic, know the price of everything and the value of nothing: education for the most part only sheds light, it is culture that furnishes perspective; the difference is almost that between knowledge and understanding. And without wide, unselfconscious culture there must result (at whatever level) an oppressive provincialism, a collection of small inbred "cultures," each vitiated by particular snobberies, shibboleths, and taboos, each a Holy City instead of an intellectual capital.

Perhaps the surest sign of this provincialism is its self-approvingness; its not really wanting to know how the other half lives; its becoming defensively aggressive about its tastes, noisily moral about its prejudices. In the current criticism that should be doing most to determine values, far too much seems provincial, far too much (what is even worse) seems prig-ridden. Its concern is so much less with what is beckoning in art than with what is baffling: in its opinion, it is only agitated waters than run deep. Every age of criticism, to be sure, rejects as compulsively as it rediscovers, tending to fix its values by its needs. Yet the basis of today's provincialism seems to me a neurotic desire not simply to specialize, but to exclude and excommunicate. And with it there promptly emerges a need to find language that, while pretending to be judicial, will actually prove dismissive.

Once this process gains ground, we have always to be weighing the name against the thing, appearance against reality. Take the most obvious of current examples—that of "highbrow" and "middlebrow," which, excellent as a rough-and-ready contrast, is coming to be viewed as solemnly and absolutely as "Aryan" and "non-Aryan" among racists. Hence what might be called practicing highbrows must be always walking among eggs, must be constantly thumbing the literary Social Register. Each season they must discover whether Sartre, say, or Hemingway, is in society or not; they mustn't be caught napping when, thanks to a couple of formidable hostesses, a Tennyson is once more "received"; right now they are perhaps a little sullenly getting used to the idea that George Eliot may any minute become the rage.

I'm not exaggerating much; for most of this arises from such very simple provincial motives as snobbery, bigotry, a longing for rules of guidance. The desire to exclude—whether from a golf club or a bookcase—destroys any real desire to evaluate; so that we get, not a sound and workable cultural hierarchy, but a system of untouchables. Each, moreover, has the comfort of his own half- and quarter-truths. The philistine snorts that a lot of Melville and Henry James isn't any good. The pedagogue points out how much of Faulkner's prose lacks syntax, how many of Dickens's novels lack structure. The disease spreads, furthermore, until each group, rampant with exclusiveness, has little more of a historical than a geographical perspective.

The number of literary people one meets who seem to know little beyond the current fashions of their particular world is quite staggering. "Who now reads Bolingbroke?" asked Burke on a well-known occasion; today—judging by the critical reviews—the same questions might be asked of half the classics. And who, indeed, can be expected to read Molière or Meredith or Heine while there are drama critics who have never read Aristotle, connoisseurs of wit who are strangers to Peacock?

It is true that in an age of mass-culture, when everything is abridged, adapted, adulterated, and Philistia's loud-

speakers are incessantly braying, one can't help wanting
a congenial and private nook. In other days, all the same,
a Heine, an Arnold, a Wilde, a Shaw went forth to harry
the philistine with a very telling slingshot; today's critic
goes at him, if at all, with sugar tongs. And does today's
critic, despite his fondness for the word, have a real eye
for the thing? As Leslie Stephen once said, "philistine" is
what a prig calls anything he dislikes. And the prig, on his
side, offers us so cramped a shelf of favorites, requiring so
much bulkier a shelf of commentary. At his worst, indeed,
he is a disguised anthropologist or psychoanalyst or moral
philosopher who quite ignores the central functions of art
for an important special function: he is like those schools
that are really only interested in their problem children.
The drawback, even so, is less his lack of balance than his
lack of verve.

But if (using the words on a rough-and-ready basis)
highbrow is bad, middlebrow is decidedly worse. If highbrow's yardstick of value is too often mere complexity,
middlebrow's is almost always freedom from strain. Highbrow can fall for humbug; but middlebrow, so long as
something is plausible and engaging, doesn't even *ask*
whether it is false. Though middlebrow sanctimoniously
condemns slickness as a word, he loves it as a thing. He
has a bourgeois feeling for tidiness; sees art as for the most
part a kind of charmingly furnished drawing-room and, at
intervals, as a beautifully run "rough camp." Middlebrow
loves to be surprised, but hates to be really shocked; loves
to tour, but hates to explore; is all tastefulness and no
taste.

Nor has middlebrow any of highbrow's real, however
misguided, seriousness; any of its concern with how far
literary criticism must be social and cultural as well. It is
a concern that poses a kind of paradox. The exclusively

literary critic performs a very narrow function, yet must have the broadest possible sympathies—must in theory be as eclectic as an auctioneer. He cannot let personal quirks or philosophical or political theories blur the precision of his responses. The cultural critic, on the other hand, can perform a far broader function with far narrower—or at least far more personal—views, his subject-matter being in fact so large that if it isn't harnessed to a point of view it becomes unwieldy. And though even for him literature can never be merely a tract, it can be a test, it can help determine the master currents of his age.

Too much current criticism sees literature as a form of testimony rather than of talent, as something that explains far more than it enriches; as, in other words, education rather than culture. As intellectual deep-sea fishermen, many of our critics have all sorts of useful psychological and philosophical tackle and gear; what they seem to lack is a very vital artistic sense, a distinguished or even a decent command over words. So much of their criticism is exegesis and jargon—such jargon as brings to mind Crébillon's remark about "marrying words that hadn't even thought of becoming acquainted."

Perhaps, too, there is the simple matter of responsiveness. Good critics, even the lawgivers like Aristotle, strike us as in an important sense participants, wanting to account for what has charmed or excited or disaffected *them,* not for what subconsciously attracted or repelled the author. Despite magnificent special jobs of re-creation like *The Road to Xanadu,* the big thing, still, is not what went into "The Ancient Mariner" or *King Lear,* but what came out of it. What went in has its own kind of value; but modern criticism is too much in a mood to investigate, and too little to interpret and appraise; is obsessed (as it were) with the mystery of Shakespeare's sonnets and not with the artistry. So obsessed, its search tends to narrow rather than widen; its effect, however cerebral, to seem dehydrated: the critic ceases to be a person, his writing fails to possess a style.

One reason why T. S. Eliot commands so large and attentive an audience is that he so notably does possess a style; and far from flattening out the critic's role, makes it ripple with showmanship. His are very calculated audacities and snobberies. When he calls the Romantic poets "riff-raff" he may seem to be losing his temper, but he is very deliberately meaning to shock. When he had himself photographed in a white tie, he displayed in reverse the showmanship of Napoleon when he appeared among his dressed-up generals in an old dusty cloak. As a showman Mr. Eliot belongs, despite his frequent humorlessness, with the Dr. Johnsons and Byrons and Shaws: and this is meant of course, for praise. Eliot deserves his reputation because, among weightier reasons, he knows how to give pleasure: we want to read him as much for his blind spots as his insights, his manner as his matter.

Of course there is serious criticism—a lot of serious criticism—being written in America by very able critics. But in general, by its dead, priggish manner, its neglect of the pleasurable in art, serious criticism has failed of leverage and is failing of influence. More and more of our serious critics are moving into the tight, gnomelike little world of the pedagogues, carrying on endless ill-natured controversies in print, confusing purism with integrity, using every critical article as the basis for another. As a result, criticism very misguidedly denies literature any sense of allure: for criticism, after all, is the only *disinterested* form of publicity that there is.

In fact, criticism would not so often have to defend its claim to be an art had it oftener the look of one. How dazzlingly down-to-earth Dr. Johnson, suddenly shedding all his polysyllables, could be! The best short essay on Dickens I know—Santayana's—is equally the best-written. The most searching of modern theater criticism—Shaw's—is not less the most brilliant. That rusty jagged weapon "brilliant but unsound," wherewith academic dullards have always done in their betters, is now making itself a menace in criticism too. So many of our serious critics don't like brilliance; it suits their book no better than their temperaments. For brilliance is like lightning—either it flashes, or it flashes and hits something; whatever happens, there is not much to investigate.

(1950)

CHAPTER XX

The Autobiography of Thomas Wolfe

THERE has been no American first novel since the war which promised so greatly as *Look Homeward, Angel.* To be sure, it was a large, sprawling record cut down from an incredibly longer and more sprawling one. With all the vitality of a born writer behind it, it showed nothing of the discipline of a born artist. It lacked perspective; it lacked proportion; the emotions it struck were too often homesick and adolescent. But nobody reading it could fail to perceive its spendthrift power, or fail to recognize the vigor with which the Gant family was brought to life, or close the book without being aware that no such rhetoric, no such energy and rush of language, had been visited upon any other young man of our time.

Look Homeward, Angel was an autobiographical novel, the usual beginning for a young man who wrote hotly and expressively from within. Not at once did the reader grasp that this particular young man must be always an autobiographer, because his equipment—his tortured romantic egoism, his megalomaniac memory, his grandiose assimilation of life in terms of purely personal encounter—outlawed any other approach to literature. But this worship of selfhood was confirmed by Wolfe's second novel, the even more unrestrained *Of Time and the River.* Clearly the world about him existed no farther than his eye could see; and it was a world that lacked order, objective truth, social meaning. Only what he could sink his teeth in, or fling his body upon, or whirl about in his memory, was real; and even these were things he must write about with the same vehemence and ardor that he lived them.

The Web and the Rock is again autobiography, full of the same raptures and incontinences, and pondering again those poetic truisms about time and love and death which are as close as Wolfe could come to thinking, and as much philosophy as the egocentric adolescent ever needs. True, Eugene Gant is here called George Webber, and grows up in some other North Carolina community, and salutes the great city with new apostrophes, and embarks with a woman older and mellower than himself on a stormy love affair. Few love affairs in fiction have been more minutely reported. Few, I should think, have been more self-consciously lived through. Scarcely any, while exposing so much, have analyzed so little. The whole business, with Wolfe, becomes a piece of violent self-dramatization.

Wolfe's real weakness was not that he dramatized his life, but that the writer dramatized it even more than the man. The man suffered; the writer merely exulted in the suffering. The man doubted and was afraid; the writer chose to celebrate himself on the grand scale. The result was not entirely hollow or cheaply operatic, but much of it might fairly be called Wagnerian. Wolfe would, to begin with, have acknowledged Wagner's dictum that all art is a way of remembering one's childhood. He had, too, Wagner's grandiosities: used leitmotivs, operated in tetralogies, succumbed to that mystical, mindless *Nachtkultur* which pervades *Tristan* and the *Ring*. He had the Wagnerian tumidity and opulence, the love of size, the delight in effect; but though in Wagner too there are emptiness and show, Wagner knew how to work in large forms, and what Wagner created in the end—whatever we may think of it intellectually—was indeed a cosmos. Wolfe never created anything, even in disorder. He remembered, he recaptured, he elaborated on things known, and with himself for substructure threw up a great shapeless edifice. Even his prose is not really created; it is only superbly improvised. His best writing is possibly magnificent, but even his best writing is not solid; and there is hardly one paragraph in all he wrote that is not self-indulgent. His worst prose (and there is a great deal of it) is unspeakable.

The whole body of Wolfe's work, marvelous as fragments of it are, betrays the amateur and the adolescent. One regrets the want of cerebration, the addled values, in much of Hemingway; but as a *writer*, Hemingway is altogether professional, always knows exactly what he is doing. Wolfe knew nothing of the sort, and would never have known. It was not for him to curb his excesses by learning his trade. What he was, what he achieved, resulted from a heady, untamable personality—with the bit in his mouth, he would have turned dumb. Real passion he did not have, for he was too ungovernable to be truly intense. His energies, like his perceptions and his attachments, were adolescent. For home and the home country and the family life he had outgrown, Wolfe was insistently nostalgic. City life and the great world fascinated him to the end, I should guess, because they had fascinated him when he was growing up. "A man spends his youth dreaming out," says a mountain character in a Lola Ridge play, "and the rest of his life dreaming back." Of no one is that truer than of Wolfe.

He never acquired, of course, any values—either intellectual or moral—that were worth consideration. He had enough experience of life, and enough sensibility, to recognize what was narrow, parochial, absurd in the life he quitted; he was so carried away by romanticism that in moments of recoil he could perceive its shams, and look with some suspicion on the individualist codes it produced. But of man's place in the hard, downright living world he knew little, for to a writer so inward-looking the world and himself were one. The great arcana—time and death and fate—fascinated him; but even these, from his incorrigible habit of words, he ended by exploiting and vulgarizing.

Wolfe belonged to the high-pitched, unreal 1920's; their injunction to live fully, to seize all experience, perfectly fitted his need. When he died, young as he was, he had lived too long. For the soberer life that came after the twenties, when the accent fell not on the individual but on society, was something Wolfe could not understand. The fruits that one after another he thirstily sucked in gave him their flavor but no nourishment. One can glibly lament the awful sense of waste about his career; yet one knows, really, that it could not have been otherwise—that his talents were wasteful by nature, that his energies were so wonderful just because they were so unharnessed. One more book of Wolfe's will be published next year. Meanwhile, what remain are the symphonic fragments of language; the tortured soul seen through the angry tumults; the brightly unrolling memory; and the vast wonder of a boy.

(1939)

A NOTE ON THE TYPE
IN WHICH THIS BOOK IS SET

The text of this book is set in Caledonia, a Linotype face designed by W. A. Dwiggins. Caledonia belongs to the family of printing types called "modern face" by printers—a term used to mark the change in style of type-letters that occurred about 1800. Caledonia borders on the general design of Scotch Modern, but is more freely drawn than that letter.

The book was composed, printed, and bound by
THE PLIMPTON PRESS, NORWOOD, MASSACHUSETTS